For Kathy —
Great to ___ ___ ___ you!
Hope you ___ ___ ___.
Warmly,
Leslie

COME FOR
DINNER

COME FOR DINNER

Memorable Meals
to Share with Friends

Leslie Revsin

WILEY

John Wiley & Sons, Inc.

Library of Congress Cataloging-in-Publication Data:

Revsin, Leslie.
    Come for dinner: memorable meals to share with friends / Leslie Revsin.
        p. cm.
Includes index.
    ISBN 0-471-42010-7 (Cloth)
1. Cookery. 2. Entertaining. I. Title.
    TX714 .R493 2003
    642' .4—dc21   2002151814

Printed in the United States of America

10 9 8 7 6 5 4 3 2 1

for
Giulietta
Masina

✿ Acknowledgments

There can't be enough thank-you's for each of you who has contributed to this book. Your help and suggestions were invaluable, running the gamut from recipe retesting and organizational tips to promotional brainstorms (and just plain listening). You are my special community joined by the web of this project. My heart goes out in thanks to:

Philip, my soulmate.

My precious daughter Rachel, great cook, great Mom, and top-notch consultant; Bob, in your own right and for your enthusiasm for food; and our beloved Max and Henry.

Ethan, my favorite brother; and Sue, a true friend in sister-in-law form.

Cynthia, your smarts and humor show me what I'm made of.

Cecile, for your generosity and inspiration.

Kate and Marie, for so many years of love and friendship.

Ruth, Carol, and Liz, for all your love and help.

Katherine, my dear junkaholic gardening buddy.

Raquel and Lear, for your generosity and warmth.

Rita Sherman, for genuinely being there.

My other wonderful friends and neighbors: Claudia and Joel, Susan and Steve, Beth and Jay, Pen and Amanda, Pam and Matt, Marion and Alan, Doris, Marc, Chiaheng, Jon, Maureen and Mel, Nancy and Chuck, Emily and Frank, Laurie, Kevin, and in memory of Barry.

The "Psychotic Women's Group"—Lynne, Shoshana, Pam, Rutie, and Ruth, for your companionship and our hysterical evenings.

Joseph Piazza, for your dead-on sense of what food (and haircuts) should be.

Meg Simon, for being my one-woman public relations force.

More tons of thanks to:

Judy Kern

Annie Leuenberger

Michael Anastas

Abbie Gonzalez

Daniel Swee

Alicia Ng

Monique Calello

Dee and Kate Munson of The Food Professionals; Susan Boyer and Mark Munger of Driscoll's; Martha Holmberg, Sarah Jay, Susie Middleton, Joanne Smart, Jennifer Armentrout, and Amy Albert of *Fine Cooking*; and Stephen Michaelides, all of whom make business what it can be, a pleasure. And of course Chef Arno Schmidt, who had the vision to hire me at the Waldorf Astoria so many years ago.

And finally, two Susans: Susan Ginsburg, my wonderful agent and friend, and Susan Wyler, my great editor, for truly caring; and thank you to Christopher Hirsheimer, whose eye turned ideas and emotion into stunning pictures. I have been blessed to work with you all.

❖ Contents

❉ Introduction

"Truly good food can only be made with love," my dear friend Kate reminds me. When your heart is in the process, your hands carry the message into the cutting, the measuring, the stirring, the pouring, the roasting, the baking. Mundane jobs, perhaps, yet somehow they are transformed by this special resonance of feeling, which penetrates the lamb chops and the string beans and the salad and the chocolate cake and feeds us deeply.

In a former life as a professional chef, I spent my days and nights in a kitchen equipped with an amazing batterie of industrial equipment. Now in my kitchen I have a well-used, and well-built, 30-year-old, regular home gas range that sits across from a perfectly fine, but nothing fancy, refrigerator. Lots of old ceramic bowls run around a narrow shelf, which juts out a ways below the ceiling and encircles much of the room. Pots and pans hang everywhere, and jars of dried mushrooms, chiles, beans, and assorted rices and spices, as well as a pair of ancient electric mixers, cover the counters.

My husband says, "There are no surfaces left in this house!" Which is true. But I like my worn kitchen with all its stuff because good things happen there.

Our kitchen is the hub of the house, and from it flows the everyday meals, new creations, and dinners for friends who come to share food and stories around the table. So many meals have been cooked there and so much time spent there with the favorite people in my life that by now the room has an aura of celebration all its own, even when the lights are out and only the low hum of the refrigerator can be heard.

Whatever the occasion, the food I love to make is simple and pure, with a sophistication that doesn't bonk you over the head. I don't hold with any silly torturing of ingredients or any fancy doo-dads on the plate.

Here are my cooking basics

1. Buy the freshest and best ingredients.

2. Combine them so that each genuinely enhances the other.

3. Present the dish without contrivance, letting the natural shapes and colors beguile the eye and the delicious aromas create their magic.

When I tell you I prefer small get-togethers, it might be easy to imagine it's because I had to cook for legions in my restaurant days. But it's really because inviting fewer people means more time with each friend—more time to hear about her life right now, encouraging closeness, getting to know him better.

As for dressing up the house when company comes, I keep it as relaxed as can be. An armful of fresh flowers and music to set the mood are all that's needed. I rely on the warmth of our welcome, the mutual affection, and as much laughter as possible.

How do I accomplish all this since there's only so much time and energy in the day and so many things I want to do in addition to cooking? And, most important, how do I serve wonderful food and still stay a part of the party? Very simple: I cook ahead.

I plan my menus so that every dish can be completely or at least partially done in advance, and I spread the preparation over days and sometimes even weeks. This gives me the leeway I need and lets me comfortably decide how much last-minute cooking I want to do. Here's an example.

In a week with a deadline looming and company coming, I cook or prep something whenever I can fit it in. I whisk together a shallot vinaigrette on one day (which could sit in the refrigerator for weeks); roast and marinate squash on another (to serve at room temperature). I brown the short ribs so they can braise while I work at my desk. I measure the ingredients for chocolate chunk cookies one day and bake them the next. And finally, I mash potatoes with butter and cheese and pack them into a gratin dish, so all they will need is a hot oven to turn them golden and crisp before serving.

This do-ahead dinner (leaving the lettuce to wash that morning and two dishes to reheat that night) suits me perfectly and opens up a whole evening for fun. And though there are plenty of times when I plan a meal with a dish that needs last-minute attention, I can still relax knowing everything else is ready to go.

Freed from the restaurant edict of serving every dish "piping hot" or "ice cold," I serve food warm, or cool, or at room temperature (which actually means about 65° or 70°F). Not only do many dishes taste just as good or better when their heat dissipates or their chill wears off, but it puts less day-of-the-party demand on the oven, and reduces my need to juggle.

When it's time to serve, these do-ahead options give me the knack to pull it all together so much more easily. I can gleefully spoon food into bowls, set it on plates, lay it on platters, or just bring the pot to the table. When the food is arrayed before us, with me at my place and a stack of dishes on my left, I serve my friends with generosity and joy. But when it's time for seconds, it's every man for himself.

The chapters in the book are grouped by traditional courses—such as appetizers, main courses, and side dishes—which make hunting for a new recipe easy and direct. And because my focus is on entertaining, planning the menu is key—and that's the part I find really creative.

I love to conjure up all sorts of dishes, from old favorites or variations on a theme to surprising new ideas. I imagine one dish with another and think about how their tastes and textures will play off one another. I mull over whether I want dinner to be on the delicate side, and therefore more elegant, or more rustic and earthy. But whichever direction the meal takes, for me the process is wonderfully satisfying. And long before I start cooking, I taste it all in my mind and take pleasure from imagining the joy it will give.

To that end, interspersed with the recipe chapters, I've included three sections of menus. Each section contains ideas for categories of dinners, such as Alfresco Menus from the Grill, Simplest Dinner Menus, and Do-Ahead Dinners. And each menu offers my choices for a very doable two- or three-course meal, and then some more ideas *For a Bigger Feast*, in case you wish to be a bit more elaborate.

Use the menus just as they are, or pick and choose and mix and match among the book's recipes as your heart desires, letting the menu suggestions be just that—jumping-off points and ideas to inspire you to create your own dinners—for that's my aim.

COME FOR
DINNER

SOME MENUS FOR MEMORABLE MEALS

Great Home Cooking

O ne of the greatest pleasures of cooking at home is its utter lack of pretense. When I ask friends to come for dinner, I'm inviting them for more than food; I'm welcoming them into my home. Eager to feed them and wrap them in the warmth of friendship, I cook the kind of satisfying dishes I know will nurture and hearten as well as entertain.

I'm likely to have a chicken or two sizzling in the oven turning brown and crisp, or meaty beef short ribs with ginger and garlic braising slowly to succulence. There might be big, meaty lamb shanks turning fork-tender in red wine and a spiced broth sweetened with dates, or old-fashioned meat loaves formed into individual portions, baking to juicy goodness.

Because I love sweets so, there is always a special dessert, plain or fancy. It might be my Buttermilk Cake with Orange Mascarpone Cream and Chocolate Glaze (page 234), which everyone adores, or an assortment of buttery cookies or brownies. I often make an old-fashioned pudding filled with the tartness of lemon or perfumed with ambrosial vanilla.

No matter whether they're foods we remember from childhood or newer creations that please in the same sort of way, there's no mistaking the comfort that home cooking provides. And for me, dinner with friends always turns a house into a home. Here is an assortment of menus that epitomize the best of home cooking for me.

Three Homey Menus

Mini Meat Loaves (*page* 152)

Roasted Carrots with Orange (*page* 180)

Cheese Mashed Potatoes (*page* 200)

Lemon sorbet or fresh fruit

For a Bigger Feast

Hearts of Romaine with Sherry-Basil Dressing to start (*page* 48)

Hot Fudge Sundae instead (*page* 283)

Veal Meatballs with Fresh Dill (*page* 142)

Mesclun with Cucumbers, Mushrooms, and Sweet Onions
(and roasted beets) in Cider Honey Vinaigrette (*page* 42)

Buttered egg noodles or buttered short-grain rice

Chocolate or raspberry sorbet

For a Bigger Feast

Lemon Rice Pilaf with Dill in place of the noodles or rice and
sprinkling the dill over all (*page* 211)

Double Chocolate Cream Cheese Brownies (*page* 246)

Rachel's Shepherd's Pie (*page* 160)

Tossed greens with mustard vinaigrette

Dark Chocolate Chunk Cookies with Macadamia Nuts (*page* 241)

For a Bigger Feast
Roasted Beets with Orange-Balsamic Butter (*page* 175)

Three Falling-off-the-Bone Menus

Lamb Shanks with Red Wine and Green Olives (*page* 162)

Swiss Chard with Browned Onions and Feta Cheese (*page* 184)

Warm flatbreads or buttered rice

Chocolate Mousse (*page* 274)

For a Bigger Feast
Potatoes Fried in Olive Oil with Fresh Garlic Salt and Pepper (*page* 204)
– or –
Cheese Mashed Potatoes in place of the bread or rice (*page* 200)

Braised Beef Short Ribs with Chinese Flavor (*page 166*)

Mashed potatoes (without the cheese) from
Rachel's Shepherd's Pie (*page 160*)

Stir-fried snow peas or cabbage with Chinese black forest mushrooms

Hot Fudge Sundae (*page 283*)

❧

Veal Stew with Mushrooms and Potatoes (*page 168*)

Hearts of Romaine with Sherry-Basil Dressing, using dill,
parsley, or watercress leaves for the basil if it's unavailable (*page 48*)

Chocolate frozen yogurt or sorbet with strawberries, raspberries,
or blackberries

The Simplest Dinner Menus

The menus that follow are for the kind of casual dinners that come close to being last-minute but still leave time to cook something a little special. Think of them for when friends blow into town out of the blue; when you're up to your elbows in work but long for an evening of fun and food at home; or when you run into a friend, get to talking, and hear yourself exclaim, "Why don't you all come to our house for dinner!" Or when you simply want to have friends over to share a meal with the least amount of fuss.

Purchasing an item or two for an hors d'oeuvre or appetizer (see the suggested hors d'oeuvres on pages 286–291), or buying a dessert from a good bakery, makes the doing all the easier, and you can feel comfortable knowing that your delicious homemade cooking will take care of the rest. Remember that spanking-fresh ingredients often need nothing more than a generous seasoning of salt, a grinding of fresh pepper, a dab of sweet butter or drizzle of olive oil, and sometimes a sprinkle of fresh herbs to show off their excellence. If you'd like to do a little more, however, here are six menus to guide you.

Three Seafood Menus

Steamed dumplings or fried wontons or egg rolls (purchased)

Stir-Fried Shrimp with Mint-Ginger Sauce and Mango (*page* 108)

Milk Chocolate Parfait with Strawberries (*page* 269)

❖

Thai-Style Halibut with Lime, Scallions, and Crushed Chiles (*page* 96)

Vegetables with Ginger Butter from Restaurant Leslie (*page* 192)

Steamed jasmine or basmati rice

Berries with fromage blanc or cream (whipped or poured)

For a Bigger Feast
Raspberry (or other fruit) Shortcakes in place of the berries (*page* 264)

❖

Grilled Salmon with Fresh Tomatoes and Basil (*page* 98)

Minty New Potatoes with Summer Herbs, without the basil (*page* 203)

Glazed Berries with Orange, Lemon, and Lime (*page* 248)
— *or* —
Strawberry Sauté (*page* 268)

For a Bigger Feast
Summer Corn Chowder, without its tomato garnish and
not serving new potatoes (*page* 22)

Grilled Vegetables in Asian Vinaigrette (*page* 198)

Blueberry Crisp in place of the berries (*page* 256)

Three Simple Meat Menus

Grilled Pork Chops Teriyaki (*page* 132)

Grilled vegetables and potatoes

Sliced mango and pineapple garnished with berries
– *or* –
Sliced peaches with cream

For a Bigger Feast
Chilled Melon Soup with Lemongrass and Mint (*page* 20)
to start if not serving fruit for dessert

Double Chocolate Cream Cheese Brownies (*page* 246)

Roast Pork with Black Forest Mushrooms (*page* 130)

Stir-fried snow peas with red pepper julienne

Asian noodles (or steamed rice) tossed with butter and
a few drops of sesame oil

Raspberry or orange sorbet

For a Bigger Feast
Add slivered red cabbage to the snow peas and peppers

Sugar Yeast Crisps (*page* 239)
– *or* –
Warm Apple-Walnut Crumble instead of the sorbet (*page* 240)

Lamb Burgers with Chinese Five-Spice Powder and
Slivered Garlic Butter (*page* 140)

Arugula Salad with Yogurt Dressing (*page* 39)

Chocolate ice cream with sliced strawberries

For a Bigger Feast
Turnip Puree with Caraway Seeds, Scallions, and Bacon (*page* 190)
— *or* —
Israeli Couscous with Red Peppers and Shallots (*page* 217)

Brown Sugar Chocolate Sauce for the ice cream (*page* 238)

Just Good Food

Sometimes food refuses to be pigeonholed into a rigid category, and these menus are like that. The dishes cover a range of tastes and styles. Many of them would be appropriate in almost any season. You'll find a small slew of menus for chicken, plus one for lamb chops, and an earthy tortilla, bean, and chile casserole. Each chicken dish has its own signature seasonings, such as smoky Spanish paprika, Indonesian coconut milk with ginger, and one with the quiet notes of pine nuts and honey.

It's food that is a little casual at heart but can easily be turned into something fancier depending on the accompaniments and the dinnerware. The breast of chicken "deviled" with Dijon mustard and the lamb chops resting on a bed of Provençal tomatoes, for example, are more informal when served on pottery plates with a simple accompaniment. But placed on lovely china with a special side dish or two, the dinner becomes instantly elegant with little extra effort on the part of the cook.

Five Chicken Menus

Double Breast of Chicken with Two Mustards (*page* 112)

Roast Zucchini with Herbes de Provence (*page* 196)

Roasted potatoes

Little Chocolate Spice Cakes with Strawberries and
Warm Mocha Sauce (*page* 228)

For a Bigger Feast
French Lentil Soup (*page* 36)
— *or* —
Red and Green Lettuces with Shallot Vinaigrette, Tomatoes,
and Goat Cheese to start (*page* 44)

Mashed Potatoes with Caramelized Onions in place of
the roasted potatoes (*page* 202)

Chicken Cutlets with Fresh Tomato-Shallot Sauce (*page* 114)

Browned Asparagus in Buttery Lemon Sauce (*page* 174)

Rachel's Chocolate Truffle Ice Cream Sundaes with Raspberry Sauce (*page* 280)

For a Bigger Feast
Sliced prosciutto drizzled with extra-virgin olive oil and seasoned
with fresh pepper to start

Caesar Salad with Sun-Dried Tomatoes (*page* 41)

Chicken Breasts Roasted with Honey Pine Nuts, and Thyme (*page* 116)

Baked Acorn Squash with Rosemary-Garlic Butter (*page* 189)

Strawberry Sauté (*page* 268)

For a Bigger Feast
Tender Green Beans with Olive Oil and Thyme (*page* 185)

✤

Broiled Chicken with Coconut Milk, Ginger, and Chiles (*page* 118)

Glazed Carrots with Cardamom (*page* 179)

Buttered couscous with scallions

Lemon or lime sorbet

For a Bigger Feast
Aromatic Yellow Rice in place of the couscous (*page* 210)

Pistachio Sugar Cookies (*page* 244)

✤

Lemon-Garlic Roast Chicken with Smoked Paprika (*page* 124)

Roasted Carrots with Orange (*page* 180)
— or —
Roast Zucchini with Herbes de Provence (*page* 196)

Bitter Greens with Lemon-Anchovy Vinaigrette (*page* 46)

Raspberries with Vanilla Bean Custard (*page* 276)

For a Bigger Feast
Feta Cheese with Tahini and Walnuts to start (*page* 60)
— or —
Mom's Potato Rolls with the main course (*page* 220)

Mediterranean Lamb Dinner

Lamb Chops with Provençal Tomatoes (*page 136*)

Cauliflower with Olives, Anchovies, and Capers, without the olives (*page 181*)

Warm focaccia or herbed grilled or toasted bread

Lemon Cloud Pudding with Blueberries, with raspberries or blackberries (*page 273*)

For a Bigger Feast
Cheese and Black Pepper Pasta to start (*page 59*)
— or —
Potatoes Fried in Olive Oil with Fresh Garlic Salt and Pepper (*page 204*)

Rustic Mexican Meal

Black Bean Tortilla Casserole with Ancho Chiles (*page 170*)

Sliced avocados garnished with lime wedges and fresh cilantro leaves

Fruit sorbet with mango and raspberries

For a Bigger Feast
Sautéed zucchini with corn and jalapeños

Cinnamon sugar cookies sprinkled with cocoa

Soup Dinners

As the nippy breezes of fall settle into the harsh weather of the winter months, there's little better than sitting around the table with friends enjoying a savory soup, particularly when you ladle it, steaming, into bowls right from a tureen or from its pot, plunk right at the table.

All you need are bowls to fit the occasion, like stoneware or pottery, or anything homey and welcoming, big cloth napkins that generously cover your lap, and nice big soupspoons. Just an accompaniment or two make the meal complete, such as a vegetable or salad, bread with character, and of course a terrific, simple dessert.

For me, soup for dinner is the perfect way to entertain when I want to spend an evening with friends and don't want to turn myself inside out with cooking. And how wonderful that this meal-in-a-pot can be made days ahead, since its flavor just keeps getting better as it sits; or even weeks ahead and stashed in the freezer. Soup combines the best of comforts from the kitchen: it's nurturing, it's delicious, and it can conveniently bubble away at the back of the stove while you go about other tasks . . . all done whenever you need it.

Soup Under an Italian Influence

Arugula Salad with Yogurt Dressing (*page 39*)
— *or* —
Caesar Salad with Sun-Dried Tomatoes (*page 41*)

White Bean Soup with Rosemary (*page 28*)

Ice cream, gelato, or sorbet with Pine Nut Cookies (*page 240*)

A Classic Mexican Sopa

Mexican Tortilla Soup (*page 30*)

Corn cooked in butter with a little chopped garlic and
cream (with diced zucchini too, if you want)

Roasted Pineapple with Rum Cream (*page 262*)
— *or* —
Black Skillet Banana Cake with Rich Chocolate Sauce (*page 237*)

Hearty and Comforting

Split Pea Soup with Ham (*page 38*)

Big tossed salad with tomatoes
— *or* —
Swiss Chard with Browned Onions and Feta Cheese (*page 184*)

Sourdough bread

Double Chocolate Cream Cheese Brownies (*page 246*)
— *or* —
Dark Chocolate Chunk Cookies with Macadamia Nuts (*page 241*)

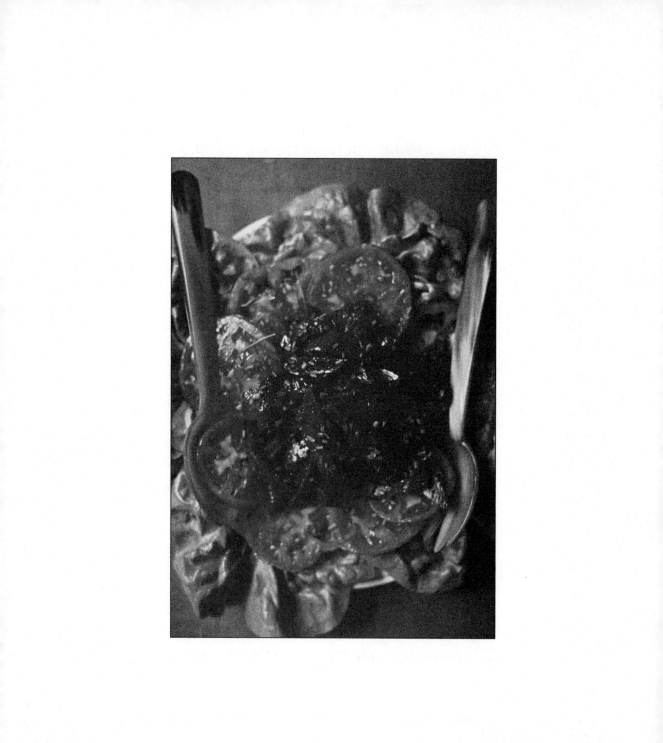

SOUPS, GREEN SALADS, AND OTHER STARTERS

SOUPS

❖ Chilled Melon Soup with Lemongrass and Mint

This simple soup is the ethereal essence of melon suffused with the gingery citrus quality of lemongrass. A cool bowl of it provides a lovely, refreshing beginning to a summer meal. 4 TO 6 SERVINGS

---

2 to 3 lemongrass stalks or 6 slices of fresh ginger, coarsely chopped, plus 8 strips of lemon zest, each about 1 x 2 inches

1/2 cup dry white wine or white vermouth (see page 117)

1 1/2 to 2 tablespoons sugar

1 to 2 ripe melons, such as honeydew, cantaloupe, Galia, or crenshaw

2 to 3 tablespoons freshly squeezed lime juice

Salt and freshly ground white pepper

2 tablespoons sour cream or crème fraîche

1 tablespoon mint leaves, cut into fine strips

1 Trim the lemongrass stalks about 2 inches above the bulbous ends. Peel away the tough outer layers to expose the pale inner cores and very thinly slice enough of the cores to measure 1/4 cup; save any extra for another use.

2 Simmer the lemongrass (or ginger and lemon zest) with the wine and 1 1/2 tablespoons sugar in a very small saucepan set over low heat, covered, for about 5 minutes, stirring occasionally. If the melon isn't sweet enough, add up to 1/2 tablespoon more sugar. Remove the pan from the heat and keep covered.

3 Cut a thin slice off both ends of the melon(s) and stand on a flat end. Placing your knife at the top just behind the rind, cut down with a slight sawing motion to remove a section of rind. Continue cutting in the same fashion until all the rind has been removed. Cut the melons in half, scoop out and discard the seeds, and cut enough into 2-inch chunks to measure 6 cups; save any extra for another use.

4 Place the melon in a blender or food processor (a blender purees more smoothly), strain the lemon-

Do-Ahead Options

◆ Make and refrigerate the syrup up to 2 days ahead.

◆ Make the soup up to a day ahead.

grass syrup into the container, and add 2 tablespoons of lime juice. (All the melon may not fit in the blender at once, but as you puree, the volume decreases and you can add the rest.) Puree the melon until smooth, 1 to 2 minutes, season with salt and up to 1 more tablespoon lime juice, and chill well.

5 Stir the cold soup to reincorporate any solids that have risen to the top and ladle the soup into chilled bowls. Grind a little pepper over the top of each serving. Stir the sour cream or crème fraîche in a small bowl to liquefy it slightly and drizzle over the soup. Sprinkle with the mint and serve good and cold.

❖ Summer Corn Chowder

The fresher and sweeter the corn, the better the chowder, because all you really want to do is highlight the simple beauty of corn. By simmering the kernels in milky cob broth with creamy potatoes, soft sautéed onions, and fresh thyme, you're barely messing with it. If you prefer a meatless chowder, omit the bacon and begin with Step 2. Use 4 tablespoons butter in Step 3. **6 TO 8 SERVINGS**

---

5 strips of bacon

6 ears of fresh corn, husked

4½ cups chicken broth

2 to 3 tablespoons butter

4 medium onions, thinly sliced (3¾ cups)

1 medium red bell pepper, finely diced (1 cup)

12 sprigs of fresh thyme tied with string, plus 2½ teaspoons thyme leaves, for garnish

Salt and freshly ground pepper

3 large garlic cloves, minced

2 tablespoons plus 1 teaspoon flour

2 medium to large boiling potatoes, peeled and cut into ½-inch dice (3 cups)

1½ cups milk

⅓ cup heavy cream (see Note)

Tabasco sauce

Diced tomatoes and minced fresh chives, for garnish

1 In a large skillet, cook the bacon over medium-low heat until the strips are brown and crisp, turning them once, 8 to 10 minutes. Drain the bacon on paper towels and reserve for garnish. Reserve 3 tablespoons of the bacon fat.

2 One at a time, stand the ears of corn on end and cut down each cob to remove the kernels. Then, with the dull side of the knife, scrape down the cobs to release the remaining pulp and milk. Score the cobs as deep as possible with a large knife and snap into 3 to 5 pieces each or chop apart with a cleaver. Place the cobs and chicken broth in a large saucepan, cover the pan, and simmer for 30 minutes. Drain the cobs in a colander set in a larger bowl and reserve 3⅓ cups of the broth (saving or discarding any extra, or adding enough hot water to bring the liquid to 3⅓ cups). Discard the cobs.

3 Heat the reserved bacon fat with the butter in a large pot set over medium heat. Add the onions, bell pepper, and thyme bundle and season lightly with salt and pepper. Cook without letting the vegetables brown until the onions turn translucent, 8 to 10 minutes, stirring frequently and adjusting the heat if necessary. Stir in the garlic and cook for 30 seconds more. Stir in the flour and cook for 1 more minute, stirring constantly. Remove the pot from the heat.

Do-Ahead Options

⬦ Cut the vegetables, potatoes, and corn, and prepare the cob broth up to a day ahead.

⬦ Make the chowder up to 3 days ahead and reheat it over low heat. Garnish when serving.

4 Meanwhile, bring a large pot of generously salted water to a boil over high heat. Add the potatoes and cook at a low boil until they're slightly underdone, about 5 minutes. Drain them in a colander and run cold water over them to stop their cooking. Drain well.

5 Set the pot with the vegetables back over low heat and gradually stir in 3 cups of the chicken-corn broth, reserving the remainder. Increase the heat to medium and bring to a boil, whisking, if necessary, to smooth out any lumps. Reduce the heat to low, partially cover the pot, and simmer until the onions are soft, about 12 minutes. Stir in the corn kernels and pulp, and cook for 2 to 3 minutes more, partially covered, until the kernels are cooked but still a little crunchy. Stir the milk and cream into the soup. Add the potatoes and simmer for 5 minutes more, or until tender.

6 Discard the thyme bundle and puree about 1¼ cups of the chowder in a blender or food processor until smooth, then stir it back into the pot. If the chowder is too thick, add as much of the reserved corn broth as you think it needs. Season with salt, pepper, and Tabasco to taste.

7 Ladle the chowder into a warm tureen or soup bowls. Garnish with tomatoes and crumbled bacon, and sprinkle with thyme leaves and chives. Serve steaming hot.

NOTE: If you prefer a leaner chowder, omit the cream and increase the milk to 1¾ cups.

White Gazpacho with Almonds and Basil

Though not as familiar as the red, white gazpacho is just as terrific in a different way. Genuinely Spanish in origin and usually utterly smooth in consistency, it is generally delicate in taste and often the color of cream. This one, though, turns a pale green from green pepper and basil, has more texture, and is surprisingly feisty with garlic and vinegar. 6 SERVINGS

---

1 cup plus 2 tablespoons dry bread crumbs

1/3 cup whole blanched almonds (see Note)

2 to 3 garlic cloves, sliced

1 large green bell pepper, coarsely chopped (1 cup)

1 large cucumber, peeled, seeded, and sliced (2 1/4 cups), plus 2 tablespoons finely diced cucumber

1/2 cup lightly packed basil leaves, plus more for garnish

4 1/2 tablespoons aged Spanish sherry vinegar or white wine vinegar

3/4 cup extra-virgin olive oil, plus more as desired

Salt and freshly ground white pepper

6 ice cubes

18 red or green seedless grapes, cut in half

1 Preheat the oven to 350°F with a rack in the center. In a small mixing bowl, moisten the crumbs with 1/2 cup plus 1 tablespoon water and let them sit for about 10 minutes. Meanwhile, toast the almonds on a baking sheet in the oven until golden, 8 to 10 minutes. When cool, chop them coarsely.

2 Place the almonds and garlic in a food processor and finely chop. Add the moistened crumbs, green pepper, sliced cucumber, 1/3 cup of the basil, and the vinegar. Process as fine as possible, scraping down the sides of the bowl once, 1 to 2 minutes. With the machine on, gradually add the 3/4 cup oil.

3 Transfer the gazpacho to a large mixing bowl, stir in 1 1/4 to 1 1/2 cups of cold water, or enough to make a light-bodied soup. Season with salt and white pepper, cover, and chill thoroughly.

4 When the gazpacho is cold, taste it for seasoning and add more salt, pepper, and olive oil if you like. Ladle the soup into chilled shallow soup plates and place an ice cube in each; if the bowl is shallow, you will see the cube glisten beautifully. Garnish with the diced cucumber, grape halves, and remaining basil torn into pieces. Serve right away.

Do-Ahead Options

◈ Toast and chop the almonds and cut up the vegetables up to a day ahead.

◈ Make and refrigerate the gazpacho up to 2 days ahead and garnish it when serving.

NOTE: If you don't have blanched almonds, add natural almonds (with the skins on) to a small pot of boiling water. Turn off the heat and let them sit for a minute or two, or until the skin of one easily slips off. Drain and when cool enough to handle, slip off the skins between your fingers and discard them. Let the almonds dry on paper towels for at least 5 minutes before toasting.

Roasted Tomato Gazpacho with Cumin and Garlic Croutons

This cooked tomato gazpacho jumps out of the pack with its sensual richness and haunting flavor. It's perfect, of course, served chilled on a sweltering day, but it's just as good heated up in the fall. And if you have no intention of turning on the oven to roast the tomatoes during the dog days of summer, try grilling them instead. **6 SERVINGS**

- 3 pounds ripe plum tomatoes, rinsed and dried
- 3 cups 1/2-inch dried bread cubes cut from country-style white bread, crusts trimmed
- 1/2 cup plus 2 1/2 tablespoons extra-virgin olive oil
- 3 medium garlic cloves, finely chopped
- 1 1/2 tablespoons aged Spanish sherry or other vinegar, or to taste
- Salt and freshly ground pepper
- 1 generous teaspoon cumin seeds

1 Preheat the oven to 500°F with a rack at the top. Roast the tomatoes in one layer on a large baking pan (or use two) until blistered and very soft, 20 to 30 minutes, depending on their size. Transfer them, and any skins that have popped off, to a bowl to cool. Reduce the oven temperature to 325°F and lower the rack to the center, leaving the door ajar to cool down faster.

2 Meanwhile, toss the bread cubes in a large bowl as you drizzle them with 1 1/2 tablespoons of the olive oil. Spread them out on a cookie sheet and bake, turning with a metal spatula occasionally, until they are light gold, 10 to 12 minutes. Sprinkle the chopped garlic over the croutons, toss to combine as best as possible, and continue baking until the garlic is just beginning to take on color, 2 to 4 minutes. Remove the pan from the oven and let cool.

3 Place the tomatoes and their accumulated juices in a blender or food processor with the remaining 1/2 cup plus 1 tablespoon oil and the vinegar. Puree until the mixture is somewhat smooth but retains a slightly nubby texture, 1 to 2 minutes. Transfer the gazpacho to a large bowl and stir in 2 1/4 cups cold water (it will thicken as it chills). Add salt to taste, cover, and chill.

4 Toast the cumin seeds in a small dry skillet set over very low heat, shaking the pan occasionally, until their aroma begins to rise and they turn a shade darker, 1 to 2 minutes. Remove from the heat.

5 The gazpacho should be lightly but nicely thickened. If it is too thick, stir in up to ¾ cup more cold water. Season with salt and more vinegar, if you like. Ladle the gazpacho into chilled bowls, grind pepper over the top, and garnish with the toasted cumin seeds and garlic croutons. Serve cold with the rest of the croutons on the side.

❖ White Bean Soup with Rosemary

Hearty but not heavy, this bean soup owes its levels of taste to the slow cooking of vegetables and herbs and the flavor imparted by a few chunky pieces of prosciutto. If you keep Parmesan rinds in the freezer or can cut one off a wedge you have in the fridge, slip one or two into the simmering soup to add another subtle, enriching dimension. 8 SERVINGS

---

3 tablespoons butter

2½ tablespoons olive oil

One 6- to 8-ounce piece of prosciutto (cut from the shank end), cut in 2 to 3 pieces, or 1 smoked ham hock

3 medium onions, thinly sliced (2½ cups)

6 medium carrots, peeled and sliced into ½-inch rounds (2 cups)

3 celery stalks, cut into ½-inch pieces (1½ cups)

5 to 6 garlic cloves, chopped

1 cup dried cannellini beans, rinsed and soaked overnight

6 cups chicken broth

1 bay leaf

1 to 2 imported Parmesan rinds, each roughly 2 x 2 inches (optional)

1 loaf of country-style bread, sliced ½-inch thick

1 small head of radicchio, cut in ½-inch pieces (1½ cups)

Salt and freshly ground pepper

1 Melt the butter with 1½ tablespoons of the olive oil in a large, heavy soup pot set over low heat. Add the prosciutto and cook, stirring occasionally, until lightly browned, about 10 minutes. Stir in the onions, carrots, celery, and garlic. Cover and cook over medium heat, stirring occasionally, until the vegetables begin to soften, about 15 minutes.

2 Drain the beans and add them to the pot. Add the broth, bring it to a boil, skim off the froth that rises, and reduce the heat to low. Add the bay leaf and Parmesan rinds, if using them. Partially cover and let the soup simmer about 45 minutes, or until the beans are almost tender. Preheat the oven to 325°F with a rack in the center.

3 Cut enough bread into pieces about 2 x 1½ inches to make 24 croutons. Lightly brush both sides with the remaining 1 tablespoon oil and bake on a cookie sheet until golden, turning them once, 15 to 20 minutes. Set them aside.

4 When the beans are almost tender, add the radicchio and continue simmering, partially covered, 20 minutes more, or until the beans are very tender but still intact. Discard any cheese rinds and the pieces of prosciutto. Puree 1 cup of soup in a blender, then stir it back into the pot; the soup should be lightly thickened but not porridge-like. Add a little more broth, if nec-

1¾ teaspoons minced fresh rosemary, or ¾ teaspoon dried

¼ cup chopped parsley

Freshly grated imported Parmesan cheese

Do-Ahead Options

☞ Cut the vegetables up to a day ahead and bake the croutons up to 3 days ahead. If the croutons have gotten stale, recrisp them in a low oven.

☞ Make the soup up to 5 days ahead or freeze it for up to 2 months.

essary, and season with salt and pepper to taste. (If using a ham hock, cut off the meat and stir it into the soup, and discard the cartilage and bone.)

5 Stir in the rosemary and parsley and ladle the soup into warm bowls. Float 2 croutons on top of each serving, sprinkle with cheese, and serve very hot, with the remaining croutons and grated cheese on the side.

✤ Mexican Tortilla Soup

One of my favorite soups in all the world, tortilla soup, is best of course when served in the context of all things Mexican. But this version is so deeply satisfying that it thrills me far north of the border. And not surprisingly, the richer the chicken broth you use, the better the soup will be. You can double the recipe without any problem and, if you want, let it become dinner on a blustery fall or winter night. For a more authentic flavor, use half vegetable oil and half lard to fry the tortillas. **6 SERVINGS**

---

1 pound ripe tomatoes
(2 medium to large)

3 Mexican dried ancho chiles

6 corn tortillas

½ cup vegetable oil

2 garlic cloves, coarsely
chopped

½ cup thinly sliced onion

6 cups chicken broth

Salt and freshly ground
pepper

1 skinless, boneless chicken
breast (6 to 8 ounces), cut
into thin strips, or 1 cup
bite-size pieces of cooked
chicken

Garnishes of your choice:
diced avocado, sour
cream, grated queso
blanco or Cheddar cheese,
cooked chorizo, coarsely
chopped cilantro

1 Preheat the oven to 450°F with the rack at the top. Set a baking sheet lined with a double layer of paper towels near the stove. Rinse and dry the tomatoes and cut out the cores. Cut the tomatoes in half and place them, cut side down, on a baking sheet. Roast them until soft and blistered or even slightly blackened, about 15 minutes; set aside.

2 Meanwhile, with a paring knife, make a slit along both sides of the chiles, open them up, remove and discard the seeds and stems, and set them aside.

3 Cut the tortillas in half and then across into ½-inch-wide strips. Heat the vegetable oil in a medium skillet set over medium heat. When the oil is hot, fry the tortilla strips in small batches until crisp and golden, about 2 minutes each batch, draining them on the paper towel–lined baking sheet as they're done. Reduce the heat to low, fry the chiles in the same pan for about 5 seconds each side (watch closely so they don't burn), and drain them on the same baking sheet. Reserve 1 tablespoon of oil in the skillet.

4 Place the roasted tomatoes, garlic, onion, and 4 of the chile halves in a blender or food processor and puree until the mixture becomes a smooth sauce, about 2 minutes. Set the skillet with the oil back over very low heat and gently simmer the sauce, stirring

- Cut and fry the tortilla strips up to 2 days ahead and store them at room temperature.
- Prepare the tomato-chile sauce up to 5 days ahead or freeze it.
- Prepare the soup up to 5 days ahead or freeze it for up to 2 months. Add the chicken and garnish it when serving.

occasionally, for 8 to 10 minutes, to thicken it slightly and cook the onion and garlic.

5 Heat the broth in a large pot set over low heat. Stir in the sauce and simmer for about 10 minutes to combine the flavors, skimming off any impurities that rise to the surface. Season with salt and pepper.

6 Meanwhile, crumble the 2 reserved chile halves and place your choice of garnishes into small serving bowls. Stir the chicken strips into the soup (or the cooked chicken) and cook about 1 minute or until just cooked through. Stir in the tortillas, ladle the soup into warm bowls, and serve piping hot, letting each person garnish his or her own.

COCOONING

Snow had begun to fall. I could see it coming down through the panes of the kitchen windows, drifting over the garden and settling on the winter skeleton of the shrubs. The flower stalks and seed heads I'd left for the birds were becoming delineated, too. I knew they would make a spare and lovely drawing against the season's monotone backdrop. Crystalline flakes already lined my trellises in white like the freshly painted rungs of a ladder, and the sound of the quiet that comes with snow was gathering.

"Great," I said, because I was inside making soup—lots of it—in my big black iron pot, and our friends didn't have to come too far. I knew earlier in the day that we would lay a fire in the fireplace, but now I smiled because its warmth would be all the more inviting. I envisioned hors d'oeuvres and drinks in front of the hearth, then dinner in the dining room with its windows backlit by the falling snow. When we were happy and done with food, we'd go back and talk in front of the fire until all that remained were embers, glowing orange and hot.

Rich Chicken Broth

One 4-pound whole chicken or fowl, or a mixture of chicken backs, necks, and trimmings including any roasted bones, if you have any

1 large unpeeled onion, cut into eighths

2 large unpeeled carrots, rinsed, trimmed, and cut into 2-inch pieces

2 celery stalks, cut into 2-inch pieces

2 unpeeled garlic cloves

3 or 4 leek greens (optional)

1 small bunch of parsley stems

1 bay leaf

½ teaspoon dried thyme or a few sprigs of fresh thyme

12 black or white peppercorns

When you make the broth with a whole chicken, its meat becomes falling-apart tender, perfect for garnishing soups such as the Mexican Tortilla Soup on page 30. Just discard the skin, pull the meat from the bones, and tear or cut it into bite-size pieces.
MAKES ABOUT 3½ QUARTS

1 Place the chicken in a large stockpot, cover with cold water by about 2 inches, and set it over high heat. Add the onion, carrots, celery, garlic, leek greens, if using, and parsley stems.

2 When the water boils, immediately reduce the heat to low and skim off the impurities that have risen to the surface. Add the bay leaf, thyme, and peppercorns. Simmer the liquid very slowly, uncovered, for about 4 hours, skimming occasionally, or until the broth is flavorful and the chicken is falling apart.

3 Remove the chicken from the broth and set it aside. Strain the broth and reduce it, if necessary, over medium heat, skimming occasionally, until it's rich and flavorful. Let cool, then refrigerate. The broth will keep up to 5 days, or freeze it for up to 3 months.

❋ Puree of Potato Soup with Dill

This comforting soup has pure potato taste with a subtle, sweet undertone of vegetables.
But it's not a rustic sort of potato soup; it's smoothly elegant and perfectly completed by
crunchy, buttery rye croutons—and/or the shreds of onion from Chewy Red Onions,
page 34. **8 FIRST-COURSE SERVINGS**

---

4 tablespoons butter

4 medium onions, thinly sliced
(4 cups)

2 medium carrots, peeled
and thinly sliced (2/3 cup)

1/3 small fennel bulb or 1
small celery stalk, thinly
sliced (2/3 cup)

4 large garlic cloves, chopped

2 1/2 pounds boiling
potatoes, peeled and
thinly sliced (6 cups)

7 cups chicken broth

1 large bay leaf

1/2 teaspoon dried thyme

4 slices of rye or sourdough
bread

2 tablespoons olive oil

Salt and freshly ground white
pepper

1 1/2 to 2 tablespoons
chopped fresh dill or
fennel greens

Do-Ahead Options

- ❧ Cut the vegetables up to a day
  ahead.
- ❧ Bake the croutons up to 3 days
  ahead; reheat to recrisp, if necessary
- ❧ Make the soup up to 5 days
  ahead or freeze up to 2 months.

1 Melt the butter in a large, heavy soup pot set over
  medium heat. Add the onions, carrots, fennel, and
garlic; cover and cook, stirring occasionally, until the
onions begin to turn translucent, about 10 minutes.

2 Stir in the potatoes. Add the broth and bring the
  liquid just to a boil, then reduce the heat to low.
Add the bay leaf and thyme, and continue to simmer,
partially covered, until the potatoes and vegetables
are very tender, 20 to 25 minutes. Meanwhile, preheat the oven to 325°F with a rack in the center.

3 Trim off the bread crusts and cut the slices into 3/4-
  inch cubes—you should have about 2 cups. Place
them in a bowl and drizzle with olive oil as you toss
them. Spread out in a single layer on a cookie sheet and
bake until golden and crisp, turning them occasionally
with a metal spatula, 15 to 20 minutes. Set aside.

4 Discard the bay leaf and puree the soup in batches as necessary in a blender or food processor (a
blender gives smoother results) until very smooth;
return it to its cooking pot. The soup should have good
body but not be porridge-like. If it's too thick, stir in
additional broth or water. Reheat the soup over low
heat and season it generously with salt and pepper.

5 Stir in the dill or fennel green to taste and serve
  the soup piping hot in a warm tureen or bowls
with some of the croutons scattered over the top and
the rest on the side.

Chewy Red Onions

2 medium red onions

Salt and freshly ground pepper

⅔ cup olive oil

When you simmer a small heap of sliced red onions in olive oil, they turn so sweet and chewy you could almost call them candied. The oil becomes deeply flavorful, too, and between the two of them, there are countless ways to use them. (For some ideas, see page 35.) The onions can sit at room temperature for up to a week and the oil for who knows how long. MAKES ABOUT ½ CUP

1 Slice the ends off the onion, peel, and cut it in half lengthwise. Lay the halves flat side down and slice enough ¼-inch thick to fill 2 somewhat packed cups, saving any extra for another use.

2 Place the onion in a heavy medium skillet set over medium-low heat and salt it generously. Stir in the olive oil and cook slowly, pressing the onions into the oil and stirring occasionally until light gold, 20 to 30 minutes; reduce the heat at any point if they begin to brown too rapidly.

3 Continue to cook, stirring frequently, until they become deeply golden and translucent, about 5 minutes more, watching closely at this point (see Note).

4 Drain the onions in a strainer set over a bowl and let cool. Pepper to taste and store the onions and oil separately at room temperature.

NOTE: Once I cooked these onions several minutes too long and they quickly turned from golden brown to deep brown, almost black. They weren't ruined but were crisply chewy with a definite, but pleasing, charred quality.

USES FOR
CHEWY RED ONIONS

The onions and their oil make a great garnish or flavoring for lots of simple foods. Here are some ideas:

USING THE ONIONS AND OIL TOGETHER

- Baked potatoes drizzled with the oil and topped with onions

- Pasta tossed with the oil, grated Romano cheese, onions, and herbs

- Cooked grains such as rice or couscous cooked in the oil and sprinkled with onions

- Steak or burgers, veal, pork, lamb, chicken breasts, salmon, or tuna moistened with the oil, grilled or broiled, and topped with onions and a drizzle of oil

USING THE ONIONS ALONE

- Stirred into yogurt, sour cream, and feta, goat, or blue cheese for a dip

- As a garnish for soups, Caesar Salad (see page 41) and other tossed salads, vegetable purees like carrot or turnip (see page 190), or pastas with a cream or tomato sauce

USING THE OIL ALONE

- Brushed on grilled bread (or for croutons) with or without herbs

- For sautéing meat or fish, potatoes, and vegetables

- For cooking the vegetables or browning the meat in a soup or stew

- For frying eggs

French Lentil Soup

There's nothing French about this soup except the lentils—the small, green-brown legumes with a disc-shaped physique. Even when tender they hold their shape, and in your mouth they give themselves over with a soft pop and a rich, distinctive taste. There's just enough curry powder to deepen the flavor, but not enough to make it taste "curried." 6 TO 8 SERVINGS

---

2 tablespoons butter

2 medium onions, thinly sliced (2 cups)

1 small celery stalk, cut into ³/₄-inch pieces (¹/₂ cup)

3 to 4 large garlic cloves, coarsely chopped

2 teaspoons curry powder

1 cup canned crushed tomatoes or chopped, canned plum tomatoes

1 cup French lentils (*lentilles de Puy,* available in some supermarkets, specialty stores, and by mail order), rinsed and drained

3 cups chicken or vegetable broth

1 bay leaf

¹/₄ cup coarse bulgur wheat (optional)

Salt and freshly ground pepper

1¹/₂ to 2 tablespoons freshly squeezed lemon juice

¹/₂ cup sour cream, crème fraîche, or plain yogurt, for garnish

¹/₃ cup thinly sliced scallions

1 Melt the butter in a large soup pot set over medium heat. Stir in the onions, celery, and garlic; cover the pot and cook the vegetables without browning for about 5 minutes, stirring occasionally. Stir in the curry powder and cook, stirring, for about 30 seconds. Add the tomatoes, raise the heat to high, and cook for 1 to 2 minutes more. Stir the lentils into the pot.

2 Add the broth and 2 cups water, and bring to a simmer. Add the bay leaf, partially cover the pot, and simmer until the lentils are almost tender, about 30 minutes.

3 Stir in the bulgur wheat, if using it, and continue to simmer, partially covered, until the lentils are tender and the bulgur is tender-firm, about 10 minutes more. (If the soup is too thick, add a little more broth.) Season the soup generously with salt and pepper.

4 Stir up to 2 tablespoons lemon juice into the soup and serve it steaming hot in a warm tureen or bowls. Stir the sour cream to liquefy it slightly and drizzle about 1 tablespoon over the top of each serving. Give each a good grind of pepper, sprinkle with scallions, and serve very hot.

VARIATION
Lentil Stew

This lentil soup started out life as a stew. Looking to make a simple, earthy, meatless meal one evening, I decided I would play around with lentils and bulgur wheat, knowing I wanted to flavor the dish with tomato and curry. (My daughter Rachel had inspired me by saying she was making chicken curry for dinner with lots of tomato.) To my delight, the stew was rich and earthy, and really good.

So, if you'd like lentil stew, prepare the soup as directed but use 3 cups of broth diluted with 1½ cups water and increase the bulgur to ½ cup. Finish it just like the soup with the lemon juice and garnishes.

HOW TO SLICE AN ONION

You might be wondering why I'm bothering to tell you how to slice an onion since it seems like a no-brainer. But in a professional kitchen we have a technique that's safe and efficient, and just as doable for home cooks. Here's the most efficient and safest way to peel and slice an onion:

First, slice off about ½ inch from both ends. Make a cut lengthwise through the papery skin and the first layer, going from one trimmed end to the other. Slip your fingers into the cut to get under the first layer and peel it off in one circular piece.

Stand the onion on end and cut it in half from top to bottom. Lay the halves flat side down and cut them lengthwise along the natural lines that run along the top; they'll fall into even, thin slices. For short lengths, cut each half across its width before slicing.

❖ Split Pea Soup with Ham

When done, this soup is satiny in texture, lush with chunks of tender, smoky meat, and rich with the taste of peas. But before this happens, a nice amount of onions, celery, carrots, and garlic are slowly simmered in butter (or olive oil) to coax out their natural sweetness. Then the ham, peas, and broth follow, and they all bubble together at a leisurely pace. It's enough soup for a small army, but if you haven't invited one, you can freeze the rest or just make half a recipe. **8 TO 10 MAIN-COURSE SERVINGS**

---

3 tablespoons butter or olive oil

2 medium-large onions, chopped (2½ cups)

2 medium carrots, peeled and thinly sliced (¾ cup)

3 celery stalks, thinly sliced (1⅔ cups)

4 to 5 garlic cloves, smashed and peeled

1½ to 1¾ pounds smoked pork shoulder butt, cut into 2-inch chunks (available in supermarket meat section)

1 pound green split peas

3½ cups chicken broth

1 large bay leaf

1 teaspoon dried thyme

Freshly ground pepper

Do-Ahead Options

❧ Cut the vegetables and ham up to a day ahead; refrigerate them separately.

❧ Make the soup up to 5 days ahead or freeze it for up to 2 months. As the soup sits it thickens, so add more water when it needs it.

1 Melt the butter (or heat the olive oil) in a large pot set over low to medium heat. Stir in the onions, carrots, celery, and garlic; cover the pot and cook the vegetables without browning until the onions begin to turn translucent, about 10 minutes, stirring occasionally. Stir in the ham and cook, uncovered, stirring occasionally, until its surfaces look moist and slightly swollen, 2 to 4 minutes.

2 Rinse and drain the peas (don't rinse them until the last minute or they'll stick together) and stir them into the ingredients, coating them with the fat and any juices, 1 minute. Add the broth and 3½ cups hot water. Stir, increase the heat to high, and bring to a boil. Immediately reduce the heat to low, skim off the froth, and add the bay leaf and thyme. Gently simmer the soup, partially covered, until the peas are falling apart and look sludgy, about 1 hour and 15 minutes.

3 Remove the soup from the heat and, using tongs or a slotted spoon, transfer the ham to a plate and cover it. Discard the bay leaf and proceding in batches, puree the soup in a blender until satiny smooth, returning it to the cooking pot. Stir the ham back into the soup and reheat over low heat. Season with pepper and serve good and hot.

GREEN SALADS

❖ Arugula Salad with Yogurt Dressing

Creamy and slightly tangy, yogurt dressing brings out the best in peppery arugula. And amazingly, you can dress the salad, then refrigerate it overnight, and it will still be crisp for lunch the next day (perfect for when you have leftovers). The dressing is also good as a sauce, spooned over sliced tomatoes, cooked potatoes, chicken breasts, or fillets of sole or red snapper. **6 SERVINGS**

2 tablespoons freshly squeezed lemon juice

2 teaspoons Dijon mustard, preferably French

¼ cup olive oil

½ cup plain yogurt

Salt and freshly ground pepper

2 teaspoons chopped mixed fresh herbs, such as chives, tarragon, parsley, basil

12 very loosely packed cups arugula, mesclun, or other salad greens, washed and dried (see page 40)

1 Place the lemon juice in a small bowl, whisk in the mustard until smooth, and gradually whisk in the olive oil to make a lightly thickened vinaigrette. Gradually whisk in the yogurt 1 tablespoon at a time to make a slightly thick dressing. Season generously with salt and pepper and stir in the herbs.

2 Place the greens in a large salad bowl and toss with enough dressing to lightly coat the leaves.

Do-Ahead Option
◆ Refrigerate the dressing for up to a week.

Roasted Beet and Tomato Salad

Roasted beets in vinaigrette set on a bed of sliced summer tomatoes make a glistening jewellike salad. I prefer to cut the beets into somewhat thick little sticks, but they're just as pretty sliced into rounds, if you'd rather. When you've peeled, cut, and dressed the beets beforehand, this pretty salad takes only a few minutes to pull together. 6 SERVINGS

---

2 to 3 large roasted beets (page 176), **peeled and cut into sticks about 1½ x ⅜ inches**

⅔ cup Shallot Vinaigrette (page 44)

Salt and freshly ground pepper

8 large Boston or red-tipped lettuce leaves

3 large ripe tomatoes, sliced

Torn fresh basil leaves or minced chives, for garnish

Do-Ahead Options

- Make the Shallot Vinaigrette up to 2 weeks ahead.
- Roast the beets up to 5 days ahead. Refrigerate them in their skins. Peel, cut, and toss them in the vinaigrette up to a day ahead.

1 Place the beets in a large bowl and toss with 2 to 3 tablespoons Shallot Vinaigrette, or enough to coat and flavor them nicely. Season with salt and pepper to taste.

2 Lay the lettuce leaves on a platter so their frilly ends make an attractive border all around. Arrange the tomato slices on top so each slice overlaps. Then mound the beets in the center and sprinkle both the beets and tomatoes with basil or chives. Serve the salad right away, with the remaining vinaigrette on the side for spooning over each serving.

HOW TO WASH LETTUCE AND OTHER LEAFY GREENS

Washing lettuce (or greens like chard or spinach) seems easy enough, and it is, but the most effective way to do it is in a clean sink or a huge bowl. When the leaves float on top of a large amount of water you can plunge them up and down with your hands, letting the grit drop to the bottom. When you lift the leaves out after letting them rest for a few minutes, the sediment remains at the bottom. Sometimes, depending on how dirty the leaves are (and how crinkly—which makes good hiding places), it's necessary to wash them more than once, using fresh water each time.

✤ Caesar Salad with Sun-Dried Tomatoes

Caesar salad is one of life's basic needs. I find it nigh to impossible to ignore its siren call: the promise of crunchy leaves of romaine lettuce slicked with punchy lemon-garlic dressing, then gentrified with freshly grated imported Parmesan cheese. Serve it with restraint as a traditional first course for dinner or pile on big plates for lunch, gussied up, if you want, with smoked mozzarella and Chewy Red Onions (page 34). **6 FIRST-COURSE SERVINGS**

---

1 loaf French baguette or Italian bread

¾ cup olive oil

3 heads of romaine lettuce

2 tablespoons plus 1 teaspoon freshly squeezed lemon juice

1 tablespoon Dijon mustard, preferably French

1½ teaspoons Worcestershire sauce

2 teaspoons coarsely chopped garlic

Salt and freshly ground pepper

⅔ cup freshly grated imported Parmesan cheese

9 pieces sun-dried tomatoes, drained and quartered

Do-Ahead Options

✤ Bake the croutons up to 3 days ahead and recrisp them in a low oven if they've gotten a little stale.

✤ Make the vinaigrette up to 2 weeks ahead and take it out of the refrigerator an hour before using.

1. Preheat the oven to 325°F with the rack in the center. Cut 12 slices of bread about ½ inch thick on the diagonal, saving the rest for another use. Brush both sides of the slices with 2½ tablespoons of the olive oil and bake them on a cookie sheet, turning once, until crisp and golden, 15 to 20 minutes. Set them aside.

2. Meanwhile, remove the dark green outer leaves of the lettuce (saving them for another use). Cut or tear enough of the crisp, lighter colored inner leaves into pieces to measure 11 to 12 lightly packed cups and wash and dry them (see page 40).

3. In a blender, briefly combine the lemon juice, mustard, Worcestershire, and garlic. With the machine still running, gradually add the remaining olive oil to make a somewhat thick dressing. (Or finely chop the garlic and whisk it in a bowl with all the ingredients except the oil, then gradually whisk in the oil. It will make a thinner dressing.) Season with salt and pepper and set it aside.

4. Place the lettuce in a very large salad bowl, spoon the dressing over the top, toss to evenly coat the leaves, sprinkle with cheese, and toss again. Serve the salad right away with 2 croutons next to each, and place the sun-dried tomatoes on top.

Mesclun with Cucumbers, Mushrooms, and Sweet Onions in Cider Honey Vinaigrette

The tiny lettuces that make up mesclun are brought to life by this lightly honeyed dressing. In addition to the vegetables that are already in the salad, sometimes I toss in roasted beets as well. Their taste ties in with the honey and their glistening garnet color looks so pretty with the red lettuces in the mix. **6 SERVINGS**

2 tablespoons apple cider vinegar

1 tablespoon honey

1 teaspoon minced fresh rosemary

⅓ cup olive oil

Salt and freshly ground pepper

15 cups very lightly packed mesclun, washed and dried (see Note)

18 thin slices peeled cucumbers

3 large white mushrooms, thinly sliced

½ cup Vidalia or red onion, cut into small dice

Do-Ahead Option

◈ Refrigerate the vinaigrette for up to 3 weeks and take it out at least 30 minutes before using.

1 Whisk together the vinegar, honey, and rosemary in a small bowl until smooth. Gradually whisk in the olive oil and season with salt and pepper to taste.

2 Place the mesclun in a large salad bowl and add the cucumbers, mushrooms, and onion. Drizzle with enough of the vinaigrette and toss to lightly coat the leaves; save any leftover for another use. Serve right away.

NOTE: Even though many mesclun mixtures tout themselves as prewashed, I do it again to rehydrate the leaves, which can be slightly wilted (and to pick out any in sorry shape). After washing and drying, I refrigerate the mixture for at least 1 hour so the leaves will crisp up nicely.

❋ Maureen's Garden Salad

My friend Maureen makes the loveliest salad from her garden. She sends her husband, Mel, out with scissors to harvest tender, young lettuces like arugula, Bibb, and red leaf and handfuls of herbs like basil, dill, chives, and two kinds of parsley. (Mel tells me he cuts only the dill with the scissors, plucking everything else carefully by hand.) The leaves are so beautiful, only their best olive oil and vinegar are allowed to dress them. **6 SERVINGS**

5½ to 6 cups very lightly packed mixed Bibb or Boston and red leaf lettuces torn into pieces

3 cups arugula, long stems trimmed

1½ cups very lightly packed watercress, coarse stems trimmed

3 cups lightly packed mixed herbs, such as basil and mint leaves, flat and curly parsley, small dill sprigs, and chives cut into 1-inch lengths

1 tablespoon aged balsamic or Spanish sherry vinegar

3 tablespoons extra-virgin olive oil

Salt and freshly ground pepper

1 Wash the lettuces, arugula, watercress, and herbs together (see page 40) and let them soak while you prepare the vinaigrette.

2 Place the vinegar in a small bowl. Gradually whisk in the olive oil and season with salt and pepper to taste, and more vinegar or oil, if you like. Set the vinaigrette aside.

3 Dry the lettuces and herbs thoroughly and place them in a large salad bowl. Whisk the vinaigrette to recombine, spoon it over the greens, toss gently until all the leaves are lightly coated, and serve the salad right away.

Do-Ahead Option

◇ Prepare the vinaigrette up to 5 days ahead and store it at room temperature.

Red and Green Lettuces with Shallot Vinaigrette, Tomatoes, and Goat Cheese

This is my favorite salad born at Restaurant Leslie, my tiny, grandly rustic bistro on Cornelia Street in New York's Greenwich Village. We tossed big red-tipped and green lettuce leaves in a vinaigrette of balsamic vinegar, good olive oil, and handfuls of minced shallots, then showered the salad with chunks of snowy goat cheese. At the end of each dinner service, when the customers had gone, the staff and I devoured a huge communal bowl of the salad. When the restaurant shut its doors and I moved on to other kitchens, the salad came with me.

There are two important things to know for this vinaigrette: cut the shallots into tiny pieces with a sharp knife—chopping or processing them makes them taste unpleasantly strong (see page 45), and let the vinaigrette rest in the refrigerator for at least 2 days so that "the shallots become almost cooked by the vinegar," as James Beard put it, after munching on this salad. **6 SERVINGS**

¼ **cup balsamic vinegar**

⅔ **cup plus 1 tablespoon extra-virgin olive oil**

1 large garlic clove, lightly crushed and peeled

⅓ **cup finely diced shallots, about** ⅛ **inch (see page 45)**

¼ **teaspoon coarsely ground black pepper**

Salt

2 large ripe tomatoes

15 cups lightly packed mixed green and red lettuces, such as Boston, red leaf, Bibb, radicchio, and watercress, washed and dried (see page 40)

1 Place the vinegar in a medium bowl and gradually whisk in the olive oil. Stir in the garlic, shallots, pepper, and salt to taste. Cover the vinaigrette and refrigerate for at least 2 days. Let return to room temperature before serving.

2 Cut each tomato into 9 slices. Place 3 slices on each of 6 chilled plates at 12, 4, and 8 o'clock positions.

3 Place the lettuces in a large salad bowl. Whisk the dressing to recombine it as much as possible. Drizzle about ½ cup over the greens and toss to coat. (Refrigerate the remaining vinaigrette for future use.) Place the salad on the plates so that the tomato slices peek out. Scatter the goat cheese over the top and serve right away.

1¼ cups firm, tangy goat cheese in ½-inch chunks (about 6 ounces)

Do-Ahead Option

✧ The vinaigrette needs to be made at least 2 days ahead, but it can be refrigerated for up to 2 months. Take it out of the refrigerator at least 30 minutes before using it.

HOW TO DICE SHALLOTS AND ONIONS

Chopping shallots and onions with a dull knife is more like hammering them into submission than cutting them. This bludgeoning, though well meant, makes them taste somewhat like gasoline. To avoid this sad start, use a sharp knife and follow these steps for dicing shallots and onions:

1. Cut a thin slice off the top and bottom of the shallot or onion.

2. Score through the skin and first layer, then peel and discard them (or save for a broth).

3. Cut the shallot or onion lengthwise in half and lay the halves cut side down, parallel to you.

4. Hold the top of one (so it doesn't slide) and, starting from the bottom, make horizontal cuts at equal intervals (⅛ to ¼ inch or wider, depending on the size dice you want), cutting up to but not through the end.

5. From the top, cut down but not through the end at ⅛- to ¼-inch (or wider) intervals.

6. Finally, cut crosswise at ⅛- to ¼-inch (or wider) intervals and watch it fall into dice. Cut the end into small pieces and repeat the process with the other half.

As you can see, the size of the dice is determined by the width of the cuts. Once you get the hang of it, it's easier to do than to read about.

Bitter Greens with Lemon-Anchovy Vinaigrette

My new appreciation for anchovies was sparked in Rome, where I ate one of their favorite winter greens, puntarelle (see page 47), dressed in a brazen anchovy–olive oil mix. While I'd never been a fan of the salty little fish except as a kind of "you'll never know it's there" enrichment, it worked in that salad because it was so well balanced by lemon and the vigor of the greens. On our side of the Atlantic, try the vinaigrette with bitter greens, which can also hold their own.

2 medium Belgian endive

1¾ teaspoons anchovy paste, or 3 to 4 anchovy fillets, chopped then smeared smooth with the flat side of a knife

1 medium garlic clove, crushed and smeared to a paste (see page 47)

4 teaspoons freshly squeezed lemon juice

¼ cup extra-virgin olive oil

Salt and freshly ground pepper

9 to 10 cups loosely packed mixed bitter greens, such as watercress, radicchio, and frisée torn into small pieces, washed and dried (see page 40)

Grape or cherry tomatoes (optional)

1 Cut the endive in half lengthwise, lay the halves flat, and slice them into long strips about ½ inch wide. Wash, drain, and dry them well. Place in a large salad bowl.

2 Whisk the anchovy, garlic, and lemon juice together in a small bowl. Gradually whisk in the olive oil to make a slightly thickened vinaigrette and season with salt and pepper.

3 Add the mixed greens to the endive and toss them with enough vinaigrette to coat. Serve the salad right away, garnished with tomatoes if you like, and grind more pepper on top of each.

WHAT IS PUNTARELLE?

Puntarelle vaguely resembles a bunch of celery (before it's cut into spearlike strips for salad). It has the fleshy, succulent bitterness of Belgian endive, only with a lot more character. Its availabilty in the United States is limited.

HOW TO MAKE GARLIC PASTE

Chopped garlic is easily turned into a paste by sprinkling it generously with coarse salt, then smearing it repeatedly with a large knife held at a slight angle to the chopping board.

HOW TO BUY AND STORE WATERCRESS

Buy the greenest watercress you can find; reject any bunches with yellowing leaves and broken stems.

A lot of markets don't know how—or don't take the time—to store watercress properly, and yet it's so simple. At home, merely submerge the bunch leaves down in a bowl of cold water, enclose the whole deal in the plastic bag you brought the watercress home in (to keep the stems moist), and put it in the refrigerator. Depending on its state when you bought it, the watercress will be fine for 3 or 4 days.

Hearts of Romaine with Sherry-Basil Dressing

The satisfying crunch of crisp inner leaves of romaine lettuce makes the perfect counterpoint for this light and creamy basil-infused dressing. 6 SERVINGS

½ cup less ½ tablespoon extra-virgin olive oil

6½ tablespoons mayonnaise

3 tablespoons aged Spanish sherry vinegar (available in some supermarkets, specialty stores, and by mail order) or other wine vinegar

Salt and freshly ground pepper

3 tablespoons finely diced shallots (see page 45)

1 small garlic clove, minced

¼ cup fresh basil, torn into bite-size pieces

3 hearts of romaine lettuce or whole heads

1 Place the olive oil, mayonnaise, and vinegar in a blender or food processor and combine them on low speed until smooth and creamy, about 1 minute. Pour the dressing into a bowl, season it with salt and pepper, and stir in the shallots, garlic, and basil. Cover and refrigerate until ready to use or for at least 10 minutes to allow the basil flavor to permeate the dressing.

2 Meanwhile, if you have only whole heads of romaine, remove the dark green, coarse outer leaves, saving them for another use, to reach the lighter colored, crisp ones at the core. Trim and discard the root ends. Figuring six to seven medium leaves per person, separate enough of the leaves. Wash and dry them well (see page 40).

3 Arrange the leaves on plates slightly overlapping, stir the dressing to recombine if it has separated, and drizzle it over the lettuce. Grind a little pepper over the top of each salad and serve right away.

Do-Ahead Option

◆ Refrigerate the dressing for up to a week. If it has separated, whisk it well to recombine, but either way, it will still taste fine.

OTHER STARTERS

✤ Avocados Stuffed with Tropical Fruit and Berries

On a frigid day when I was longing to knock back rum punches under a leafy canopy on a tropical beach, instead I tossed the usual vinaigrette suspects of mustard, vinegar, and olive oil (with a little honey) into a blender with raspberries and came up with a creamy vinaigrette for fruits destined for a short life in the cavity of an avocado. It was great to look at, tasted fresh and lush, and was perfect as a starter or for brunch. **8 SERVINGS**

⅔ cup fresh raspberries

2½ teaspoons Dijon mustard, preferably French

2 tablespoons balsamic vinegar

1 tablespoon honey

½ cup olive oil

Salt and freshly ground pepper

2½ cups mixed berries, such as blueberries, sliced strawberries, and raspberries or blackberries

1 cup peeled diced tropical fruit, such as mango, papaya, cherimoya, pineapple, kiwi, or melon

4 ripe avocados, preferably Hass variety

Do-Ahead Option

✎ Prepare the raspberry dressing up to 4 days ahead, taking it out of the refrigerator about 15 minutes before dressing the fruit.

1 Puree the ⅔ cup raspberries with the mustard, vinegar, honey, and olive oil in a blender until smooth, thick, and creamy, about 1 minute. Push the dressing through a strainer to remove the seeds, season with salt and pepper, and set it aside.

2 Place the mixed berries and fruit in a large bowl. Gently fold in enough dressing to coat them lightly and transfer the remainder to a sauceboat. Cut the avocados in half, discard the pits, and slice a sliver off the bottom of each so they sit flat. Season lightly with salt and pepper and set them on plates or a platter. Spoon the fruit into the cavities, letting it overflow attractively. Serve with the remaining dressing on the side.

Artichokes with Roasted Red Pepper and Olive Dip

In our house, we adore artichokes for their singular yet elusive flavor—part asparagus, part nut, part smoke, all pleasure. Some of their spell, I'm sure, lies in how they're eaten: biting and scraping off the nubs from each leaf in a steady, tantalizing progression as you get closer and closer to the prize: a thick, fleshy saucer of a bottom with thrilling, concentrated taste. Not to be outdone, the dip is also excellent drizzled over grilled shrimp, salmon, or chicken and as a sauce for roast pork. **6 SERVINGS**

---

6 large globe artichokes

3 thin slices of lemon

1 bay leaf

1 cup coarsely chopped roasted red bell peppers (see Note and page 63)

3 tablespoons coarsely chopped Piquillo peppers (optional; see Note and page 51)

2 generous tablespoons Dijon mustard, preferably French

½ cup plus 1 tablespoon extra-virgin olive oil

Freshly squeezed lemon juice or wine vinegar, if needed

Salt and freshly ground pepper

2 generous tablespoons coarsely chopped pitted ripe Mediterranean olives, such as Alphonso, Kalamata, or Gaeta (see page 51)

Tabasco sauce, if needed

1 Set a pot of generously salted water large enough to hold all the artichokes over high heat with the lemon slices and bay leaf. Meanwhile cut off a 1-inch section from the top of each artichoke with a serrated knife and cut the stems flush with the bases. Cut off the thorny end of each leaf with scissors and set the artichokes aside.

2 When the water reaches a boil, add the artichokes. Cover and cook at a low boil for 20 to 25 minutes, depending on their size. They are done when a leaf pulls out with very slight resistance.

3 Place the roasted red peppers and Piquillo peppers, if using them, with the mustard and olive oil in a blender or food processor. Puree until thick and somewhat smooth, about 2 minutes, scraping down the sides once or twice. (If using freshly roasted peppers, you may want to add a few drops of lemon juice or vinegar to give them a little edge.) Season the dip with salt and pepper, transfer it to a bowl, stir in the olives and, if not using Piquillo peppers, add a few drops of Tabasco, then set aside.

4 When the artichokes are done, drain them upside down in a colander. As soon as they are

Do-Ahead Option

⇨ The dip can be prepared up to 4 days ahead and the artichokes up to 1 day. Take them both out of the refrigerator a good hour before serving.

cool enough to handle, gently squeeze their sides to remove excess water. Serve hot, warm, or at room temperature, on plates with a spoonful of dip next to each or in individual tiny bowls. Place several empty bowls on the table for the discarded leaves.

NOTE: If you don't have Piquillo peppers, increase the roasted peppers to 1 cup plus 3 tablespoons. Also, jarred roast peppers vary greatly in quality. Look for ones that are very red, appear firm, and don't have citric acid listed on the label.

HOW TO PIT OLIVES

Press the flat side of a large knife on top of a few olives at a time and exert a little pressure until they split open enough to pull out the pits. The softer flesh of the purple and black ones make them a little more accommodating than the green ones, but either way it's simple to do.

SPANISH PIQUILLO PEPPERS

Spanish Piquillo peppers are a gorgeous cardinal red with a charming triangular shape and remarkable depth of flavor—sweet with a touch of heat. In Spain they are roasted over a wood fire and stored in their own juices. Luckily, we can buy them here in cans and jars in specialty stores and by mail order. For mail order sources, see page 296.

❖ Baked Vegetable Antipasto

This dish was inspired by the vegetables I tasted in Italy, which were never foolishly dressed up unsuitably. Simply seasoned, they rang with their own flavor. Our peppers, broccoli, onions, and mushrooms, too, seem to develop greater taste when baked with fruity olive oil, a bit of vinegar, and eaten at room temperature.

8 SERVINGS

---

2 large green bell peppers

2 large red bell peppers

2 large stalks of broccoli

1 medium to large red onion

4 very large white mushrooms, or 32 button white or cremini mushrooms, rinsed, dried, and quartered, if large

Salt and freshly ground pepper

½ cup extra-virgin olive oil

2 teaspoons balsamic vinegar

3 tablespoons plus 1 teaspoon red wine vinegar

8 to 10 sprigs of flat-leaf parsley or mint, leaves picked, washed, and dried

1 Preheat the oven to 375°F with the rack in the center.

2 Cut the peppers in half lengthwise and discard the stems, seeds, and ribs. Trim the broccoli stems 1 to 2 inches below the crowns so that the head stays in one piece, saving or discarding the stems (see page 178). Cut each head into two 4-inch florets, reserving any extra for another use. Peel and cut the onion into quarters (leaving a little of the root end to hold them together) to form wedges about 2 inches wide at the thickest part.

3 Place the peppers cut side up along with the other vegetables, also grouped by kind, in one layer in a heavy roasting pan or other ovenproof baking pan. (They should bake somewhat close together so the pan juices won't evaporate.) Season generously with salt and pepper, then drizzle with olive oil, balsamic vinegar, and 2 tablespoons of the red wine vinegar.

4 Cover the pan tightly with foil and bake until the vegetables are almost tender when pierced with a wooden skewer or fork, 18 to 25 minutes. Remove the foil, tip the juices out of the peppers into the pan, turn the broccoli over, stir the mushrooms once, and bake, uncovered, until they are tender but still firm, 5 to 10 minutes more. If they have browned a little, all the better.

5 Transfer the vegetables to a platter and reserve the pan and juices. Stir the remaining 1 tablespoon plus 1 teaspoon red wine vinegar into the juices and season with more salt and pepper to taste. Spoon the juices over the vegetables, loosely cover them, and let them cool.

6 Cut the peppers in half lengthwise to make 16 pieces. Cut the broccoli in half lengthwise to make 8 pieces. Arrange the vegetables on plates or on a platter. Sprinkle with the herbs, placing a few leaves in the pepper cavities, and serve.

Gratinéed Eggplant, Lasagne Style

With the remarkable simple beauty of Italian food, this layered eggplant, ricotta, mozzarella, and tomato casserole, with its golden crust of crumbs and Romano cheese, emerges bubbling from the oven. Just be sure to bake it in a shallow dish on the top rack of the oven so that it browns easily (and if you have a great, rustic-looking oven-to-table dish, use it here). 6 TO 8 SERVINGS

- **2 medium eggplants, about 1 pound each**
- **1/2 cup plus 2 tablespoons extra-virgin olive oil**
- **2/3 cup ricotta cheese, preferably fresh**
- **Salt and freshly ground pepper**
- **1 1/2 pounds plum tomatoes, very ripe but not soft**
- **3 large garlic cloves, cut into very thin slices**
- **1/2 teaspoon dried oregano**
- **1/3 cup freshly grated pecorino Romano cheese**
- **1/3 cup dry bread crumbs**
- **1 1/2 tablespoons butter, melted and cooled**
- **1 cup shredded mozzarella cheese (6 ounces), preferably fresh**

1 Preheat the oven to 450°F. Trim and discard both ends of the eggplants. Preparing one at a time, cut lengthwise slice about 3/8 inch thick and lay the eggplant flat side down, then cut into long slices 1/3 inch thick. Lay the slices in a single layer on 2 cookie sheets, brush both sides with 6 tablespoons of the olive oil, and roast until tender but not mushy, about 20 minutes, turning them once midway. If they brown somewhat, all the better.

2 Meanwhile, place the ricotta in a small bowl, season with salt and pepper to taste, and set aside. Remove the eggplant when it is done, but leave the oven on.

3 Holding each tomato with the stem end facing your palm, grate enough tomatoes on the large perforations of a box-type grater to measure 2 cups pulp. (This is a handy technique; you'll see as you grate that the tomato flattens out, and its skin protects your hand.) Discard the skin.

4 Place the remaining 1/4 cup olive oil in a medium saucepan set over low heat, and when hot, cook the garlic, stirring, for about 30 seconds. Add the tomatoes and oregano, increase the heat to medium, and cook the sauce, stirring occasionally, until thickened and reduced to about 1 1/3 cups, 10 to 15 minutes. Season generously with salt and pepper.

Do-Ahead Options

- The eggplant can be roasted and the sauce prepared up to 2 days ahead.
- The crumbs can be seasoned up to 3 days in advance.
- Assemble the dish up to 6 hours ahead and let it come almost to room temperature before sprinkling it with crumbs and baking it.

5 Combine the Romano cheese and bread crumbs in a small bowl and stir in the butter until the mixture looks like moist, coarse sand.

6 Spread about 3 tablespoons of the tomato sauce over the bottom of a shallow, 1½-quart oven-proof casserole. Lay one-third of the eggplant over the sauce (it won't completely cover), season with salt and pepper, top with half of the ricotta, spreading it to cover as best possible. Cover the ricotta with half of the remaining tomato sauce, followed by half of the mozzarella. Add another layer of eggplant and repeat the process with the remaining cheeses and sauce. Add the final layer of eggplant (which may not completely cover).

7 Spread the crumb mixture as evenly as possible over the top and bake on the top rack until golden brown and bubbling, about 20 minutes.

✤ Roasted Mushrooms with Lemon Oil

When roasted in a very hot oven with shallots and olive oil, a mixture of unusual cultivated mushrooms (along with some genuinely wild types such as morels, chanterelles, porcini, or hen-of-the-woods, whenever you're lucky enough to get them) become an enticing woodsy mixture. However, if the selection at your market is less than inspiring, regular white mushrooms will work just fine for all, or some, of the more heady ones. (And without the lemon oil, you can toss them with pasta, stir them into Rachel's Shepherd's Pie on page 160, or serve them as a side dish.)

6 APPETIZER SERVINGS OR 8 SIDE-DISH SERVINGS

1½ pounds mixed mushrooms, such as portobello, shiitake, cremini, oyster, and/or white mushrooms

¾ cup thinly sliced shallots (about 4 large)

4½ tablespoons olive oil

3 tablespoons chicken or vegetable broth

Salt and freshly ground pepper

1 tablespoon freshly squeezed lemon juice

1 tablespoon chopped fresh dill, thyme leaves, or snipped chives

1 Preheat the oven to 500°F with the rack at the top holding a large roasting pan (see Note).

2 If you are using portobellos, snap off the stems and trim and discard their dirty ends. Slice the stems lengthwise ½ inch thick and place them in a large bowl. Rinse the top of the caps, rubbing lightly with your fingers to remove any encrusted dirt, and dry them with paper towels. Slice them ½ inch thick and add them to the bowl.

3 Briefly rinse the cremini and white mushrooms, dry on paper towels, and trim the stem ends slightly if they are dirty. Cut them into halves or quarters if they are large and add them to the bowl.

4 Trim and discard any tough stems from the oyster mushrooms, if using them. If they're large, tear them into ½-inch-wide pieces, or if small, into 1-inch clusters. Add them to the bowl.

5 Trim the stems off the shiitakes flush with the caps and discard them. Cut the caps into halves

Do-Ahead Options

➢ Prepare the lemon oil up to a day ahead and remove it from the refrigerator an hour before serving.

➢ Roast the mushrooms up to 3 days ahead and take them out of the refrigerator an hour before serving. Or reheat them gently in a skillet and serve them warm.

or quarters if they are large and add them to the bowl.

6 Mix the shallots with the mushrooms, drizzle with 3½ tablespoons of the olive oil, toss, drizzle with the broth, and toss again. Finally, season them generously with salt and pepper.

7 Distribute the mushroom mixture over the bottom of the preheated pan and roast them, stirring once, until tender and any moisture has evaporated, 10 to 15 minutes.

8 Meanwhile, place the lemon juice in a small bowl and gradually whisk in the remaining 1 tablespoon olive oil. Season with salt and pepper.

9 Remove the mushrooms from the oven and divide them among warm plates. Drizzle a circle of lemon dressing around them, sprinkle with herbs, and serve hot, warm, or at room temperature.

NOTE: The mushrooms should roast in no more than 1½ layers; any deeper, and they will steam in their juices. However, if the mushrooms have too much space, their juices will evaporate too quickly and they may burn, so if that's the case, lower the heat to 450°F and check them sooner.

Asparagus with Olive Oil and Herbs

Asparagus belongs to spring, which is the only time I'll eat it unless someone else serves it to me. That the vegetable rises up through God's green earth in the company of daffodils, tulips, and burgeoning lilac buds is no accident. The magical, delicious spears are all the more flavorful when relished within their own true time. This makes just as good a side dish as a first course. **6 SERVINGS**

2¼ pounds medium to large asparagus spears

¼ cup chopped parsley, preferably flat-leaf

2 medium garlic cloves, minced

4½ tablespoons extra-virgin olive oil

Salt and freshly ground pepper

2¼ teaspoons dried mint, or ½ cup lightly packed mint leaves, rinsed, dried, and chopped (see Note)

2½ tablespoons freshly squeezed lemon juice

Do-Ahead Options

◆ Snap and peel the asparagus up to a day ahead and refrigerate it rolled in damp paper towels inside a zipper-seal plastic bag.

◆ Prepare the dish up to 3 days ahead; take it out of the refrigerator an hour before serving.

1 Snap off the woody ends of the asparagus. Rinse and dry the spears and set them aside or lay them in a pan of cold water to soak for 10 to 15 minutes if you think they may be sandy.

2 Briefly chop the parsley and garlic together to mingle the flavors; set aside.

3 Place the asparagus in a skillet large enough for them to lie flat in no more than two layers, or use two skillets. Toss them with the olive oil and the parsley mixture and season generously with salt and pepper. Cover the skillet—that's right, no water—set over medium-high heat, and as soon as you hear sizzling, reduce the heat to low. Cook until the asparagus spears are tender but not mushy, 10 to 20 minutes depending on their thickness.

4 Transfer the asparagus to a platter, and sprinkle the spears with the fresh or dried mint, tossing gently. Stir the lemon juice into the pan juices (combining the juices in one pan, if you used two), add more salt and pepper if you like, and pour over the asparagus spears. Serve them hot, warm or at room temperature.

❋ Cheese and Black Pepper Pasta

When you lay eyes on this less than showy pasta, you may think, "What's the big deal?" But when it reaches your mouth, you're rewarded with the potent taste of milky sharp Romano cheese and tingling pepper. It's my take on a shepherd's dish from Italy called la gricia, and if you use an older and drier cheese (which won't completely melt), the dish is close to the original; because the specks of cheese that coat the strands add satisfying texture. Do grate the cheese and grind the pepper close to serving time, since the pasta depends on their vibrancy. **6 SERVINGS**

Salt

¾ pound dried spaghettini, linguini fini, or other long pasta

1½ tablespoons extra-virgin olive oil

2½ teaspoons butter, softened

¾ teaspoon freshly ground black pepper, plus more for garnish

½ cup plus 1 tablespoon freshly grated pecorino Romano cheese

1 Set a very large pot of water over high heat to come to a boil for the pasta. When the water reaches a boil, salt it generously and add the pasta. Cook until al dente, about 6 minutes. Drain thoroughly in a colander.

2 Return the hot pasta to its warm cooking pot. Mix in the olive oil and butter, lifting and tossing the pasta to do so. Sprinkle it with the pepper, lifting and tossing to mix it in. Lastly, sprinkle the pasta with cheese and mix again, lifting and tossing.

3 Divide the pasta among warm plates, grind more pepper over the top, and serve right away.

Feta Cheese with Tahini and Walnuts

This dish began life as an almost-instant hors d'oeuvre for company practically on the doorstep. I scanned the cupboard and refrigerator shelves, hoping for something to catch my eye and fixed on two Mediterranean stalwarts: feta cheese and tahini. Hurriedly, I tossed them into the food processor, and they made their debut as a dip for raw vegetables. Another night I took it a step further and turned the dip into a first course in the form of a rich, nutty mound perched on a pretty leaf speckled with red radish, just as it is here. If you're serving this as a dip and it's too stiff, stir in just enough water, wine, or milk to make it slightly more fluid. Garnish with crumbled feta and grated radish when serving. **8 SERVINGS**

⅔ cup tahini

1 cup crumbled feta cheese

1½ teaspoons paprika, preferably Spanish smoked *pimentón dulce* or sweet Hungarian

⅓ to ½ cup extra-virgin olive oil

½ cup lightly toasted walnuts

2 teaspoons *herbes de Provence*, or a mixture of other dried herbs such as thyme, rosemary, and oregano

1½ to 2 tablespoons aged Spanish sherry vinegar or other wine vinegar

Salt and freshly ground pepper

8 red leaf or Boston lettuce leaves, rinsed and dried

1 Place the tahini, feta, and paprika in the bowl of a food processor and process for 1 minute. Gradually add ⅓ cup olive oil until combined, 1 to 2 minutes. (If the mixture seems very stiff, add more oil, a little at a time.) Add the walnuts and process again until the nuts have become small pieces. Add the *herbes de Provence* and enough vinegar to give the mixture a gentle acid edge, and continue processing until the mixture is well amalgamated but the walnuts are still in tiny pieces. Season generously with salt and pepper and set aside. (If the mixture looks separated when it comes out of the processor, chill it well, then stir it vigorously.)

2 Set one lettuce leaf on each plate, spoon one-eighth of the mixture on top of each leaf, grate the radish over using the large holes of a box-type grater, and sprinkle with parsley. Toast the bread, place 2 slices on each plate (or in a napkin-lined basket), and serve right away.

6 to 8 small radishes,
trimmed, rinsed, and dried

2 teaspoons chopped
parsley, preferably flat-leaf

16 small slices of country-
style or sourdough bread

Do-Ahead Option

⬦ Make the mixture up to a week
ahead and take it out of the
refrigerator an hour before
serving.

HOW TO MEASURE TAHINI

When you buy tahini, most of the time it has separated in
the jar and it's a pain to stir together. Instead, spoon all of it
into the bowl of the food processor and process just until it is
blended well. Then make the dip without washing the
bowl—just be sure to leave only the amount needed for the
recipe.

Roasted Sweet Peppers with Olive Vinaigrette

As it is, or with slices of fresh mozzarella, this is a simple-to-put-together, colorful way to start off dinner. 6 SERVINGS

1 tablespoon white wine vinegar

¾ teaspoon grated lemon zest

2½ teaspoons freshly squeezed lemon juice

2½ teaspoons Dijon mustard, preferably French

½ cup extra-virgin olive oil

2 tablespoons coarsely chopped pitted black Mediterranean olives such as Kalamata, Alphonso, or Gaeta (see page 51)

Salt and freshly ground pepper

6 roasted large bell peppers in different colors (see page 63), peeled and seeded, or jarred roasted peppers

2½ cups packed small salad greens, such as mesclun, frisée, watercress, or other lettuces torn in small pieces, washed, and dried

8 to 10 basil leaves torn into bite-size pieces, or 1 tablespoon chopped fresh dill

1 Whisk together the vinegar, lemon zest, lemon juice, and mustard in a small bowl. Gradually whisk in the olive oil to make a lightly thickened dressing. Stir in the olives, season with salt and pepper, and set the vinaigrette aside.

2 Tear the peppers in half lengthwise and place them in a medium bowl (if they're drippy from sitting in their juices, pat them dry with paper towels first). Drizzle them with about 1½ tablespoons of vinaigrette.

3 Place the lettuce in a bowl, toss with about 1½ tablespoons of vinaigrette, and season lightly with more salt and pepper, if you like. Lay 2 pepper halves opposite one another on each plate to meet in the center. Place a serving of lettuce at the meeting point, sure it doesn't cover the peppers by more than half, drizzle everything with the remaining vinaigrette, sprinkle with herbs, and serve cool.

HOW TO ROAST PEPPERS

Home-roasted peppers have more flavor than the ones you buy already roasted (though there are some good brands), even if the process is a little time consuming.

To roast them, place the whole peppers directly on the stovetop burners over a low flame and turning them with tongs, char all the surfaces. Or cut them in half, remove their stems, ribs, and seeds, flatten them slightly with your hand, and broil them on a lightly oiled cookie sheet. Transfer the charred peppers to a covered bowl so that they steam and cool at the same time (the steaming helps the skins come off easily).

When the peppers are cool enough to handle, peel off and discard the skins, but don't be tempted to rinse the peppers as you're doing it (or after) because rinsing dilutes their flavor.

Shrimp with Golden Garlic Vinaigrette

I had a salad of Bibb lettuce in Spain years ago that I'll never forget, and it was the vinaigrette that made it special. The dressing was nothing more than garlic simmered in olive oil until it turned pale gold, then simply mixed with a little vinegar.

That vinaigrette, or my rendering of it here, dresses sautéed or grilled shrimp, which lie on top of sliced tomatoes, which, in turn, cover toast. The shrimp and tomato juices combine with the dressing to turn parts of the toast deliciously soggy, while the edges keep a crunchy contrast. It's a great way to start off dinner, but it also makes the perfect lunch for shrimp and garlic lovers. 6 SERVINGS

---

6 thin slices of country-style bread, each about 2½ x 4½ inches

3 to 4 garlic cloves

5½ tablespoons extra-virgin olive oil

½ teaspoon paprika, preferably Spanish *pimentón dulce* or sweet Hungarian

1½ tablespoons aged Spanish sherry or red wine vinegar

2½ teaspoons freshly squeezed lemon juice

Salt and freshly ground pepper

12 thin slices of ripe tomato

3 dozen large shrimp, peeled and deveined (see page 65)

2 teaspoons fresh thyme leaves

1. Preheat the oven to 425°F with the rack in the center for the bread. Toast the bread directly on the oven rack until golden (the center of the slices won't brown as well as the edges), 7 to 10 minutes, and let them cool on a rack.

2. Cut the garlic into very thin lengthwise slices, arrange them into several stacks, cut through each stack into long, thin julienne strips, then cut the strips across to make tiny pieces (see Note). Measure out 1 tablespoon of the garlic, saving any extra for another use, and put it in a small, heavy skillet with 4½ tablespoons of olive oil. Set the skillet over very low heat and cook, stirring frequently, until the garlic is pale gold, 2 to 3 minutes. (It will continue to cook from the pan's retained heat.) Remove the pan from the heat and stir in the paprika. Let cool, then stir the vinegar and lemon juice into the garlic-oil mixture. Season generously with salt and pepper.

3. Cover each toast with 2 slices of tomato, overlapping them if necessary. Season generously with salt and pepper and set them aside to allow their juices to flavor the toast while you cook the shrimp.

Do-Ahead Options

➥ Pick the thyme, chop the garlic, and prepare the vinaigrette up to a day ahead.

➥ Toast the bread up to several hours ahead.

4 Dry the shrimp well on paper towels. Heat the remaining 1 tablespoon olive oil in a large skillet set over medium-high heat and when it's hot, add the shrimp. Season them with salt and pepper and sauté, stirring occasionally, until they are white throughout, 3 to 4 minutes, cutting one in half to check if done. Remove the skillet from the heat.

5 Place the tomato toasts on plates and cover each with its share of shrimp, spooning over any juices. Stir the vinaigrette to blend it, spoon it over the shrimp, sprinkle with thyme, and serve right away.

NOTE: Cutting the garlic this carefully makes more even pieces and therefore more even cooking.

HOW TO CLEAN SHRIMP

When I clean shrimp, first I pull off their shells. Then I lay them, one at a time, on a paper towel and make a shallow cut down the middle of the back to expose the black (and once in a while pink) intestine. This I pull out with the tip of my paring knife and scrape it onto one end of the towel. Or you could flush out the intestine by running the backs under cold water. Whichever way you do it, unless you're going to boil the shrimp, it's important to dry them well on paper towels before you cook them.

Orzo "Risotto" with Roasted Tomatoes and Hot Sausage

Orzo is the diminutive Italian pasta that looks like rice (or the tiniest footballs imaginable). Cooked until just al dente, its comforting grains roll on your tongue like silken beads. Here, plenty of Parmesan cheese stirred in at the end of cooking makes it creamy like risotto. 8 SERVINGS

1½ pounds ripe plum tomatoes, rinsed and dried

⅓ cup olive oil

1 medium onion, thinly sliced (1 cup)

3 garlic cloves, minced

4 links hot or sweet Italian sausage (about ¾ pound)

1½ cups dried orzo, preferably Italian

1 cup chicken broth

Salt and freshly ground pepper

1 cup freshly grated imported Parmesan cheese, plus more for garnish

Torn fresh basil leaves, coarsely chopped flat-leaf parsley, or coarsely chopped fresh oregano, for garnish

1 Preheat the oven to 500°F with the rack at the top. Roast the tomatoes in one layer on a large baking pan until blistered and very soft, 20 to 25 minutes, depending on their size. Transfer them, with any skins that have popped off, to a plate. Let cool, then coarsely chop the tomatoes, skin and all (to measure about 1½ cups).

2 Meanwhile, set a large heavy skillet over low heat with the olive oil. When it's hot, add the onion and cook, stirring frequently, until tender and slightly golden, about 8 minutes. Stir in the garlic, cook for 1 minute more, and remove the pan from the heat.

3 Peel off and discard the sausage casing. Break enough of the meat into small pieces to measure 2 generous cups.

4 Bring a large pot of water to a boil, salt it generously, and cook the orzo until al dente, 8 to 10 minutes.

5 Reheat the onion mixture over low heat, add the sausage, and cook, stirring occasionally, until the meat is half done, about 3 minutes. Stir in the tomatoes and cook 2 to 3 minutes more, stirring occasionally. Stir in the broth, season with salt and pepper, and remove the skillet from the heat. When the orzo is

Do-Ahead Option

↝ Chop the garlic a day ahead.

↝ Roast and chop the tomatoes up to 3 days ahead.

ready, drain it in a colander and give it several good shakes to eliminate as much water as possible.

6 Return the orzo to its cooking pot set over low heat and dry it for about 30 seconds, stirring. Stir in the tomato-sausage mixture and heat for about 1 minute, stirring frequently. Stir in 1 cup of the cheese. Spoon the orzo onto warm plates, sprinkle with herbs, if using them, and serve right away with more grated cheese on the side.

Shrimp Roasted in Olive Oil with Rosemary and Lemon

Plump shrimp, spiked with rosemary and baked with savory companions that may already be in your pantry, make a good, light lunch or first course for dinner. It can also be put together quickly, particularly if the shrimp are already cleaned. **4 SERVINGS**

¼ cup freshly squeezed
lemon juice

¼ cup plus 2 tablespoons
extra-virgin olive oil

1 tablespoon drained capers,
lightly chopped

3 tablespoons canned
crushed tomatoes or
drained and chopped
whole tomatoes

¼ teaspoon crushed hot red
pepper, or more to taste

Salt and freshly ground
black pepper

1½ pounds large shrimp,
peeled and deveined
(see page 65)

6 small sprigs of fresh
rosemary

4 lemon wedges

1 Preheat the oven to 400°F with the rack in the center. Place the lemon juice in a medium bowl, gradually whisk in the olive oil, and stir in the capers, tomatoes, and hot pepper. Season generously with salt and black pepper.

2 Dry the shrimp on paper towels and add them to the bowl. Toss with the vinaigrette. Pour the contents into a shallow baking dish or other ovenproof pan so the shrimp lie in a single close layer; be sure to scrape out all the vinaigrette with a rubber spatula and add to the pan. Tuck in the rosemary sprigs so they are covered by either the vinaigrette or the shrimp. Roast the shrimp, turning them once, until just cooked through, about 10 minutes.

3 Spoon the shrimp with its sauce into warm shallow soup plates, grind pepper over the top of each, and garnish with a rosemary sprig. Serve hot, warm, or cool, with wedges of lemon.

Do-Ahead Options

◆ Prepare the vinaigrette and clean the shrimp up to a day ahead.

◆ Prepare the finished shrimp up to 2 days ahead. Take them out of the refrigerator an hour ahead and serve them with wedges of lemon alongside.

MORE MENUS FOR EASY ENTERTAINING

A Little Grander

While casual entertaining is a pleasure that makes life easier on the cook — eschewing fussy recipes and elaborate presentation — there are times when even an informal meal calls for food that's a bit more special. On those occasions, I think back upon my professional cooking career, because coming up with a dish for a restaurant menu always means that no matter how basically simple it is, it has to appear elegant, with a nod to style. And although I love homey, old-fashioned cooking, finesse was — and still is — just as important an element to me, because I see that extra something as an indication of real caring, and, of course, as an expression of culinary skill. The eight main courses in the menus that follow have, to one degree or another, a kind of dual sensibility. While some are grander than others, they all dress up for a special occasion and still keep a toe in the comfort zone.

There is delicate sea bass, sumptuous loin of lamb, buttery filet mignon, and stately standing rib roast of beef complete with Yorkshire pudding, not to mention slow-roasted duckling and pork, the latter as both cutlets with olives and feta and as tenderloin with mustard and tomatoes.

Putting all this in fashion terms, the success of a good outfit often depends on how it's accessorized. To help make your meal as much of a dressed-up event as you'd like it to be, I've given special suggestions for first courses, side dishes, and desserts. However, just as with fashion, more doesn't necessarily mean better — or more elegant. A carefully chosen appetizer and a distinctive accompaniment (or two) to the main course, along with a great dessert to finish, easily make the most memorable, stylish meal.

Two Menus on the Grander Side

Grilled Loin of Lamb with Ginger Yogurt *(page 138)*

Grilled asparagus and fennel with orange wedges

Wild rice
— or —
Basmati Rice with Olives, Lemon, and Nutmeg *(page 214)*

Peaches Sautéed with Butter and Cinnamon Sugar *(page 258)*

For a Bigger Feast
Shrimp with Golden Garlic Vinaigrette to start *(page 64)*
— and/or —
Rich Chocolate Gateau instead of the peaches *(page 226)*

◆

Filet Mignons with Gorgonzola-Porcini Butter *(page 150)*

Baked Vegetable Antipasto as a side dish *(page 52)*
— or —
Roast Zucchini with Herbes de Provence *(page 196)*

Mashed Potatoes with Basil Oil *(page 199)*

Pecan-Apricot Roulade *(page 230)*
— or —
Buttermilk Cake with Orange-Mascarpone Cream and Chocolate Glaze *(page 234)*

For a Bigger Feast
White Bean Soup with Rosemary, without the mashed potatoes *(page 28)*
— and/or —
Bitter Greens with Lemon-Anchovy Vinaigrette *(page 46)*
after the main course (without the antipasto)

A Classic Roast Beef Dinner

Roast Standing Rib of Beef with Potatoes and Carrots and Yorkshire Pudding
(page 154)

Chocolate ice cream or frozen yogurt with Raspberry Sauce *(page 280)*
and Frosted Almonds *(page 282)*

For a Bigger Feast
Caesar Salad with Sun-Dried Tomatoes to start *(page 41)*
– and/or –
Warm Apple-Walnut Crumble instead of the sundae *(page 249)*

A Dinner Rich with Flavors

Slow-Roasted Duckling with Black Currant Sauce *(page 157)*

Sautéed sugar snap peas or snow peas

Saffron Couscous with Dried Cranberries, Pistachios,
and Fresh Herbs *(page 216)*

Fresh pineapple, served drizzled with Grand Marnier (or other orange liqueur)
and topped with a small scoop of raspberry sorbet

For a Bigger Feast
The turnip puree (without the garnish) from Turnip Puree with Caraway Seeds,
Scallions, and Bacon in place of the peas *(page 190)*
– and/or –
Poached Pears with Vanilla Bean and Lemon in place
of the pineapple *(page 260)*

Two Light Menus Full of Flavor

Roasted Sweet Peppers with Olive Vinaigrette (*page* 62)

Chilean Sea Bass with Shallots (*page* 102)

Boiled new potatoes in their jackets

Orange sorbet garnished with chunks of bittersweet chocolate

For a Bigger Feast

Swiss Chard with Browned Onions and Feta Cheese (*page* 184)

Rachel's Chocolate Truffles instead of the chocolate chunks (*page* 281)
— *or* —
Poached Pears with Vanilla Bean and Lemon instead of the sorbet (*page* 260)

Chicken Breasts Stuffed with Asiago Cheese in Lemon and Sage Sauce (*page* 122)

Swiss chard or spinach with butter
— *or* —
Broccoli rabe with garlic and oil

Arborio Rice Pilaf with Mushrooms (*page* 212)

Strawberries in Raspberry-Balsamic Glaze (*page* 253)

For a Bigger Feast

Artichokes with Roasted Red Pepper and Olive Dip (*page* 50)
— *or* —
Orzo "Risotto" with Roasted Tomatoes and Hot Sausage
to start, without the pilaf (*page* 66)
— *or* —
Arugula Salad with Yogurt Dressing in place of
the chard or broccoli rabe (*page* 39)

Two Menus for Cool Weather

Port Cutlets with Black Olives, Feta Cheese, and Basil *(page 127)*

Tossed greens with toasted walnuts with the vinaigrette from Maureen's Garden Salad before or after the main course *(page 43)*

Mashed Sweet Potatoes with Maple Syrup *(page 206)*

Raspberry sorbet

For a Bigger Feast

Asparagus (in season) with Olive Oil and Herbs to start, instead of the salad *(page 58)*

— or —

Roasted Mushrooms with Lemon Oil as a first course
(in the fall) *(page 56)*

Sugar Yeast Crisps *(page 239)*

Pork Tenderloin with Mustard and Tomatoes *(page 128)*

Arugula Salad with Yogurt Dressing, without the herbs *(page 39)*

Mashed Potatoes with Basil Oil *(page 199)*

Chocolate Shortbread *(page 242)*

For a Bigger Feast

Baked Vegetable Antipasto to start, without the salad *(page 52)*

Raspberries with Vanilla Bean Custard *(page 276)*

Alfresco Dinners from the Grill

Grilling is one of America's favorite forms of entertaining, and mine, too. Here are twelve menus with main courses of fish, chicken, pork, lamb, veal, and beef for cooking — and perhaps eating — outside when the weather is welcoming. There are three chicken menus and two kinds of kebabs. Some of the side dishes are done on the grill, too, and those that are cooked indoors can be prepared earlier, ready to bring out when the barbecue is ready. Of course, you can mix and match any of the suggestions (not to mention whatever else from the book) and put together an all-done-ahead dinner.

AN ODE TO FIREFLIES

Twilight is a magical time. As daylight dwindles to dusk and fireflies begin to blink, we sit on the patio under the spreading canopy of the euonymous tree. The air has softened in the warmth of summer and our little piece of paradise feels embraced as we watch the sunset colors of pink and orange turn to pale lavender and parakeet blue, then deepen to velvet black.

Chicken, which I've rubbed with rich spices, is grilling over coals, and we're becoming intoxicated with its aroma. Little red potatoes tossed in olive oil with salt and fresh pepper are tucked into the belly of the grill, roasting in its indirect heat. And as the food cooks, uttering a sputter or spit now and then, the fireflies have begun their dance.

They rise and glow just long enough to throw off a wink of sharp hot gold before turning off to glimmer again in another place. They hang in mid-air like tiny sprites, each aloft in its moment, marking real then vanishing spots throughout the garden. They light over the paths, among the flowers, beneath the trees, and just above the picket fence like a *corps de ballets* of miniscule dancers spread across a stage, reminding us of the sun and welcoming the moon.

When they end their show and we are surrounded in darkness, broken by the flickering flames of kerosene lamps, throughout the night in the close, humid air and occasional breeze, we talk and laugh and eat. Spoonfuls of chocolate mousse have never tasted more lush, and bites of buttery cookies let sugar drift like snow onto the table.

A gentleness pervades the night garden, and the sound of our voices has a surprising clarity. Save for the barking of a dog, the insistent song of the cicadas, and the rare voice of a neighbor in a nearby house, all you can hear is us — a small party of close friends — and the clink of our glasses and plates.

Three Menus for Fish on the Grill

Grilled Catfish with Ginger-Garlic Vinaigrette (*page* 100)

Glazed Carrots with Cardamom (*page* 179)

Lemon Rice Pilaf with Dill (*page* 211)

Strawberry or raspberry sorbet and a big bowl of
cherries with ice cubes

For a Bigger Feast
Hearts of Romaine with Sherry-Basil Dressing (*page* 48)
– and/or –
Rachel's Chocolate Truffles (*page* 281)

Cumin-Rubbed Grilled Skate Wings with Bacon
and Lemon Oil (*page* 104)

Tender Green Beans with Olive Oil and Thyme (*page* 185)

Grilled or boiled potatoes

Roasted Pineapple (done on the grill) with Rum Cream (*page* 262)

For a Bigger Feast
White Gazpacho with Almonds and Basil (*page* 24)

Grilled Tuna with Roasted Red Pepper Pesto (*page 106*)

Slow-Sautéed Broccoli (*page 177*)

Ciabatta or other crusty bread and grissini

Strawberries in Raspberry-Balsamic Glaze (*page 253*)

For a Bigger Feast

Bitter Greens with Lemon-Anchovy Vinaigrette (*page 46*)

Arborio Rice Pilaf with Mushrooms (*page 212*)

Dark Chocolate Crème Caramels in place
of the strawberries (*page 270*)

Three Great Grilled Chicken Menus

Chicken Roasted with Indian Spices
(*see page 84 for menu*)

Broiled Chicken with Coconut Milk, Ginger, and Chiles
(*see page 14 for menu*)

Barbecued Chicken Breasts
(*see page 84 for menu*)

Sizzling Meat on Skewers, Two Menus

Soy and Spice Marinated Grilled Lamb (*page* 134)

Grilled corn on the cob

Pita breads spread with garlic butter, wrapped in foil, and heated on the grill

Milk Chocolate Parfait with Strawberries (*page* 269)
— *or* —
Brown Sugar Bananas in Phyllo (*page* 250)

For a Bigger Feast
Sautéed Corn and Summer Squash in Tomato Butter with Basil
instead of corn on the cob (*page* 186)
— *or* —
Saffron Couscous with Dried Cranberries, Pistachios, and Fresh Herbs,
without the sautéed corn and squash (*page* 216)

❧

Grilled Rib-Eye Kebabs, Satay Style (*page* 148)

Grilled Vegetables with Lemon-Basil Oil (*page* 194)

Aromatic Yellow Rice (*page* 210)

Vanilla ice cream with Raspberry Sauce (*page* 280)

or Brown Sugar Chocolate Sauce (*page* 238)

For a Bigger Feast
Roasted Carrots with Orange, served warm or at room temperature,
instead of the grilled vegetables (*page* 180)

Rachel's Chocolate Truffles on the sundae (*page* 281)

Two Menus for Steaks and Veal Chops

Grilled Steak with Shiitake Mushrooms in Whole-Grain Mustard Sauce (*page 146*)

Grilled Vegetables in Asian Vinaigrette (*page 198*)

Grilled rye bread (or sourdough), buttered, as a bed for the steak

Chocolate Mousse (*page 274*)
— *or* —
End of the Summer Upside-Down Plum and Blueberry Cake (*page 233*)

For a Bigger Feast
Hearts of Romaine with Sherry-Basil Dressing (*page 48*)

Grilled Veal Chops with Tarragon Gremolata (*page 144*)

Artichokes with Roasted Red Pepper and Olive Dip as a side (*page 50*)
— *or* —
Grilled Vegetables with Lemon-Basil Oil (*page 194*)

Lightly buttered orzo
— *or* —
Olive-oiled and grilled ciabatta or other crusty bread slices

Rachel's Ice Cream Sundaes (made with coffee ice cream) with Caramel Sauce
and Toasted Hazelnuts (*page 278*)

For a Bigger Feast
Gratinéed Eggplant, Lasagne Style in place of the artichokes, but as a
first course when serving grilled vegetables (*page 54*)

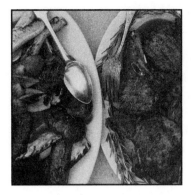

Do-Ahead Dinners

The menus in this section offer dishes that let you join your own party without sacrificing an iota of deliciousness. Some of these recipes can be done entirely ahead and served warm or, later, at room temperature. Some need a few minutes of last-minute cooking while others require just a reheat. There are lots of suggestions in the two vegetarian and antipasto menus that follow, so, if you like, think about serving small portions of each, or go the other route and make fewer dishes in larger amounts. And, finally, there's a menu that lets your friends control their own dinner-destiny by giving them a selection of main courses, accompaniments, and desserts that you've made and set out attractively, something like your own salad bar, writ large — in other words, a buffet.

Do-ahead is the only way I entertain anymore (whether in all or in part). I love this sort of food because it makes my evening so pleasant, but I also think of it as food that can travel. A portable dinner party allows you to have dinner with friends stuck without a baby-sitter, or supper, ready to eat, after a long drive to the country. Here are some possibilities.

Two Menus with
Richly Seasoned Chicken

Barbecued Chicken Breasts *(page 120)*

White and Sweet Potato Salad *(page 208)*

Sliced tomatoes with vinaigrette, sprinkled with fresh tarragon and chives

Roasted Pineapple with Rum Cream *(page 262)*

For a Bigger Feast
Roasted Tomato Gazpacho with Cumin and Garlic Croutons,
without the tomato salad *(page 26)*

Buttermilk Biscuits *(page 218)*
– or –
Corn Muffins *(page 222)*

Peaches Sautéed with Butter and Cinnamon Sugar in place
of the pineapple *(page 258)*

Chicken Roasted with Indian Spices *(page 110)*

Roasted Eggplant with Garlic and Mint *(page 188)*

Warm pita *or* naan breads

Lemon sorbet with mango *or* other fresh fruit

For a Bigger Feast
Buttered basmati rice *or* Aromatic Yellow Rice *(page 210)*

Sugar Yeast Crisps *(page 239) or* Pistachio Sugar Cookies *(page 244)*

Roasted Tomato Gazpacho with Cumin
and Garlic Croutons *page 26*

ABOVE Artichokes with Roasted Red Pepper and Olive Dip *page 50*

OPPOSITE Roasted Beet and Tomato Salad *page 40*

ABOVE **Grilled Salmon with Fresh Tomatoes and Basil** *page 98*

OPPOSITE **Stir-Fried Shrimp with Mint-Ginger Sauce and Mango** *page 108*

OPPOSITE **Lemon-Garlic Roast Chicken with Smoked Paprika** *page 124*

Grilled Pork Chops Teriyaki *page 132,*
served with **Grilled Vegetables with Lemon-Basil Oil** *page 194*

Gratinéed
Eggplant,
Lasagne Style
page 54

Two Menus for Cool Weather

Roasted Salmon with Mustard and Black Olives (*page 97*)

Slow-Sautéed Broccoli (*page 177*)

Crusty sourdough bread

Chocolate ice cream *or* frozen yogurt

For a Bigger Feast
Puree of Potato Soup with Dill (*page 33*)

Brown Sugar Chocolate Sauce for the ice cream (*page 238*)

Pine Nut Cookies (*page 240*)

❧

Sausages with White Beans and Ham Hocks (*page 164*)

Tossed greens with balsamic vinegar and oil *or* the Yogurt Dressing (*page 39*)

Italian, French, or peasant-style bread

Scoops of two flavors of gelati

For a Bigger Feast
Corn Muffins instead of bread (*page 222*)

Raspberry Sauce with the gelati (*page 280*)

A Vegetarian Table

Carrot, White Bean, and Eggplant Salad *(page 182)*

Grilled Vegetables with (or without) Lemon-Basil Oil with portobello mushrooms
and tomatoes in the warm months *(page 194)*
— or —
French Lentil Soup when it's cold *(page 36)*

Mesclun salad or bitter greens with Yogurt Dressing
on the side *(page 39)*

Basmati Rice with Olives, Lemon, and Nutmeg *(page 214)*
— or —
Lemon Rice Pilaf with Dill in the cooler months *(page 211)*

Basket of warm whole wheat pitas or other flatbread

Bowls of strawberries or raspberries with whipped cream and
a plate of chocolate cookies during the warm months
— or —
A selection of little pastries such as fruit tartlets and
éclairs in cooler weather

For a Bigger Feast
Double Chocolate Cream Cheese Brownies instead
of cookies with the berries *(page 246)*

An Antipasto Dinner

Baked Vegetable Antipasto (*page 52*)

— *or* —

A leek and basil frittata

Platter of sliced prosciutto, salamis, and cured meat such as
mortadella, coppacolla, soppresata, and bresaola

Plate of Italian canned or bottled tuna in olive oil,
broken into chunks, and garnished with thinly sliced rounds
of red onion with lemon wedges and capers

Plate of fresh fennel sticks with a dipping bowl of extra-virgin
olive oil well seasoned with salt and pepper

Cauliflower with Olives, Anchovies, and Capers (*page 181*)

Caesar Salad with Sun-Dried Tomatoes (*page 41*)

Basket of two or three Italian breads such as ciabatta,
focaccia, grissini, and herb-garlic toasts

❧

Fruit salad of mixed berries and seasonal fruit, such as sliced peeled peaches and
plums moistened with orange and a little lemon juice, with bowls of mascarpone or
fromage blanc and toasted chopped almonds alongside

— *or* —

Slices of apple torte, ricotta cheesecake, or one large Dark Chocolate Crème
Caramel with a bowl of whipped cream in the cool months (*page 270*)

For a Bigger Feast

Asparagus (in season) with Olive Oil and Herbs, instead
of the antipasto, artichokes, or frittata (*page* 58)

Small steaks of Grilled Tuna with Roasted Red Pepper Pesto, without
the artichokes in Roasted Red Pepper and Olive Dip
and the tinned tuna (*page* 106)

Pine Nut Cookies, without serving almonds with the fruit salad (*page* 240)

Make Your Own Dinner Party

There are a number of ways of going about this. All the dishes could be done ahead and simply set on the table. Main courses could be cooked to order (depending on what you're making, of course), with everything else already done. Or, if you've got the grill stoked up, you could let your friends grill their own food (if you're comfortable with that).

Bowls of arugula, mixed greens or mesclun, and hearts of romaine

Yogurt Dressing (*page 39*), Cider Honey Vinaigrette (*page 42*),
or Caesar dressing (*page 41*)

Side dishes of garlic croutons, red onion rings, sliced cucumbers, wedges of tomato,
freshly grated imported Parmesan cheese, and chunks of feta, goat, or blue cheese

Grilled or sautéed boneless chicken breasts

Roasted (or grilled) pork tenderloin
— or —
Center-cut roasted or grilled tenderloin of beef

Small roasted or grilled fillets of salmon
— or —
Stir-fried shrimp

Mint-Ginger Sauce (*page 108*)

Shiitake Mushrooms in Whole-Grain Mustard Sauce (*page 146*)

Lemon-Basil Oil (*page 194*) or Roasted Red Pepper Pesto in the summer (*page 106*)
— or —
Provençal Tomatoes when it's cold outside (*page 136*)

Basket of breads and rolls

Minty New Potatoes with Summer Herbs, as a salad in the summer (*page 203*)
— or —
Cheese Mashed Potatoes when it's cold outside (*page 200*)

Purchased small pastries such as eclairs and tartlets

Bowls of berries, cherries, and fresh figs, in the summer
— or —
Baked apples or pears

For a Bigger Feast
Roasted Mushrooms without the lemon oil, with the salads (*page 56*)

Double Chocolate Cream Cheese Brownies and
cookies instead of the pastries (*page 246*)

Just Desserts

A dessert party can be a thrilling prospect for those of us with a hankering for sweets. It's the perfect opportunity to show off your skills in a fun way and a crowd-pleaser any time of year.

I've suggested three menus, and with the exception of a couple of dishes, all the recipes can be done ahead. Each menu offers five different sweets, from cake to cookies to fruit to puddings. Because all the recipes are for six to eight servings, that means a lot of dessert. So stick with it, if you're inclined, and turn your party into a bigger bash or keep it intimate and cut the recipes in half wherever feasible. Needless to say, you can always make fewer than five desserts, or make two or three yourself and buy a couple more to round out your menu.

A Dessert Menu for the Warmer Months

Buttermilk Cake with Orange-Mascarpone Cream and Chocolate Glaze (*page* 234)

Strawberries in Raspberry-Balsamic Glaze (*page* 253)

Blueberry Crisp (*page* 256)

Raspberries with Vanilla Bean Custard (*page* 276)

Chocolate Shortbread (*page* 242)
— *or* —
Sugar Yeast Crisps (*page* 239)

A Dessert Menu for the Cooler Months

Pecan-Apricot Roulade (*page* 230)

Bowl of tangerine and/or orange segments in place of the
garnish for the roulade

Brown Sugar Bananas in Phyllo (*page* 250)

Chocolate Mousse (*page* 274)

Pistachio Sugar Cookies (*page* 244)
— or —
Dark Chocolate Chunk Cookies with Macadamia Nuts (*page* 241)

An Over-the-Top Chocolate Menu

Rich Chocolate Gateau (*page* 226), with cocoa-flavored whipped cream, if you like

Strawberry Sauté (*page* 268)
— or —
Milk Chocolate Parfait with Strawberries (*page* 269)

Dark Chocolate Crème Caramels or one large custard (*page* 270)

Rachel's Chocolate Truffles (*page* 281)

Double Chocolate Cream Cheese Brownies (*page* 246)

MAIN COURSES

SEAFOOD

✤ Thai-Style Halibut with Lime, and Scallions

The lime sauce here is vibrant and a little hot, and it goes with lots of other fish, from more delicate, white-fleshed sorts — such as bass, grouper, and sole — to richer types such as salmon or tuna, particularly when they're grilled. Soft-shell crabs in season are a great match, too. **6 SERVINGS**

½ cup plus 1 tablespoon freshly squeezed lime juice (from about 6 limes)

3 ¾ tablespoons Asian fish sauce, such as *nuoc nam* or *nam pla*

1 packed teaspoon light brown sugar

½ teaspoon crushed hot red pepper flakes, or to taste

2 medium garlic cloves, minced

2 tablespoons vegetable oil

6 halibut fillets, about 7 ounces each, cut ¾ inch thick

Salt and freshly ground pepper

Flour, for dredging

⅓ cup very thinly sliced scallions (white part only)

¾ cup cilantro leaves

Do-Ahead Option

➤ Prepare the sauce up to 4 days ahead and take it out of the refrigerator an hour before serving.

1 Preheat the oven to 400°F with the rack in the middle. Stir the lime juice, fish sauce, brown sugar, hot pepper, and garlic together in a small bowl and set the sauce aside.

2 Set 2 large, ovenproof skillets over low heat and divide the oil between them. Dry the fish fillets on paper towels, season with salt and pepper, and lightly dredge them in flour, tapping off the excess.

3 Increase the heat under the skillets to high and when the oil is hot, add the fillets, rounded side down. Sauté for 2 to 3 minutes, until browned on the bottom. Turn the fish over and transfer the skillets to the oven.

4 Roast until the fillets are just cooked through, 5 to 8 minutes. To check, place the end of the metal spatula in the thickest part of one fillet and gently push it open to see if it's white throughout. If not, cook for 1 to 2 minutes more. Remove from the oven.

5 Stir the scallions into the sauce, pour it into a serving bowl, and float a few cilantro leaves on top. Transfer the fillets to warm plates and serve them hot with the sauce and remaining cilantro on the side.

Roasted Salmon with Mustard and Black Olives

Salmon does well with the tangy tastes in this dish, because they cut through its richness and enhance its flavor at the same time. The fillets can be sautéed or grilled (or poached or broiled) instead of roasted with the vinaigrette served on the side.

6 SERVINGS

---

3 tablespoons freshly squeezed lemon juice

1½ tablespoons Dijon mustard, preferably French

¾ cup olive oil

2½ teaspoons capers, preferably the tiny ones called nonpareil

9 to 10 pitted Kalamata olives or other ripe Mediterranean olives, cut into thin strips (see page 51)

Salt and freshly ground pepper

6 salmon fillets, 7 ounces each, about 1 inch thick at the thickest part

⅓ cup coarsely chopped mixed basil and mint leaves

Do-Ahead Options

⬧ Prepare the vinaigrette up to a week ahead and take it out of the refrigerator 30 minutes before using it (or an hour if you're serving it on the side).

⬧ Cook the dish up to a day ahead and take it out of the refrigerator a good hour before you serve it.

1 Preheat the oven to 425°F with the rack in the middle. Place the lemon juice in a small bowl, whisk in the mustard, and gradually whisk in the olive oil to make a thickened vinaigrette. Stir in the capers and olives, season with salt and pepper, and set aside.

2 Season the fillets with salt and pepper and place them in a large enough roasting pan or other baking pan for each to be separated by about 1 inch. Spoon 1 tablespoon of the vinaigrette over each fillet.

3 Roast the salmon until the sides of the fillets are slightly springy when gently pressed, 10 to 12 minutes. Roast for 2 to 3 minutes more if you prefer well done, the sides will feel firm when gently squeezed and the flesh will be opaque throughout.

4 Transfer the salmon to warm plates (see Note), spoon a little more vinaigrette over each fillet, sprinkle with the basil and mint, and serve with any remaining vinaigrette on the side. Or serve warm or at room temperature.

NOTE: If the skin sticks to the pan, slide a metal spatula between the skin and the bottom of the fillet. Lift out the fillet, leaving the skin in the pan.

Grilled Salmon with Fresh Tomatoes and Basil

When grilled to a golden hue, salmon fillets have an irresistible charm all by themselves. But when topped with tomatoes that have been tossed in lemon brown butter and sprinkled with basil, they get even better. The tomatoes are cooked for seconds — just warmed, really — so they remain fresh and vibrant and release just enough of their juices to create a slightly creamy bond with the butter. It's a perfect dinner for a sticky-hot night when gorgeous garden tomatoes are in season. **6 SERVINGS**

- **6 salmon fillets, 7 ounces each, about 1 inch thick at the thickest part**
- **Salt and freshly ground pepper**
- **2 tablespoons olive oil**
- **6 tablespoons butter**
- **4½ tablespoons freshly squeezed lemon juice**
- **3 to 4 ripe medium tomatoes, cut into ¾-inch dice** (4½ cups)
- **⅛ teaspoon Tabasco sauce, or to taste**
- **12 to 15 basil leaves, torn into bite-size pieces**

Do-Ahead Option

◆ Squeeze the lemon juice and cut the tomatoes up to 2 hours ahead, draining the tomatoes of their accumulated water before using.

1 Prepare a medium fire in the grill. About 10 minutes before cooking, heat the grate 4 to 5 inches above the coals (see page 147). Brush the top of the grate with vegetable oil just before grilling to help prevent sticking.

2 Dry the salmon fillets with paper towels, season with salt and pepper, and moisten with olive oil. Place them skin side up on the grill and cook without moving them for 5 to 6 minutes, until they form a golden brown crust. (This helps prevent sticking.) Turn them and grill the other side 3 to 4 minutes more; the fillets should be just slightly underdone at this point. To check, insert a paring knife into the thickest part of one and gently push it open. If you prefer more well done, cook for 1 to 2 minutes more. Transfer the fillets to a warm platter or plates.

3 Set a medium skillet over medium-high heat and melt the butter until it turns light brown, 30 to 60 seconds. Add the lemon juice and swirl the pan as it froths up. Immediately add the tomatoes and warm them for 5 to 10 seconds for very ripe tomatoes and 15 to 30 seconds for firmer ones. Remove the skillet from the heat and stir in the Tabasco sauce and salt and pepper to taste.

4 Spoon the tomatoes over the salmon, sprinkle with the basil, and serve right away.

FRANK AND NINA

Our friends Nina and Frank have been married for over fifteen years, and we've known them for ten. They are favorites of ours, and I bet we've fed them more times than anyone else. Nina doesn't like to cook, and she doesn't mind saying she doesn't know how. But Frank is another story. He probably owns every kitchen gizmo, large and small, that was ever invented, and he uses every single one.

They are both endlessly enthusiastic and adventurous. Their only flaw, if I can call it one, is being too big-hearted. When they come for dinner, they're laden with gifts, even if I have announced we might be having only a plate of pasta. Our reward will far outweigh the effort.

Frank likes to bake bread. And when they arrive at the door, his long skinny arms are outstretched in front of him with an offering of a huge round loaf, deeply browned and crusted (with patches of black, which I love) and looking like it was just flown in from some bakery in France where they're still making bread the old way. But it's the France of his own little brick oven located just a few miles up the road behind their house. In the summer, Nina is likely to be carrying straw bags filled with peaches or strawberries or melons, and vegetables from the country, somehow also managing an armload of sunflowers, purple delphinium, or peonies still smelling of the sun.

After they transfer their bounty into our arms, they break out what they call "the real gift," which has been stashed in Frank's worn leather shoulder bag. It might be two seats behind the first base line for the World Series or an invitation to a private screening of the new Robert Altman film. Yes, they are too generous, but it comes from the bottom of their hearts.

Frank and Nina eat at our house a lot, as I've told you. They've been there in every season (as we have at their house) and for every kind of meal and for holidays and the big events of our lives. They've eaten through a sizable portion of my repertoire, and when it comes to style of food, there's nothing that I cannot feed them. For me, they are perfect from the culinary standpoint, as they welcome an elegant and delicate sea bass with shallots just as much as something more rustic with chiles or chorizos. Just as long as the cooking is delicious and, heaven knows, not fussy, they're there.

Grilled Catfish with Ginger-Garlic Vinaigrette

Catfish, a mild, sweet-tasting fish, is underappreciated for what it can be beyond cornmeal coated and fried. Unlike other white fillets, which often stick and fall apart on the grill, catfish is firm and easy to handle, so it can reap the smoky benefits of cooking over coals. Bass, halibut, red snapper, or salmon — grilled, sautéed, broiled, or baked — also take kindly to this Asian-influenced vinaigrette. **6 SERVINGS**

4½ **tablespoons rice vinegar**

1½ **tablespoons hoisin sauce**

2½ **teaspoons soy sauce**

¼ **cup plus 2½ tablespoons vegetable oil**

1 **tablespoon minced garlic**

2 **tablespoons finely chopped ginger** (see page 101)

Salt and freshly ground pepper

6 **catfish fillets, 7 to 8 ounces each, cut ¾ inch thick**

⅔ **cup thinly sliced scallions** (white part and tender green)

1 Prepare a medium fire in the grill. About 10 minutes before cooking, preheat the grate 4 to 5 inches above the coals (see page 147).

2 Meanwhile, combine the vinegar, hoisin sauce, and soy sauce in a small bowl. Gradually whisk in 4½ tablespoons of the oil. Stir in the garlic and ginger, and season with salt and pepper to taste. Set the vinaigrette aside.

3 Season the fillets with salt and pepper, moisten with the last 2 tablespoons of oil, and grill them, rounded side down, for 5 to 6 minutes or until golden. Turn them and cook until they are white and opaque throughout, 3 to 4 minutes more. To check, slightly separate the flesh in the center of one fillet with a metal spatula. If necessary, grill them 1 to 2 minutes more.

4 Transfer the fish to a warm platter or plates. Stir the scallions into the vinaigrette, spoon some over each fillet, and serve the rest on the side.

Do-Ahead Option

◇ Prepare the vinaigrette up to 5 days ahead. Take it out of the refrigerator an hour before serving and stir in the scallions at the last minute.

HOW TO STORE GINGER

You can store unpeeled fresh ginger in a paper bag with its top folded over in the crisper of your refrigerator for a number of weeks before it starts to shrivel. The paper protects it from drying out while allowing it to breathe at the same time. I know it's recommended that you peel ginger and store it in sherry, but I'm not a fan of that method because I think it dilutes the flavor.

HOW TO CHOP FRESH GINGER THE CHINESE WAY

Everyone who has seen this way of chopping ginger loves it. First, peel as much of the ginger as you think you need. Then cut it into very thin slices across the grain. Lay the slices in a row across one half of a large piece of plastic wrap; fold the other half over the slices. Pound them — let 'em have it — with the flat side of a cleaver, meat mallet, or the back of a small skillet. The slices will separate into natural fibers. And the thinner you've sliced the ginger in the first place, the finer the pieces will be. Scrape them together, give them one or two quick chops with a large knife or cleaver, and use them wherever chopped ginger is called for.

Chilean Sea Bass with Shallots

Chilean sea bass (which really isn't a bass at all but a Patagonian toothfish, a name that conjures up all sorts of images, don't you think?) has big, white, satiny flakes and surprisingly rich flavor for a white-fleshed fish. This recipe underscores its lusciousness in an understated, elegant way. You might also try sable fish (black cod) done this way if you see it around. It's similar to sea bass, but with a more delicate taste and lighter texture. **6 SERVINGS**

---

4 tablespoons butter

8 large shallots, thinly sliced (2 cups)

3 large garlic cloves, very thinly sliced

Salt and freshly ground pepper

6 Chilean sea bass fillets, about 7 ounces each, cut ¾ to 1 inch thick

Juice from 1 lemon

¾ teaspoon dried thyme

3½ teaspoons aged Spanish sherry vinegar, or 1¾ teaspoons red wine vinegar mixed with 1½ teaspoons balsamic vinegar

1½ teaspoons chopped fresh dill

1 Preheat the oven to 400°F with a rack in the middle. Melt 3 tablespoons of the butter in a medium skillet set over medium heat and cook the shallots and garlic, stirring frequently, until they are softened and a little brown, about 3 minutes. Season them with salt and pepper and set aside to cool slightly.

2 Season the fish fillets on both sides with salt and pepper, moisten them with lemon juice, rubbing it in lightly, and sprinkle with the thyme. Lay the fillets in a single layer in a baking pan large enough for them to be separated by about 1 inch. Spread the shallot-garlic mixture over and around the fillets, sprinkle them with the vinegar, and dot with the remaining 1 tablespoon butter.

3 Roast the fish until it is cooked through, 15 to 20 minutes. To check, make a small cut in the thickest part of one fillet to see if it's white and opaque throughout. If not, cook several minutes longer.

4 Transfer the fillets to a platter or warm plates. Spoon the shallots and garlic, and any juices, over the fillets, sprinkle with the dill, and serve hot.

Do-Ahead Option

◈ Slice the shallots and garlic,
squeeze the lemon, and chop
the dill up to a day ahead.

ABOUT HEAVY COOKWARE

You may notice that many recipes in this book give a range of baking and roasting times. Besides the fact that everyone's stove is slightly different, an exact number of minutes can't be set in stone because a lot depends on the pan. Cooking really starts when the pan itself gets hot and begins to transfer the heat to the food. And if the pan is heavy (my preference), it takes longer for the pan to heat up, but when it does, it cooks evenly and reliably.

Range-top cooking also works best with heavyweight pans. I'm happiest when cooking with old-fashioned black iron pots and pans, porcelain-coated ironware, French copper pans lined with either tin or stainless steel, and heavy-gauge aluminum.

Cumin-Rubbed Grilled Skate Wings with Bacon and Lemon Oil

Skate, a flat, triangular fish shaped something like a kite, sweeps gracefully along the ocean floor by waving its broad wings. And those elegant wings are the mild, sweet-tasting part that we eat. This simple grilled preparation is a celebration of smoky flavors from cumin to paprika (particularly if it's Spanish pimentón*) to bacon — and not least, the smoke cooking, which pulls it all together. The thin edges of the skate, cartilage and all, turn succulent, brown, and crusty and are wonderful to chew on.* 6 SERVINGS

---

2 tablespoons Spanish *pimentón dulce* or sweet Hungarian paprika (available in some supermarkets, specialty stores, and by mail order)

2½ tablespoons ground cumin, preferably freshly ground

6 skinless skate wings on the bone, about 12 ounces each

Salt and freshly ground pepper

½ cup plus 1 tablespoon extra-virgin olive oil

4 to 5 thick slices of bacon, cut into ½-inch pieces

4½ tablespoons freshly squeezed lemon juice

2½ tablespoons coarsely chopped parsley, preferably flat-leaf

Lemon wedges, for garnish

1 Prepare a medium-hot fire in the grill. About 10 minutes before you're ready to cook, heat the grate 4 to 5 inches above the coals (see page 147). Brush the grate with vegetable oil just before grilling to help prevent sticking.

2 Meanwhile, combine the paprika and cumin in a small bowl. Dry the skate wings with paper towels and set them on a cookie sheet. Sprinkle both sides with the spice mixture and season with salt and pepper, rubbing it in lightly. Moisten them with 6 tablespoons of the olive oil and lightly rub it in all over. Let the fish marinate for 15 minutes.

3 Meanwhile, cook the bacon in a medium skillet set over low heat until brown and crisp. Drain it on paper towels and set aside. Reserve 3 tablespoons of its fat in the skillet, saving or discarding any extra (or if there is not enough, make up the difference with extra olive oil). Add the remaining 3 tablespoons olive oil to the skillet and set it aside.

4 Grill the wings (in batches if necessary), covered by the grill top, until the bottoms have browned and crusted (don't move them earlier or they will stick and shred). Turn them over and grill until just cooked through, 15 to 18 minutes total (moving them to a cooler part of the grill if they brown too rapidly).

They're done when the flesh is white throughout and a thin metal spatula can be gently slid back and forth between the thickest part of the meat and the cartilage that runs horizontally through the center.

5   Transfer the wings to a warm platter or plates. Set the skillet with the bacon fat and olive oil over medium-high heat and season with salt and pepper. When it's good and hot, add the lemon juice and as soon as it froths, remove the skillet from the heat. Spoon a tablespoon of the lemon oil over each wing, garnish with the bacon pieces, sprinkle with parsley, and serve hot with lemon wedges alongside.

WHAT ARE SKATE WINGS AND HOW DO YOU EAT THEM?

One skate wing has two wing-shaped fillets joined by a pliable sheath of fingerlike cartilage that runs through the center. You eat the meat by pulling it away from the cartilage with your fork. Once you've finished the top fillet, you can lift off the cartilage easily to reach the fillet on the bottom, like removing the center bone from a fish. Or you can serve the wings boned (after cooking): remove the top fillet by sliding a metal spatula between the flesh and the top of the center cartilage and lift it off in one piece. Discard the cartilage and place the fillet back over the bottom to make a serving.

For recipes other than Cumin-Rubbed Grilled Skate (page 104), which uses the bone-in wing, you can have the market fillet the skate before you take it home. To sauté them as fillets, season and lightly flour them, then cook them in olive oil over very high heat in a very large skillet, turning them once, for 2 to 3 minutes in all (or longer, depending on how thick they are). When done, they should be brown on the outside and white and juicy on the inside.

Grilled Tuna with Roasted Red Pepper Pesto

Tuna is a meaty fish that can stand up to assertive companions. Traditional pesto has a pretty powerful taste, which could overwhelm the tuna, but here it's kept in check by the gentler flavor of sweet peppers. If you can grill the fish over charcoal, great, but pan-searing or broiling works well, too. 6 SERVINGS

4½ tablespoons lightly toasted walnuts

1½ cups lightly packed basil leaves, plus about ½ cup for garnish

1 medium-large garlic clove, sliced

5 tablespoons extra-virgin olive oil

Salt and freshly ground pepper

1 large roasted red pepper, chopped (¾ cup), jarred or freshly roasted (see page 63)

Large pinch of cayenne

6 tuna steaks, about 7 ounces each, cut 1 inch thick

1 Prepare a medium fire in the grill. About 10 minutes before you're ready to cook, heat the grate 4 to 5 inches above the coals (see page 147). Brush the grill with vegetable oil right before cooking to help prevent sticking.

2 Meanwhile place the walnuts, 1½ cups basil, the garlic, and 3 tablespoons of the olive oil in a food processor. Chop them together until the mixture forms a nubby puree, about 2 minutes. Season with salt and pepper to taste and transfer the puree to another bowl.

3 Put the roasted pepper in the processor (no need to rinse), chop finely, add the basil-nut puree, and pulse several times to combine. Season with salt, pepper, and cayenne pepper to taste and set the pesto aside.

4 Season the tuna with salt and pepper and moisten both sides with the remaining 2 tablespoons olive oil. Grill the first side for 2 to 3 minutes, until browned. Turn over and cook for 2 to 3 minutes more, until browned on the second side but still pink in the center. For well done, grill 1 to 2 minutes longer on each side. Transfer to a platter or plates.

5 Coat the top of each piece of tuna with pesto, spreading it with the back of a spoon. Tear the basil leaves into bite-size pieces, scatter them over the tuna, and serve hot, warm, or at room temperature. (If not serving the fish hot, garnish with basil later.)

FETA CHEESE AND ROASTED RED PEPPER PESTO SPREAD

With very little effort, the pesto from the recipe on page 106 can be turned into a savory spread — just the thing to accompany all sorts of raw vegetables, crackers, or a sliced and toasted baguette, and it can be made several days ahead.

Puree ½ pound of feta cheese in a food processor with 3 to 4 tablespoons of the roasted pepper pesto, or enough to deeply flavor it. If the mixture is stiff in the machine, add a few tablespoons of milk, cream, or yogurt to make it creamier, but don't liquefy it — it's meant to be thick. Season with salt and fresh pepper and serve the spread at room temperature or slightly chilled. A sprinkle of good Spanish or Hungarian paprika and chopped green herbs on top is nice, too.

❋ Stir-Fried Shrimp with Mint-Ginger Sauce and Mango

All the components for this dish go right on the table — crisp juicy shrimp, sweet mango, crunchy bean sprouts, and fresh, spicy sauce. Everyone takes a big lettuce leaf, stuffs and rolls it with the goodies, and chows down. It's a participatory party. To make this a meal without using the stove at all, thread the shrimp on skewers, moisten them with oil, and cook them on the grill. **6 TO 8 SERVINGS**

---

3 pounds large peeled shrimp

1½ cups loosely packed fresh mint leaves

½ cup coarsely chopped seeded jalapeño peppers (4 to 5)

3 large garlic cloves, thinly sliced

2 tablespoons coarsely chopped fresh ginger

1 tablespoon plus 2½ teaspoons sugar

½ cup plus 1 tablespoon distilled white vinegar

1½ tablespoons Asian fish sauce (optional), *nuoc nam* or *nam pla*

16 to 18 large Boston or other lettuce leaves

1½ cups large bean sprouts

¾ cup loosely packed cilantro sprigs

2 ripe mangos, peeled and sliced thin

3 tablespoons vegetable oil

Salt and freshly ground pepper

1 One at a time, butterfly the shrimp by making a deep cut down the middle of the back but not slicing all the way through. Lift out the black intestine with the point of the knife or hold the shrimp under cold running water to flush it out. Either way, dry them well on paper towels and set them aside.

2 Put half of the mint leaves in a blender and save the rest for garnish. Add the jalapeños, garlic, ginger, sugar, vinegar, and fish sauce. Puree thoroughly until smooth, about 2 minutes. Set the sauce aside.

3 Attractively arrange the lettuce leaves, remaining mint leaves, bean sprouts, cilantro sprigs, and mango slices on a platter and refrigerate until ready to serve.

4 Add the oil to a wok or large skillet set over high heat. When it's hot, add the shrimp, season with salt and pepper, and stir-fry until lightly browned and just cooked through, 3 to 5 minutes. Transfer the shrimp to a warmed platter.

5 Serve the platters of shrimp and garnishes with the sauce on the side so everyone can make his or her own. To assemble a roll, place several shrimp down the center of a leaf top with sprouts, cilantro sprigs,

Do-Ahead Options

◆ Make the sauce up to 2 days ahead and take it out of the refrigerator 1 hour before serving.

◆ Clean the shrimp up to 2 days ahead and cook them up to 20 minutes ahead; serve them warm or at room temperature.

◆ Refrigerate the garnishes on the serving platter covered with a moist towel up to 2 hours ahead.

mint leaves, and slices of mango; and drizzle with sauce. Roll the lettuce around the filling as best as possible, pick up with your fingers, and eat.

CHICKEN

❈ Chicken Roasted with Indian Spices

Chicken tossed in a pungent mix of cumin, cardamom, garlic, pepper, and curry powder is packed off for an overnight stay in the refrigerator so the spices can do deep, penetrating work. The next day, the pieces of chicken are roasted in a hot oven (or grilled over a low fire) and come out tasting something like tandoori chicken, the evocatively spiced kind that's cooked in the blistering heat of an Indian clay oven. **6 SERVINGS**

1 tablespoon tomato paste

2½ tablespoons red wine vinegar

3 tablespoons ground cumin, preferably freshly ground

1 teaspoon curry powder

¾ teaspoon ground cardamom, preferably freshly ground

2 teaspoons freshly ground black pepper

⅛ teaspoon cayenne, or to taste

¾ teaspoon salt

¼ cup plus 2 tablespoons olive oil

6 large garlic cloves, crushed with the side of a knife, then peeled

6 pounds chicken breasts, thighs, and drumsticks, or all breasts

Optional garnishes: cilantro leaves and lemon wedges

1 Whisk together the tomato paste, vinegar, cumin, curry powder, cardamom, pepper, cayenne, and salt together in a large bowl. Gradually whisk in the olive oil, then stir in the smashed whole garlic cloves.

2 Add the chicken to the spice marinade and toss, rubbing the marinade all over to coat well. Cover the bowl and refrigerate it overnight, mixing the chicken with the marinade once again during this period, if possible.

3 Remove the chicken from the refrigerator 1 hour before cooking. Discard the garlic. Preheat the oven to 450°F with a rack in the center. Set a heavy roasting pan large enough to hold all the chicken with plenty of space around each piece in the oven (see Note). When the roasting pan is very hot, place the pieces skin side down in the pan.

4 Roast until the skin is crisp and brown, 15 to 20 minutes. Turn the pieces over. (If the chicken isn't browned yet, continue to roast without turning.) The wings and breasts may be done at this point; if so, remove them. Continue roasting the drumsticks and

thighs for 5 to 10 minutes more, turning them once or twice, until their juices run clear when a skewer is inserted in their thickest part.

5 Transfer the chicken to a warm platter or plates; reserve the roasting pan. Discard the fat in the pan, pour in ¾ cup hot water, set the pan over low heat, and scrape up the browned bits from the bottom with a wooden spatula. Season with salt to taste.

6 Serve the chicken hot or warm, sprinkled with cilantro and garnished with lemon wedges. Pass the pan juices on the side.

NOTE: If all the chicken won't fit in your roasting pan, use two pans on two racks, switching them halfway through the cooking time for even browning. In Step 5, add half the water to each pan.

ABOUT SPICE GRINDERS

The most flavorful spices are ones that have just been ground. Of course, it's not realistic to grind all your own spices, but some are so easily and quickly done that it's worth investing in a small electric coffee grinder reserved for just this use.

Whole spices, such as cumin seed, black and white peppercorns, coriander seed, cardamom seed, and fennel seed, are ideal candidates. The only requirement is that you put enough in the grinding section so that the blades don't whir in fruitless circles, but don't grind so much that you defeat your purpose. (Even leftover ground spices held for a few weeks are superior to most you'll find on a market shelf.)

Double Breast of Chicken with Two Mustards

This Restaurant Leslie classic is really a dish about two ingredients: chicken and mustard . . . but what they do together! The mustard is thickly slathered over the crisped, broiled skin of a small whole breast, which is broiled further until deep brown and finally finished in the oven. When it's ready, the mustard has become a mellow, crusty blanket sealing in all the juices. At the restaurant, we served it with sauce béarnaise mixed with minced French sour pickles, but the chicken as is stands on its own. **6 SERVINGS**

---

6 skin-on whole chicken breasts on the bone, about ¾ pound each (or use split breasts of the same weight)

Salt and freshly ground pepper

¾ cup Dijon mustard, preferably French

½ cup Pommery (whole-grain) **mustard from France, such as Maille or Bornier brands**

2 to 3 teaspoons white wine or dry vermouth

2½ tablespoons dry bread crumbs

3 tablespoons melted butter

1 bunch of watercress, stems for garnish

1 If you are using split breasts, skip this step. If you are using whole breasts, remove the center bone and cartilage; the rib bones stay in. To do this, place a breast on the counter with the broad end away from you, skin side up. Holding the broad end with two hands, bend it toward you, pushing down, until you hear the small, round-topped bone snap out underneath. Pull out the bone and with it the long, narrow piece of cartilage attached. If the bone pulls out alone, cut around the cartilage with a paring knife and pull it out, discard it, and repeat the procedure with the remaining breasts. Bend the two wide sides of each breast toward you until they snap a bit and the breast sits at about a 25-degree angle, if possible (see Note).

2 Preheat the broiler with the rack placed about 4 inches from the heat source. For either whole or split breasts, smooth the skin over the top to cover it completely if possible, and trim any long overhang. Place the breasts on a broiler pan or cookie sheet and season them generously with salt and pepper. Broil 4 to 5 inches away from the heat source until the skin is brown and crisp, about 10 minutes, moving them around in the pan to brown as evenly as possible.

3 Meanwhile mix the two mustards in a small bowl. Thin with enough of the wine or ver-

mouth to spread easily but remain very thick.

Do-Ahead Options

❧ The chicken breasts can be trimmed and readied for the broiler up to 2 days ahead.

❧ The mustard mixture can be refrigerated for almost forever.

❧ The chicken can be browned up to an hour ahead and coated with mustard. Or fully cooked up to 30 minutes ahead (keeping them uncovered) and served still warm.

4 Remove the pan from the broiler and coat the entire top of the breasts with the mustard, spreading it as evenly as possible with the back of a spoon. Sprinkle the bread crumbs over the chicken and drizzle with the melted butter. Return to the broiler to brown deeply, 8 to 10 minutes, watching them closely and turning them once or twice. (They will brown in a somewhat splotchy fashion and may even blacken a little, which is fine.)

5 Remove the pan from the broiler, reduce the oven temperature to 450°F, and roast the breasts in the oven until they're just cooked through, feel firm when pressed at their thickest part, and their juices run clear, 10 to 12 minutes. Transfer the chicken breasts to a warm platter or plates, drizzle with any pan juices, and garnish each with a small bouquet of watercress. Serve hot or while still warm.

NOTE: Removing the center bone and cartilage does two things: (1) it enables you to flatten the breast just enough so it fits under the broiler to brown more evenly; and (2) it helps the breasts to cook through more quickly.

DIJON MUSTARD

Dijon mustard from France, which was first made around the city of Dijon in Burgundy in the fourteenth century, defines the taste of true "Dijon." I recommend it for recipes calling for mustard because of its clear, sharp flavor. It also does the best job in mustard vinaigrettes because it emulsifies well, makes a thicker dressing, and holds together longer when compared to one made with a domestic Dijon-style mustard. I particularly like Maille and Bornier brands, both of which I find in the supermarket.

Chicken Cutlets with Fresh Tomato-Shallot Sauce

Chicken breasts get a mere veneer of coating when pressed au naturel into bread crumbs. Their natural moisture, boosted by a little lemon juice, allows just enough crumbs to adhere so the breasts become lightly crisp and golden when sautéed. Dressed up with a spoonful of light tomato sauce and resting on a bed of lettuce strips, they become elegant in a lovely, simple way. **6 SERVINGS**

---

3 ripe medium tomatoes, best quality available

3 large shallots, peeled

1½ tablespoons butter

5 tablespoons olive oil

½ teaspoon dried oregano

Salt and freshly ground pepper

3 tablespoons heavy cream (optional)

3 tablespoons freshly squeezed lemon juice

6 skinless boneless chicken cutlets, 2¼ pounds total

Approximately 1¼ cups panko bread crumbs (see page 115) **or other dry unseasoned bread crumbs**

5 or 6 large Boston lettuce leaves or other soft lettuce

1 One at a time, grate the tomatoes on the large perforations of a box-type grater, stem end facing your palm. (As you grate, the tomatoes flatten out, and their skin protects your hand.) Measure 1½ generous cups of pulp (saving any extra for another use) and discard the skins. Without washing the grater, grate enough of the shallots on the large perforations to measure 3 generous tablespoons.

2 Set a medium saucepan over medium heat with the butter and 2 tablespoons of the olive oil. When the butter froths, add the shallots, reduce the heat to low and cook stirring frequently, until they're softened but not browned, 2 to 3 minutes. Stir in the grated tomatoes and the oregano and simmer, stirring occasionally, until the shallots are tender and the sauce has thickened to about 1½ cups in volume, 5 to 8 minutes. Season it with salt and pepper. If using cream, stir it in now. Stir in 2 tablespoons of the lemon juice and set the sauce aside. The sauce will be light but not watery. Cook the sauce longer, if necessary, before adding the lemon juice.

3 Lay the chicken cutlets on a sheet of waxed paper. Gently flatten them with a meat mallet or the bottom of a small skillet so they are an even ½ inch thick. Season with salt and pepper and moisten with the remaining 1 tablespoon lemon juice, lightly rubbing it

Do-Ahead Options

💧 Dip the breasts in crumbs up to a day ahead and refrigerate them in a single layer on a platter, loosely covered.

💧 Make the tomato sauce up to a day ahead.

in all over. Place the bread crumbs on a platter and dredge each cutlet in the crumbs, pressing both sides firmly.

4 Set a very large nonstick skillet over medium-high heat with the remaining 3 tablespoons oil (see Note). When it's hot, brown the cutlets on one side until golden, about 3 minutes. Turn them over, reduce the heat to medium, and cook until the cutlets are firm when pressed and white in the center, about 3 minutes.

5 Meanwhile stack the lettuce leaves, roll them loosely into a fat cigar shape, and slice across into 1/4-inch-wide strips to get about 3 loosely packed cups. Scatter the lettuce over a platter or divide among plates. Reheat the sauce over low heat.

6 Lay the chicken on the lettuce, overlapping the cutlets slightly if using a platter. Top each with a dollop of tomato sauce and serve right away with the remaining sauce on the side.

NOTE: If you have only one nonstick skillet and it isn't large enough for all the cutlets, then brown them in batches and transfer them to a lightly oiled cookie sheet as they're done; finish cooking them in a preheated 375°F oven.

— ❖ —

JAPANESE PANKO BREAD CRUMBS

Panko bread crumbs look like bright white, spiky shreds. They're unseasoned except for a small amount of honey or sugar. Their claim to fame is the crisp, light coating they impart to sautéed or fried foods. Use them in their original form like any other bread crumb — for coatings, stuffings, and bindings — or whirl them in a food processor until they become fine crumbs. Once their cellophane bag has been opened, simply place it in a larger zippered type bag and store it in the pantry. The crumbs are available in Asian markets and in some supermarkets, or you can order them by mail; see page 296.

Chicken Breasts Roasted with Honey, Pine Nuts, and Thyme

Chicken breasts cooked in a mixture of honey, olive oil, and herbs emerge from the oven studded with pieces of golden nuts looking almost radiant as they await their last-minute gloss of light, syrupy pan juices. 6 SERVINGS

---

3 tablespoons honey

4½ tablespoons olive oil

2 tablespoons freshly squeezed lemon juice

¾ teaspoon Worcestershire sauce

¾ teaspoon dried thyme

¾ teaspoon dried oregano

¼ teaspoon ground mace

4½ tablespoons pine nuts, somewhat finely chopped

Salt and freshly ground pepper

6 split chicken breasts on the bone, each about ¾ pound (4½ pounds total), excess skin trimmed

½ cup dry vermouth (see page 117) or dry white wine

1 Preheat the oven to 400°F with the rack in the center and a heavy roasting pan large enough to hold all the chicken with plenty of room around each piece.

2 Mix the honey, 3½ tablespoons of the olive oil, the lemon juice, Worcestershire sauce, thyme, oregano, and mace in a medium bowl until smoothly combined. Stir in the pine nuts, season with salt and pepper to taste.

3 Dry the chicken breasts with paper towels and season them generously with salt and pepper. Set a large heavy skillet over medium-high heat with the remaining 1 tablespoon olive oil. When it's hot, brown the breasts in batches, skin side down, adding more oil if needed, until they're golden and the fat from the skin is rendered, 3 to 5 minutes per batch.

4 When all the breasts are browned, transfer them to the roasting pan, skin side up, and coat each with the honey mixture, spreading it with the back of a spoon (some will drip into the pan). Pour the vermouth around the breasts and place the pan in the oven. Roast until the chicken is just cooked through, 15 to 18 minutes (to check, make a cut in the thickest part of one breast to see if it's white in the center). If at any time the juices threaten to evaporate and burn, add a little more wine or water.

◆ Mix the honey, olive oil, Worcestershire sauce, thyme, oregano, and mace up to 2 days ahead and store it at room temperature. Stir in the lemon juice and nuts and season with salt and pepper right before cooking.

◆ Brown the breasts up to an hour ahead. Right before cooking, coat them with the honey mixture and finish them in the oven in the preheated pan.

5 Transfer the chicken to a warm platter or plates and reserve the pan. Set the pan directly over low heat (or transfer the juices to a small saucepan) and cook them down with any accumulated platter juices, stirring, until they become a flavorful, light syrup. Season with more salt and pepper if you like, spoon them over the breasts, and serve hot.

WHEN TO USE DRY VERMOUTH

You may not always have an open bottle of white wine available or want to open one for the small amount of wine used in cooking. Dry white vermouth is the answer. I always have it in my pantry, and much of the time I prefer its rich, herbal, white wine flavor because of the way it combines with food. A bottle lasts almost forever unrefrigerated, and its screw-on cap is not a sign of lesser quality; it's just how vermouth is capped.

Broiled Chicken with Coconut Milk, Ginger, and Chiles

Maybe you're looking at this recipe and thinking "spicy." Well, it's actually not, because the creamy coconut milk defangs the ginger and chiles but leaves their flavor. And under the broiler, the chicken burnishes to a golden color. This chicken is best hot, as suggested, but also good warm or even lightly chilled. **6 SERVINGS**

½ **cup canned unsweetened coconut milk** (see page 119)

2½ **tablespoons finely chopped seeded jalapeño peppers**

1½ **teaspoons grated ginger** (see page 139)

¼ **teaspoon ground cinnamon**

¼ **teaspoon freshly ground pepper**

Grated zest of 3 lemons

Salt and freshly ground pepper

6 pounds chicken breasts, thighs, and drumsticks or all breasts, trimmed of any excess skin and fat

Cilantro sprigs or thinly sliced scallions, for garnish

1 In a large bowl, thoroughly combine the coconut milk, jalapeños, ginger, cinnamon, pepper, and lemon zest. Season generously with salt. Cut the breasts in half crossways, if you like. Add the pieces to the bowl, toss in the marinade to coat evenly, cover the bowl, and refrigerate overnight.

2 Remove the chicken from the refrigerator 30 minutes before cooking. Preheat the broiler with the rack about 5 inches from the heat source. Lay the chicken skin side up on a broiling pan. Broil the pieces until crisp and golden, moving them around in the pan to brown evenly, 15 to 20 minutes depending on their size. Turn them over and cook, browning lightly, for 3 to 5 minutes more, or until their juices run clear.

3 Transfer the chicken pieces to a warm platter or plates skin side up. Pour ½ cup hot water into the pan (if it has burned, skip this step and serve the chicken without juices — it will still be good) and scrape up the browned bits. Pour the juices into a small saucepan and let them simmer over medium-low heat, skimming off the fat with a spoon as it rises to the surface, until it's reduced to about ⅓ cup. Season generously with salt and pepper and spoon over the chicken. Garnish with cilantro sprigs or scallions if you'd like, and serve right away.

USES FOR LEFTOVER COCONUT MILK

Here are three uses for leftover coconut milk, which can be refrigerated for up to 7 days, though it's best to transfer it out of the can first:

Aromatic Yellow Rice (page 210)

Grilled Rib-Eye Kebabs, Satay Style (page 148)

Milk Chocolate Parfait with Strawberries (page 269)

❖ Barbecued Chicken Breasts

*More on the tart vinegar side than sweet, this barbecue sauce does right by chicken
(or Cornish hens), but I've also used it with ribs, pork chops, and beef. It's a slightly
thin, cooked mixture that can be made as hot as you like by using more or less dry
mustard and Mexican chipotle chiles. The chipotles (which are smoked jalapeños)
add heat and a smoky dimension, but if you choose to leave them out, the sauce will
still have character.* **6 SERVINGS**

¼ **cup plus 2 tablespoons
finely chopped onion**

½ **cup ketchup**

¼ **cup plus 2 tablespoons
maple syrup**

¼ **cup plus 2 tablespoons
balsamic vinegar**

**7 tablespoons freshly
squeezed lemon juice**

**2 to 3 tablespoons
powdered mustard**

**3 tablespoons red wine or
other wine vinegar**

**2 tablespoons Worcestershire
sauce**

4 whole cloves

**Salt and freshly ground
pepper**

**6 skin-on whole chicken
breasts on the bone, about
¾ pound each** (or use split
breasts of the same weight)

2 tablespoons vegetable oil

1½ teaspoons to 1½

1 Prepare a low fire in the grill or bank the coals (see page 147) as the sauce will burn easily. Set the grill rack 5 inches above the coals about 10 minutes before you're ready to cook.

2 In a medium saucepan, combine the cloves, onion, ketchup, maple syrup, balsamic vinegar, 6 tablespoons of the lemon juice, the mustard, wine vinegar, and Worcestershire sauce. Set over high heat to come to a boil, then lower the heat and let simmer, uncovered, stirring occasionally, until the onion is almost translucent, about 10 minutes.

3 Pass the sauce through a strainer set over a bowl, pressing on the solids before discarding them. Stir in enough chipotle chiles to taste if using them, season with salt and pepper, and divide the sauce between two bowls. Set one of the bowls in a larger bowl of ice water to cool down quickly. This will be the basting sauce; it handles more easily when chilled. Set aside the other bowl to serve at the table.

4 Season the chicken generously with salt and pepper, rub with the oil and the remaining 1 tablespoon lemon juice. Set skin side down on the grill and cook for 3 to 4 minutes, until browned. Turn over and lightly brown the second side, about 3 minutes more. Turn again and baste the underside with the sauce.

tablespoons minced canned chipotle chiles, plus a little sauce from the can (available as "chipotles en adobe" or "chipotles in sauce" in specialty stores and by mail order)

Do-Ahead Options

◇ Prepare the sauce up to 3 weeks ahead, using half of it chilled for basting and taking the rest out of the refrigerator an hour before serving alongside the cooked chicken.

◇ Serve the chicken warm, cool, or at room temperature.

Turn one last time so that the skin side faces up, baste liberally with sauce, and move the breasts to a cooler part of the grill. Close the grill cover and finish cooking by reflected heat, removing the cover once or twice to baste their tops with more sauce (if you run short, steal a little from the reserved bowl). The chicken is done when it looks shiny and glazed, brown to slightly charred, and the juices run clear when pierced with a cooking fork or metal skewer, 12 to 15 minutes.

5 Transfer the chicken breasts to a warm platter or plates and serve with the reserved barbecue sauce on the side.

Chicken Breasts Stuffed with Asiago Cheese in Lemon and Sage Sauce

These chicken breasts are easy to like, but how many people do you know who aren't pushovers for melted cheese? Domestic Asiago is the cheese in the recipe (and if you're not familiar with it, you can read about it on page 123), but if you wanted a different kind, you could use Italian Fontina d'Aosta (but pass on the tasteless versions from Denmark and Sweden simply called Fontina), Swiss Emmentaler, French Gruyère, or mozzarella, either smoked or plain. 6 SERVINGS

---

6 skinless boneless chicken breasts, 2 to 2¼ pounds total

6 slices of domestic Asiago cheese, each about 4 x 1½ x ⅛ inch thick

Salt and freshly ground pepper

1 tablespoon dried whole sage leaves or 1½ teaspoons rubbed sage, or 10 to 12 large fresh sage leaves

3 tablespoons freshly squeezed lemon juice

1½ tablespoons butter plus 1½ teaspoons cold butter

3 tablespoons chicken broth

Parsley sprigs, for garnish

1 Cut a 2½-inch-long pocket through the thicker side of each breast, stopping about ½ inch from the opposite side and ½ inch from the thickest end. Lay the breasts on a sheet of plastic wrap with the pocket facing you and place a second sheet on top. Using a meat mallet or the bottom of a small skillet, lightly pound the thick ends so the breasts are an even ½ to ¾ inch thick.

2 Break or cut each piece of cheese in half and slip 2 pieces into each pocket. Season the breasts with salt, pepper, and the dried sage leaves crumbled between your fingers or the rubbed sage. (If using fresh sage, cut the leaves into medium pieces and set them aside.) Moisten the breasts with 1½ tablespoons of the lemon juice, lightly rubbing it in all over.

3 Preheat the oven to 350°F with the rack in the middle. Melt 1½ tablespoons of the butter in a very large ovenproof skillet set over medium-high heat. Brown the breasts rounded side down (scattering the fresh sage, if using it, over and around them) until golden, about 3 minutes, lowering the heat if they brown too quickly. Turn them and place the skillet in

Do-Ahead Option

◇ The breasts can be stuffed up to 2 days ahead, but rub them with lemon juice and season with salt and pepper just before cooking.

the oven until the breasts are just cooked through, 4 to 6 minutes.

4 Transfer the chicken to a warm platter or plates. Set the skillet over medium-high heat with the remaining 1½ tablespoons lemon juice, the chicken broth, and the 1½ teaspoons cold butter. Swirl the skillet by the handle as the juices come to a boil and reduce them, adding any accumulated juices from the platter, until there is about ¼ cup of well-flavored, slightly syrupy sauce. Season it with salt and pepper, if you like.

5 Spoon the sauce over the breasts (if the pieces of dried sage are large, strain the sauce over the breasts; otherwise leave the sage in the dish), garnish with parsley sprigs if using them, and serve.

ABOUT ASIAGO CHEESE

Domestic Asiago, which is somewhat like Cheddar in texture and Parmesan in flavor, is made in Wisconsin, and that's the one I've called for in the stuffed chicken recipe. However, if you're interested, you may be able to hunt down genuine Italian Asiago in a good cheese store. If you do, you'll find a completely different cheese, one that's creamier and softer in texture with a mellow, rather elegant persona. I like it best served as its own course with grapes and luscious fresh figs alongside.

Lemon-Garlic Roast Chicken with Smoked Paprika

Now that I know it exists, I can no longer imagine my kitchen without its stash of pimentón, Spain's glorious, rusty-red smoked paprika. It starts out, rather unprepossessingly, as small red peppers. But after a long, slow drying process in sheds filled with the heat and smoke of smoldering oak logs, the peppers become something greater than themselves — a powerful vegetal spice infused with the taste of wood, earth, and sun. Three slightly different, though related, peppers make three different heat levels, dulce, agridulce, and picante, from sweet to hot. **6 TO 8 SERVINGS**

---

12 large unpeeled garlic cloves, smashed with the side of a knife

2 whole chickens, 3 pounds each, rinsed and dried

1 tablespoon extra-virgin olive oil

4 teaspoons Spanish *pimentón dulce* or *agridulce* (available in specialty stores and by mail order)

1 teaspoon dried thyme

1 teaspoon dried savory (or half thyme and half crumbled rosemary)

½ teaspoon freshly ground pepper

Salt

1 large lemon, rinsed and dried

½ cup dry fino sherry, white wine, dry vermouth, or water

1 Place 6 cloves of garlic in the cavity of each bird and truss them (or tie their legs together). Moisten their tops and sides with olive oil, then sprinkle with *pimentón*, thyme, savory, and pepper, lightly patting them on. Refrigerate the birds overnight, uncovered.

2 Remove the chickens from the refrigerator 1 hour before roasting. Preheat the oven to 400°F with the rack in the center.

3 Salt the chickens generously and place them in a large, heavy roasting pan with 2 inches of space between each bird. Cut the lemon into quarters, pick out and discard the seeds, and scatter the lemons around the chickens. Roast the chickens for 1 hour to 1 hour 15 minutes, basting occasionally with the rendered fat in the pan, until the thigh juices run clear when pierced by a kitchen fork or metal skewer. Transfer the chickens to a platter and let them rest for 15 minutes.

4 Meanwhile, discard the fat from the pan and set it directly over very low heat. Add the sherry, white wine, or water, and scrape up the brown bits from the bottom. Press on the lemons to release any juice they

Do-Ahead Options

 Marinate the chicken up to 2 days ahead, loosely covering it on the second day.

 Serve the chicken warm drizzled with juices or at room temperature with or without juices.

may still have, then discard them. Simmer the juices for 1 to 2 minutes without reducing and add any accumulated juices from the chicken platter. Season the pan juices with salt and pepper to taste.

5 Carve the chickens and serve with their juices spooned over all or in a sauceboat on the side.

INDIAN SUMMER

The kitchen at the Inn at Pound Ridge, a country restaurant where I was chef, was a veritable trove of goodies, my special little store stocked with favorite foods. Feeling like a child in a candy shop, I could pick and choose what I wanted to cook. (And guess what? What I wanted to cook was mostly what I liked to eat.) I was, after all, the chef. So, lucky me, the menu reflected my taste, which meant, getting back to the first part, that I ordered the food that I liked *and* that the people who ate at the restaurant liked what I liked. What a fine arrangement!

Creating new dishes was always an interesting proposition. Much of the time I was thinking on the run because the volume of work was so considerable that even a few moments of hoped-for musing took a backseat. But there were other times when I could wander from storeroom to pastry area and from refrigerator to refrigerator communing with the bell peppers; the artichokes — so satisfyingly firm to the squeeze but threatening with their nasty, pointed leaves; the disks of goat cheese awash in olive oil and herbs; and the massive chunks of glistening swordfish awaiting the knife and marination.

Many times an idea would occur to me in the most mundane of situations — while dicing eggplant, let's say, or scraping out the soft orange flesh from just-roasted butternut squash. I would look up, in a kitchen kind of reverie, deeply into the food, and see one of the cooks pressing out tomato seeds or pitting olives or cleaning wild mushrooms. At that second, the "Oh yeah!" feeling would roll through me, and these ingredients would join in culinary harmony. It was only then that I applied my "mental" power to figure out just what this dish might be. The best dishes were always these intuitive ones.

One of them was chicken breasts stuffed with Asiago cheese. And I remember the day it got created. It was a day that you could no longer say was summer, but hadn't quite become fall. I had just gone on a break, leaving the kitchen by the back and hearing the screen door clap behind me. I headed past the deep red barn that sat on the property. The sun was warm and sparkling, and I watched it play in the trees as I walked up to the road. The leaves hadn't started to turn yet, but the edge in the air was unmistakable. This was the most evocative of seasons, that almost transcendent time when the sun's cloak still enfolded you while the knowing whiffs of air revealed the cool changes to come.

When I returned to work, I put together a chicken dish that was full of both the brightness of lemon and the more forceful, earthy tastes of sage and slightly salty cheese, speaking to the days that hold both summer and fall elegantly in their hands.

PORK AND LAMB

❋ Pork Cutlets with Black Olives, Feta Cheese, and Basil

This dish was born at Restaurant Leslie with thinly pounded scaloppine of pork and purple basil, the floral-tasting, less potent member of the family. It made a really pretty presentation with its scatterings of purple-black olives, purple-red leaves, and stark white cheese over the golden brown meat. Here, the dish remains just as good with thick, boneless pork cutlets and green basil, which is much easier to find. **6 SERVINGS**

2¼ **pounds boneless pork loin, cut into 6 pieces** ¾ **to 1 inch thick**

Salt and freshly ground pepper

¾ **teaspoon dried marjoram**

Flour, for dredging

2½ **tablespoons extra-virgin olive oil**

¼ **cup plus 2 tablespoons white wine or dry vermouth**

¾ **cup chicken broth**

Approximately 24 Alphonso or Kalamata olives, pitted and quartered (see page 51)

⅓ **cup bite-size pieces of feta cheese**

2½ **tablespoons coarsely chopped or torn basil**

Do-Ahead Option

❧ Crumble the feta and pit the olives up to 2 days ahead.

---

1 Dry the pork with paper towels and season both sides generously with salt and pepper and with the marjoram, lightly pressing them in to adhere. Dredge the chops in flour and shake off the excess.

2 Heat 1 tablespoon of the olive oil in a large skillet over medium-high heat. Add the pork and sauté until golden on the bottom, about 5 minutes. Turn over and continue cooking for 4 to 5 minutes, lowering the heat somewhat once the second sides have lightly browned, until the pork is just barely pink in the center. Or cook them 2 or 3 minutes longer for more well done.

3 Transfer the pork to a warm platter. Set the skillet over medium heat, pour in the white wine and broth, and scrape up any brown bits from the bottom. Add the remaining 1½ tablespoons of olive oil, the olives, and any accumulated meat juices from the platter. Cook the liquid over medium-low heat for about 5 minutes, until the liquid is reduced to about 3 tablespoons (don't count the olives; you want a slightly syrupy, flavorful sauce). Season it with salt and pepper to taste.

4 Transfer the cutlets to warm plates or leave them on the platter, spoon the sauce and olives over the meat, scatter the feta on top, sprinkle with the basil, and serve right away.

Pork Tenderloin with Mustard and Tomatoes

Pork tenderloin is sweet, tender, and moist when it's roasted just long enough, which isn't very long at all. (Do watch carefully, though, because when pushed beyond its limits, it takes on the texture of rope.) It's such a simple yet elegant, easy-to-use cut, which makes a great choice for entertaining. 6 SERVINGS

---

3 pork tenderloins, about 2¼ pounds total

Salt and freshly ground pepper

2 tablespoons Dijon mustard, preferably French

Approximately ⅔ cup dry bread crumbs

6 sprigs of parsley, preferably flat-leaf

6 large fresh basil leaves

6 to 8 fresh sage leaves, coarsely chopped, or ¾ teaspoon dried and crumbled

¼ cup olive oil

¼ cup plus 2 tablespoons white wine or dry vermouth

1¾ cups peeled, seeded, and coarsely chopped ripe tomatoes (see page 187)

1 Dry the tenderloins with paper towels and season generously with salt and pepper; for easier handling, cut the tenderloins in half if you like. Divide the mustard among them and spread it all over to coat lightly. One at a time, roll them in bread crumbs, pressing to adhere. Refrigerate in one layer (with a little space between each, if possible) on a cookie sheet or platter, uncovered, for at least 15 minutes or up to 2 hours.

2 Combine the parsley leaves and basil in a pile and chop them together. Measure out 2½ tablespoons of the mixture for this dish and refrigerate it, saving any extra for another use. Coarsely chop the fresh sage and refrigerate it.

3 About 15 minutes before you're ready to cook the meat, preheat the oven to 375°F with the rack in the middle. Set a large, heavy roasting pan directly over medium-high heat with the olive oil (or use two large heavy, ovenproof skillets). When the oil is hot, lightly brown the tenderloins on all sides, turning them carefully with tongs, about 5 minutes.

4 Transfer the pan to the oven and roast the tenderloins, turning them several times, until they feel somewhat firm when gently squeezed around the sides, 20 to 25 minutes for medium; cook 5 to 10 minutes longer for more well done.

5 Transfer the tenderloins to a carving board. Set the pan over medium heat, add the sage, and cook, stirring, until aromatic, about 30 seconds. Add the white wine, tomatoes, and any accumulated meat juices from the platter. Cook, stirring frequently, until the tomato juices have created a small amount of creamy sauce but the pieces are mostly still intact, 3 to 6 minutes. Remove from the heat, season with salt and pepper, and stir in about 1 ½ tablespoons of the parsley-basil mixture.

6 Slice the tenderloins on a slight bias about ½ inch thick and arrange the slices, slightly overlapping, on a warm platter or plates. Spoon the tomato sauce around the slices, sprinkle with the remaining herbs, and serve right away.

Roast Pork with Black Forest Mushrooms

Here, pork browns in a hot oven, then is roasted at a low temperature along with mushrooms and a little broth to provide an almost no work au jus. This slow, moist roasting keeps the meat tender and juicy. A top coat of hoisin, soy, ginger, and garlic imparts a sweet-tinged Asian accent. For accurate timing below, be sure to remove the meat from the refrigerator 1 hour before cooking. **6 SERVINGS**

---

8 medium dried Chinese black forest mushrooms (dried shiitakes)

1³/₄ pounds boneless center-cut pork loin about 5 inches wide x 2¹/₂ inches high, fat trimmed to no more than ¹/₄ inch thick

Salt and freshly ground pepper

2 teaspoons vegetable oil

2 tablespoons hoisin sauce

2 teaspoons soy sauce

2 teaspoons ketchup

2 teaspoons rice vinegar

1¹/₄ teaspoons minced fresh ginger (see page 101)

³/₄ teaspoon minced garlic

1¹/₄ cups plus 1 tablespoon chicken broth

3 tablespoons dry sherry

1 tablespoon thinly sliced scallion

1 Place the mushrooms in a bowl and soak them in hot water to cover until soft, about 30 minutes. Remove the mushrooms from the soaking water and discard the water. Trim the stems flush with the underside of the cap and discard them. Slice the caps about ¹/₄ inch thick and set them aside.

2 Preheat the oven to 450°F with the rack in the center holding a small (8- x 12-inch is ideal), heavy roasting pan or ovenproof skillet (see Note). Season the pork with salt and pepper, rub it with the oil, and set it aside until the oven is ready and the pan is hot.

3 Meanwhile, combine the hoisin sauce, soy sauce, ketchup, vinegar, ginger, garlic, and 1 tablespoon of the broth in a small bowl.

4 Place the pork, fat side down, in the hot pan and roast until the fat is golden, about 15 minutes. Reduce the oven temperature to 350°F, pour off any rendered fat, and turn the roast over. Coat the top and sides of the pork with about two-thirds of the hoisin mixture, spreading it with the back of a spoon, and reserve the rest. Pour the remaining 1¹/₄ cups chicken broth and the sherry around the meat and roast for 15 minutes more.

Do-Ahead Option

◇ Make the hoisin mixture and soak and slice the mushrooms up to 2 days ahead.

5 Scatter the sliced mushrooms around the meat (adding additional broth or water, if necessary, so there is no less than about ¾ cup liquid in the pan) and roast for 15 to 20 minutes more, depending on the width of the meat. Remove the meat from the oven when an instant-read thermometer reaches 140°F — it will be faintly pink in the middle. For well done, roast an additional 8 to 10 minutes.

6 There should be about ½ cup of light, flavorful juices left in the pan measured without the mushrooms. If less than ½ cup, add enough broth to make up the difference. If more, remove the meat from the pan and boil down the juices. Otherwise, let the pork rest in the pan for 15 minutes before transferring it to a cutting board.

7 Reheat the mushrooms and juices over low heat, stir in the remaining hoisin mixture, and season with salt and pepper to taste. Cut the pork into thin slices, laying them on a warm platter or plates as you go. Spoon the juices and mushrooms over the pork, sprinkle with the scallion, and serve right away.

NOTE: A larger pan will allow the broth to reduce more quickly and you may need to add more broth to keep it from burning. A smaller pan will reduce the broth more slowly so it may have to be boiled down before serving to concentrate the flavor.

✤ Grilled Pork Chops Teriyaki

Ginger, garlic, and soy sauce is an irresistible combination for flavoring pork (not to mention lamb and chicken) and adding rosemary to the mix adds another friendly note of flavor. 6 SERVINGS

---

6 pork chops, about 10 ounces each, cut 1 inch thick (3¾ to 4 pounds total)

Freshly ground pepper

3 tablespoons soy sauce

1½ teaspoons minced fresh rosemary, or ½ teaspoon dried

3 medium garlic cloves

2 teaspoons grated fresh ginger (see page 139)

1 tablespoon vegetable oil

1 tablespoon dry sherry, dry vermouth, or white wine

1 Dry the chops with paper towels. Make 3 or 4 shallow, diagonal slashes on their fatty edge to prevent them from curling, season both sides with pepper, and set them aside.

2 Place the soy sauce and rosemary in a small bowl. Squeeze the garlic through a garlic press held over the bowl. Whisk in the ginger, oil, and sherry.

3 Place the chops on a platter or other container that will hold them in one layer, pour over the marinade over the meat, and turn them in it to coat well. Refrigerate them overnight.

4 Prepare a low fire in a barbecue grill (see page 147). About 10 minutes before cooking, set the grate 5 to 6 inches above the coals.

5 Grill the chops, turning them once, until nicely browned and slightly pink in the center, 15 to 18 minutes, depending on the grill. For more well done, cook them 2 to 3 minutes more. Transfer the chops to a warm serving platter or plates and serve right away.

HOW TO GRILL
MARINATED MEATS

Grilling meats, like chops or steaks, that have been
brushed or marinated in a soy sauce mixture (or one that
includes honey, maple syrup, or sugar) should be done over a
relatively low fire. High heat will quickly brown — or burn
— the exterior, leaving the inside raw or at least underdone
(thin or small pieces can work fine, though).

If you have a gas grill, set the heat to medium and cook
the food directly over the elements. If you cook over charcoal briquettes or hardwood charcoal, you have two options:
grill directly over a low fire; or do what I do, make a medi-
um-intense fire and bank all the coals to one side. Then I
lightly brown the food (on both sides) over the coals and
pull it toward the cooler side to finish cooking (turning it
once again during that time). And when grilling anything
with an edge of fat, like chops, I face the fat toward the coals
during at least part of the grilling to crisp and brown it.

If you like the banking-the-coals idea, try grill-roasting any
large piece of meat with or without a soy marinade. Lightly
brown the roast close to or over the coals first (if it's very
large, cook it away from the coals the entire time — it will
brown as it cooks), turning it on all sides as it browns. Then
move it to the cooler side, cover the grill to turn it into an
oven, and let it cook until done (turning it occasionally).

Soy and Spice Marinated Grilled Lamb

I love to hear the skewers of lamb sizzle over the coals, watch their edges start to char, and smell the hot, smoky perfume of meat on the grill. When they're done, the outsides are a little crusty and dark, making the juicy pink insides all the more delectable. Chops, steaks cut from the leg, and butterflied legs can be cooked this way, too, and if the meat is cut into bite-size pieces, it makes great hors d'oeuvres. **8 SERVINGS**

1/3 cup soy sauce

4 teaspoons dark brown sugar

2 medium-large garlic cloves

2 teaspoons ground cumin seed, preferably freshly ground (see page 111)

1¼ teaspoons ground coriander seed, preferably freshly ground

¼ teaspoon freshly ground black pepper, or to taste

⅛ teaspoon cayenne pepper

4 teaspoons freshly squeezed lemon juice

1 teaspoon grated orange zest

3½ tablespoons olive oil

3½ pounds boneless leg of lamb, fat trimmed to a thin layer, cut into 2-inch cubes

Sprigs of fresh cilantro or mint, for garnish

Plain yogurt, as accompaniment (optional)

1 You'll need 10- or 12-inch-long wooden skewers or metal skewers for this recipe. If you're using wooden skewers, soak them in water for at least 30 minutes to prevent them from burning. Meanwhile, prepare a medium-hot fire in a barbecue grill. About 10 minutes before you're ready to cook, set the grate 4 to 5 inches above the coals (see page 147).

2 Stir the soy sauce and brown sugar together in a large bowl until the sugar dissolves. Squeeze the garlic through a garlic press into the bowl. Whisk in the cumin, coriander, pepper, cayenne, lemon juice, and orange zest, then gradually whisk in the olive oil. Add the lamb and toss to coat thoroughly. Let the lamb sit, covered, at room temperature for at least 30 minutes or refrigerate it for up to 8 hours, turning the pieces in the marinade once or twice.

3 Slide the pieces onto the skewers with the fat sides facing out to crisp and brown, leaving about ½ inch of space between each piece so they'll cook all around. Grill, turning the skewers to brown the lamb deeply on all sides to the point of slight charring. If they brown too quickly (see page 133), move them to a cooler spot on the grill to finish cooking. They'll be medium-rare to medium in about 8 minutes. Grill a few minutes longer for more well done, if you prefer.

Do-Ahead Option

◇ Refrigerate the lamb in the marinade for up to 8 hours and take it out an hour before skewering and cooking it.

4 Transfer the skewers to a warm platter and garnish with the cilantro or mint sprigs. Serve the meat hot, coated with a spoonful of the juices that have accumulated on the platter. Pass a bowl of yogurt on the side, if you like.

BLUEPRINT

One day in the dead of August, when we were discussing selling our house, my husband burst out with, "Let's have a party before we go. We'll invite a few friends." So we started to make a list, and within 90 seconds the number was already climbing into the stratosphere. "Hmm," was the only sound I uttered. The solution quickly became clear — make it an open house. While the focus of this book is intimate get-togethers, what could better illustrate the beauty of a cook-ahead approach than an almost all-day party?

As the guest list grew so did my resolve to remain a part of the experience and not merely as chef. Already I knew it would be an all-done-ahead deal, whether I bought some of the dishes or cooked them. I might serve a big bowl of zippy white gazpacho, which everyone could ladle into their own cups. Maybe the spicy barbecued chicken breasts, which always went over well, would be a good choice, though I'd probably slice them ahead and serve them at room temperature. And we could also have salmon fillets in tangy mustard and black olive dressing because it, too, tasted just as good cool as hot.

Then it hit me. I didn't know when this party would be (since the house hadn't even gone on the market). What if it was in November, or worse, January? If that was what happened, well, then there were hot plates to use and our good old chafing dishes could be dragged out of the closet for chunks of sweet, tender duck, a homey meat and vegetable stew, or a Mexican casserole chock full of tortillas and chiles. My game plan would be to have everything ready so I could slip the pots into the oven throughout the day until the last had been heated and put out.

Salads, side dishes, and cold meats would also be ready. Would I make roasted sweet peppers and wild mushrooms? A simple, creamy potato salad? String beans with olive oil and thyme? And what about lemon rice or Arborio pilaf? The possibilities swirled in my head, and it looked like I was planning to cook everything in my book at one time. But then I breathed a sigh of relief, remembering that all I had to do was pick a direction and follow the arrows.

Lamb Chops with Provençal Tomatoes

It seems like a hundred years ago that I cooked order after order of noisettes of lamb Provençal at a Manhattan bistro called P.S. 77, but its earthy flavors will still be appealing for a hundred years to come because they are so satisfying. I like to sear the chops in a hot pan so they get a good crust and then slide them into a moderate oven to finish so their middles stay pink and juicy. But if high-heat sautéing seems like too much, you can grill or broil them instead. And in cold weather or for more of a crowd, you could roast a leg or a couple of racks in place of the chops and serve them with double the tomatoes. **4 SERVINGS**

3½ tablespoons extra-virgin olive oil

4 large garlic cloves, finely chopped

1 teaspoon dried *herbes de Provence*

1 can (35 ounces) plum tomatoes, drained, then crushed or coarsely sliced

2½ tablespoons pitted and coarsely chopped Mediterranean olives, both black and green (see page 51)

¼ to ½ teaspoon hot crushed red pepper flakes

Salt and freshly ground pepper

8 loin or rib lamb chops, cut 1 to 1¼ inches thick

¼ cup dry vermouth, or dry white or red wine

Basil or sprigs of another fresh herb, for garnish

1 Preheat the oven to 350°F with the rack in the center. Heat 2 tablespoons of the olive oil in a large skillet set over high heat. Stir in the garlic and dried herbs, immediately followed by the tomatoes. Cook over high heat, stirring occasionally, until the watery liquid has evaporated but the mixture is still very moist, 4 to 6 minutes. Remove from the heat and stir in the olives. Season with the red pepper flakes and salt and black pepper to taste; cover to keep warm.

2 Season both sides of the chops with salt and pepper. Heat a very large heavy, ovenproof skillet over high heat with the remaining 1½ tablespoons olive oil. Add the lamb chops and sauté until brown on one side, about 2 minutes. Turn them over and lightly brown the second side, about 1 minute (that side will finish browning in the oven). Stand the chops on their fatty edge to crisp before turning them back to their less browned side. Discard the fat in the skillet and transfer the skillet to the oven.

3 Cook the chops 5 to 8 minutes for medium-rare to medium, or 2 to 3 minutes longer for more well done. Transfer the chops to a platter. Set the skillet

back over medium-low heat, pour in the vermouth or
wine, and scrape up any brown bits from the bottom of
the pan. Add any accumulated juices from the platter.
Boil slightly to intensify the flavor and season with salt
and pepper to taste.

4 Quickly reheat the tomatoes, if necessary. Make a
bed of the tomatoes on a warm platter or plates.
Arrange the chops on top, spoon the pan juices over
them, garnish with the basil, and serve right away.

HOW TO SAUTÉ MEATS, POULTRY, AND SEAFOOD

The word *sauté* paired with meat generally brings to mind
a browned and lightly crisped fillet, cutlet, or chop with
delicious caramelized taste. To get the technique down,
there are three key points to remember:

1. You need *high heat* and you need the pan hot *before* the
    food goes in.

2. Use *as little fat* as possible — just enough to keep the
    food from sticking.

3. Leave *room in the pan* around each piece you're sautéing. A
    crowded pan lowers the temperature of the pan, making
    food difficult to brown and causing their juices to escape
    into the pan — Not to mention the difficulty of
    manuevering food around in the pan if it's all close
    together.

Grilled Loin of Lamb with Ginger Yogurt

Loin of lamb is a really special cut, with a price to prove it, but getting your mouth around such tender succulence makes it worth the expense, at least upon occasion. The yogurt sauce does double duty — first as a marinade, which mellows as it cooks, and second as a hot and gingery condiment alongside the lightly charred, rosy slices of meat. Ask your butcher to prepare the meat for you as you won't find it in the regular meat section of your market. **6 SERVINGS**

---

5 teaspoons powdered mustard

2½ tablespoons freshly squeezed lemon juice

2½ tablespoons grated fresh ginger (see page 139)

1½ tablespoons tamari or soy sauce

⅓ cup plain yogurt

Salt and freshly ground pepper

2 loins of lamb, boned, including their fillets (each loin about 1¼ pounds), **flaps trimmed, top fat no more than ¼ inch thick, and tied**

1 Prepare a low to medium fire in the grill. About 10 minutes before you're ready to cook, set the grate 4 to 5 inches above the coals (see page 147).

2 In a small bowl, make a paste with the dry mustard and lemon juice. Stir in the ginger, tamari, and yogurt until smooth, season with salt and pepper, then reserve 2 tablespoons. Season the lamb with salt and pepper and coat all over with the ginger yogurt.

3 Set the loins fat side down on the grill to brown and char slightly, about 2 minutes. Continue to grill, turning them as they brown (and moving them to a cooler part of the grill if they begin to burn), for a total of about 15 minutes for medium-rare, or about 5 minutes longer for more well done. Transfer the meat to a platter and let it rest for 5 to 8 minutes.

4 Snip off and discard the strings, thinly slice the lamb (or cut into thick slices, like filet mignon), and transfer the slices to warm plates. Drizzle any accumulated juices from the platter over the meat and garnish each serving with a teaspoon of the reserved ginger yogurt. Serve right away. Or let the meat sit, kept just warm, for up to 30 minutes before slicing and garnishing.

HOW TO GRATE GINGER

Fresh ginger is very firm, with a smooth, slightly shiny beige skin. As it ages, the skin starts to dry up, loses its slight shine, and begins to shrink. Eventually the ginger becomes wrinkled like a prune, with a spongy feel. While firm, fresh ginger is important for both chopping and grating it's particularly important for grating because what you're going for is the mostly liquid essence (which has all the flavor), along with some of the finer fiber.

To grate fresh ginger, peel it first with a paring knife or push a teaspoon under the skin to remove it. Grate the ginger across the grain using the medium perforations of a box grater or on a made-for-the-task ginger grater. The pulp that collects inside the grater will be fine, soft, and juicy, but most of it on the outside will be coarse and fibrous. Use the inside pulp for any recipe calling for grated ginger. And keep in mind that producing an equal volume of grated ginger as chopped requires a lot more ginger.

Lamb Burgers with Chinese Five-Spice Powder and Slivered Garlic Butter

Mixing a little five-spice powder into the ground lamb before cooking adds a hint of anise, clove, and hot Szechuan peppercorn flavor, which complements the natural sweetness of the meat. Then the garlic butter — with the garlic left in slivers — takes it one step further. And if you'd rather grill the burgers than sauté them, you can make the butter in a small pan on top of the grill. 6 SERVINGS

---

3 pounds ground lamb

2½ teaspoons Chinese five-spice powder (see page 141)

Salt and freshly ground pepper

1 tablespoon olive oil

2½ tablespoons butter

6 medium to large garlic cloves, cut lengthwise into very thin slivers

1 tablespoon coarsely chopped fresh tarragon (optional)

1 Place the ground lamb in a large bowl, sprinkle it with the five-spice powder, and season it with salt and a generous amount of pepper. Combine lightly but thoroughly (using your hands or a fork) and form the mixture into six 1-inch-thick burgers.

2 Set a very large nonstick skillet over high heat with the olive oil. When the oil is very hot, place the burgers in the skillet, in batches if necessary, and cook until the first side is well browned, about 3 minutes. Flip the burgers over, pour off any excess fat in the skillet, and cook about 3 minutes more for medium-rare or 5 minutes more for medium. Transfer the burgers to a warm platter or plates.

3 Set a small skillet over very low heat with the butter and garlic and season with salt and pepper. Cook, swirling the pan occasionally, until the garlic *just begins* to turn golden in color, 1 to 2 minutes. Spoon the garlic butter over the burgers, sprinkle with the tarragon, and serve right away.

ABOUT CHINESE FIVE-SPICE POWDER

Chinese five-spice powder is a fragrant, slightly heady mixture of ground spices that generally includes star anise, cloves, fennel or aniseed, cinnamon, and ginger. When the mixture is old, it becomes stale and lifeless. Sniff the powder in your bottle: it will either be aromatic or smell pretty much like nothing if it's been around a while. The blend is sold in many stores, but if you have trouble finding it and don't want to order it through the mail, you can combine equal amounts of ground cloves, aniseed or fennel, cinnamon, and dried ginger.

VEAL AND BEEF

❖ Veal Meatballs with Fresh Dill

These mellow meatballs loll about in their creamy pan juices (though you can leave the cream out, if you must), content to do their part on a cozy evening. For a larger get-together, you can double the recipe or make whatever size batch into somewhat smaller balls and serve them as hors d'oeuvres. **4 TO 5 SERVINGS (ABOUT 32 SMALL MEATBALLS)**

1½ **tablespoons butter**

¾ **cup finely chopped onion**

Salt and freshly ground pepper

1 **teaspoon minced garlic**

1½ **pounds finely ground veal**

1 **cup lightly packed shredded carrot**

¼ **cup dry bread crumbs**

1 **egg, lightly beaten**

⅓ **cup freshly grated imported Parmesan cheese**

¼ **cup plus 1 tablespoon chopped fresh dill**

2 **teaspoons vegetable oil**

½ **cup chicken broth**

⅓ **cup sour cream, at room temperature**

1 Melt the butter in a small skillet set over low heat. Add the onion, season lightly with salt, and cook, stirring frequently, until it's tender and slightly golden, 8 to 10 minutes. Add the garlic and cook, stirring occasionally, for 1 minute. Transfer to a plate and refrigerate until cooled to room temperature.

2 Place the veal, carrot, bread crumbs, egg, cheese, ¼ cup of the dill, and the sautéed onion and garlic in a large bowl. Combine with your hands, seasoning the mixture generously with salt and pepper, until all the ingredients are well incorporated. To test for seasoning, make a tiny patty and sauté it in a little oil in a small skillet set over low heat until cooked through.

3 Pinch off walnut-size pieces of the mixture and roll them between your palms into 1½-inch balls. Place the oil in a very large nonstick skillet over medium-high heat. When the oil is hot, sauté the meatballs in batches, rolling them in the skillet, until brown on at least 2 sides. Remove them to a platter as they brown. When all are done, discard any oil in the skillet and return it to the stove over low heat.

Do-Ahead Options

- Cook the onion up to 2 days ahead.

- Form the meatballs up to 2 days ahead or freeze them for up to a month.

- Cook the meatballs up to 4 days ahead. Gently reheat them in a skillet, covered, just long enough to warm through. Turn off the heat and stir in the sour cream, if you're using it.

4 Return all the meatballs to the skillet and add the chicken broth. Gently simmer the meatballs, uncovered, turning them occasionally, until they are just cooked through and no longer pink in the center, 8 to 10 minutes.

5 Remove from the heat and stir in the sour cream. *Do not cook*, or the sour cream will curdle; the retained heat of the skillet is enough to heat it through. Transfer the meatballs and sauce to a warm serving dish, sprinkle with the remaining 1 tablespoon dill, and serve right away.

Grilled Veal Chops with Tarragon Gremolata

When you serve veal chops, you can make a luxurious impression without turning yourself inside out with work. In this case, merely marinate them overnight, then grill them until they're lightly browned and their edges are crusty (and middles slightly pink). Give them a drizzle of good olive oil and a sprinkle of parsley mixed with tarragon, garlic, and lemon zest — it's all they need. 6 SERVINGS

---

2 to 3 lemons, washed and dried

¼ cup extra-virgin olive oil

2½ teaspoons Worcestershire sauce

¾ teaspoon ground coriander, preferably freshly ground (see page 111)

Freshly ground pepper

6 loin or rib veal chops, 8 to 10 ounces each and about 1 inch thick (see Note)

1½ teaspoons minced garlic

3 tablespoons minced fresh parsley, preferably flat-leaf

1½ tablespoons coarsely chopped fresh tarragon

Salt

1 Grate enough lemon zest—colored part only, no bitter white pith — to measure 2½ teaspoons and refrigerate it. Squeeze enough lemon juice into a small bowl to measure 1½ tablespoons. Gradually whisk 2 tablespoons of the olive oil, along with Worcestershire sauce, coriander, and pepper to taste into the lemon juice.

2 Slash the fat edges of the chops in 3 or 4 places, lay them in a single layer in a nonreactive container, and pour the lemon juice marinade over them. Turn to coat completely, cover, and refrigerate overnight.

3 Prepare a medium fire in a barbecue grill. About 10 minutes before you're ready to cook, set the grate 3 to 4 inches above the coals (see page 147). Mix the lemon zest, garlic, parsley, and tarragon in a small bowl to make the gremolata.

4 Season the chops with salt and grill them, turning once, until nicely browned, a total of 7 to 8 minutes for pink centers; or cook 2 to 3 minutes longer, turning once again, for more well done.

5 Transfer the chops to warm plates, drizzle each with a share of the remaining 2 tablespoons olive oil, sprinkle with the gremolata, and serve right away.

NOTE: If you prefer bigger, thicker chops, prepare a less intense fire and grill them a few minutes longer on each side.

Grilled Steaks with Shiitake Mushrooms in Whole-Grain Mustard Sauce

A different take on steak with mushrooms, these guys are topped with shiitakes in a lush, full-bodied wine sauce with a touch of creamy yogurt for a flavor that falls somewhere between beef stroganoff and boeuf bourguignon. *When you don't want to grill (or can't, for whatever reason), you can broil or pan-sear the steaks instead. Or, serve the sauce with a beautiful hunk of roast sirloin, cut into rosy slices.* 6 SERVINGS

---

6 boneless shell steaks or other boneless cut, 8 to 10 ounces each and 1 to 1¼ inches thick

1½ tablespoons olive oil

2 tablespoons soy sauce

Freshly ground pepper

2½ tablespoons French whole-grain mustard (Pommery)

2 tablespoons tomato paste

¼ cup plus 2 tablespoons plain yogurt

½ cup plus 1 tablespoon full-bodied dry red wine

1 tablespoon minced fresh rosemary

Salt

1½ tablespoons butter

8 ounces shiitake mushrooms (about 18 medium), **stems removed, caps quartered**

1 Prepare a medium fire in the grill. About 10 minutes before you're ready to cook, set the grate 4 to 5 inches above the coals (see page 147). Rub the steaks all over with the olive oil and 1 tablespoon of the soy sauce. Pepper them generously.

2 In a medium bowl, mix the remaining 1 tablespoon soy sauce with the mustard, tomato paste, yogurt, wine, and rosemary. Season with salt and pepper to taste; set the sauce aside.

3 Melt the butter in a large skillet set over medium heat and sauté the mushrooms, stirring occasionally, until brown and tender, about 5 minutes. Set them aside in the skillet.

4 Grill the steaks, letting each side crust somewhat (watch them — soy sauce burns easily) for a total of 8 to 10 minutes for rare to medium-rare. Or cook them longer for more well done, turning once or twice and moving them to a cooler part of the grill, if necessary. Transfer the steaks to a platter and let them rest for 3 to 5 minutes.

Do-Ahead Options

◆ Season the steaks up to a day ahead and take them out of the refrigerator an hour before cooking. Trim and cut the mushrooms up to a day ahead.

◆ Make the sauce up to 3 days ahead and heat it with the just-cooked mushrooms according to the recipe.

5 Set the skillet with the mushrooms on the grill rack or over a low burner and add the reserved sauce along with any accumulated meat juices from the platter. Simmer, stirring occasionally, for 1 to 2 minutes. Transfer the steaks to warm plates, (or leave them on the platter), spoon the sauce on top, and serve right away.

OUTDOOR GRILLS AND THEIR COOKING TIMES

Each grill is unique. Whether yours is fueled by gas, hardwood charcoal, or briquettes (I use hardwood charcoal when I can get it), more times than not it's going to perform differently from your next-door neighbor's (or mine, for that matter). Each has its own hot spots, not to mention its own manufacturer's idea (if it's gas) of what hot is. An otherwise wonderful person I know has a gas grill I'd just as soon dump into the ocean as cook on — its "hot" is my barely "medium." So any grill cooking times I've given may be somewhat different from your own — only you know your grill's innermost secrets.

❖ Grilled Rib-Eye Kebabs, Satay Style

These morsels of beef get their flavor from a richly spiced, but not seriously hot, coconut-milk marinade. A little tamarind paste (from the fruit pod of the tamarind tree) adds a somewhat mysterious sweet and sour element, but if you don't have it, a squeeze of lime will add the tartness, if not the mystery. Cubes of lamb are great here, too, and either beef or lamb cut into smaller pieces makes an easy hors d'oeuvre, particularly if the grill is going anyway. **6 SERVINGS**

½ **cup plus 1 tablespoon canned unsweetened coconut milk**

1½ **teaspoons powdered mustard**

1½ **teaspoons ground ginger**

¾ **teaspoon ground turmeric**

¾ **teaspoon ground coriander, preferably freshly ground** (see page 111)

½ **teaspoon ground cumin, preferably freshly ground**

½ **teaspoon ground cloves**

1½ **medium jalapeño peppers, stemmed, seeded, finely chopped**

2 **to 3 garlic cloves, sliced**

1 **tablespoon vegetable oil**

2 **tablespoons tamarind paste** (available in specialty stores and by mail order) **or** 2 **teaspoons freshly squeezed lime juice or to taste** (optional)

1. Place the coconut milk, mustard, powder, ginger, turmeric, coriander, cumin, cloves, jalapeños, garlic, and oil in a blender with the tamarind paste or lime juice. Puree the ingredients until smooth, 2 to 3 minutes. Season with salt and pepper, reserve 3 tablespoons of the marinade, and set the rest aside.

2. Place the cubes of beef in a large bowl and season them lightly with salt and pepper, toss with the larger amount of marinade, cover, and let marinate for 30 to 60 minutes at room temperature or up to 6 hours in the refrigerator.

3. Prepare a medium-hot fire in the grill. About 10 minutes before you're ready to cook, set the grate 4 to 5 inches above the coals (see page 147).

4. Slide the beef cubes onto the skewers, leaving ½ inch between the pieces so they'll cook all over. Grill the beef, turning the skewers once or twice, until they are brown to the point of slightly charring, 4 to 6 minutes total for medium-rare to medium; move them to a cooler spot on the grill if they brown too quickly. Grill the meat a few minutes longer if you prefer it more well done.

Salt and freshly ground pepper

3 to 3¼ pounds boneless rib-eye steak, sliced 1 to 1½ inches thick, fat trimmed, meat cut into 1- to 1½-inch cubes

5 Transfer the skewers to a platter or warm plates, drizzle with the reserved marinade, and serve hot or warm.

Do-Ahead Options

- Make the marinade up to a week ahead and refrigerate.
- Marinate the meat up to 6 hours before cooking.
- Grill the skewers up to 20 minutes ahead and serve them warm.

Filet Mignons with Gorgonzola-Porcini Butter

Buttery beef tenderloin is renowned for its tenderness, though not for big, beefy taste. But when it's matched by something as lusty as this flavored butter, it's hard to beat. The filets are pan-seared to a delicious state of caramelization, but you could grill them, instead, to add a bit of smoky flavor; be careful, though, because this cut of meat is short on fat and dries out easily. I don't advise broiling unless you have a seriously hot broiler, because anything less than intense heat can turn them an unfortunate gray. **6 SERVINGS**

¾ ounce dried porcini mushrooms (about ⅓ cup)

4½ tablespoons butter, slightly softened, plus 1 teaspoon

6 tablespoons Italian Gorgonzola cheese cut into small pieces

1½ teaspoons Dijon mustard, preferably French

Salt and freshly ground pepper

1 tablespoon olive oil

6 filet mignons, 6 to 7 ounces each, cut 2 inches thick

Minced fresh chives or finely sliced scallion greens, for garnish

1 Place the porcini mushrooms in a bowl, cover them with 1½ cups of warm water, and set aside until they soften, 20 to 30 minutes. Lift the porcini out of the water (strain and save the water for another use such as the Veal Stew with Mushrooms and Potatoes on page 168, if you like), trim and discard any dirty stem ends, and rinse them in clean water once or twice. Dry them on paper towels and chop into small pieces.

2 Cream the 4½ tablespoons softened butter, with the Gorgonzola and mustard in a small bowl. Season with salt and pepper.

3 Preheat the oven to 400°F with the rack in the middle. Set a small skillet over medium heat with the remaining 1 teaspoon butter. When it has melted, add the chopped porcini and sauté, stirring, for about 1 minute. Season with salt and pepper and transfer to a plate to cool. Then, stir them into the butter mixture and add more salt and pepper, if you like. Set the porcini butter aside.

4 Set a large heavy, ovenproof skillet over medium heat with the olive oil. Dry the filets with paper towels and season generously with salt and pepper. Increase the temperature under the skillet to high, and

◈ Make the porcini butter up to a week ahead or freeze it for up to a month. Either way, let it soften again somewhat before topping the filets with it.

when the oil is hot, deeply brown the filets on one side, 2 to 3 minutes. Then turn them on their edges to brown all the way around, about 5 minutes total. Turn them onto their unbrowned side, pour off any excess oil, and transfer the skillet to the oven.

5 Cook the filets, turning once, 8 to 10 minutes for medium-rare — their sides will feel slightly springy when they are gently squeezed. Cook them 2 to 4 minutes longer, turning once again, for more well done.

6 Transfer the filets to warm plates, top each with a share of porcini butter, and sprinkle with chives. Serve hot.

❖ Mini Meat Loaves

These individual little loaves are light and juicy. Part of their secret is tiny strips of bacon added to the mix, which bastes them from inside. They're classic and comforting, and for close friends. The recipe can be doubled if you want. **4 TO 6 LOAVES**

1½ **pounds ground beef chuck** (see Note)

2½ **tablespoons butter**

¾ **cup finely chopped onion** (see page 45)

1½ **teaspoons minced garlic**

2 **slices of white or whole wheat bread, crusts removed**

⅓ to ½ **cup milk**

1 **egg**

2 **teaspoons Dijon mustard, preferably French**

¼ **cup plus 2 tablespoons ketchup**

1 **tablespoon Worcestershire sauce**

½ **teaspoon dried thyme**

3 **thin strips of bacon, halved lengthwise and cut crosswise in ¼-inch-wide pieces** (about ⅓ cup)

⅓ **cup chopped parsley**

Salt and freshly ground pepper

1 **tablespoon soy sauce**

4 **parsley sprigs, for garnish** (optional)

1 Preheat the oven to 425°F with a rack in the center. Set a medium, heavy skillet over low heat with the butter. When the butter has melted, cook the onion and garlic, stirring occasionally, until the onion is light brown and slightly translucent, 3 to 5 minutes. Let cool to room temperature.

2 Meanwhile, tear the bread into small pieces into a small bowl. Mix in enough milk to thoroughly soak it and set aside to soften.

3 Break the egg into a large mixing bowl and whisk it lightly. Whisk in the mustard, 3 tablespoons of the ketchup, the Worcestershire, and the thyme. A handful at a time, squeeze out the softened bread and add it to the bowl, tearing it into smaller pieces as you do so. Amalgamate it with a whisk and stir in the bacon, separating the pieces, if necessary.

4 Break the meat into small pieces as you add it to the bowl. Add the browned onion mixture, the chopped parsley, and a generous amount of salt and pepper. Combine lightly but thoroughly — hands do the best job — and form a teaspoonful into a patty. Set a small skillet over low heat with a few drops of oil and cook the patty. Taste it and add more salt and pepper if it needs it.

5 Divide the meat mixture into 4 parts (each about 9½ ounces in weight) and pat them into slightly flattened loaves about 4½ inches long and 1 inch high. Set them in a roasting pan or other ovenproof pan sep-

Do-Ahead Options

 ❧ Combine the egg mixture,
   prepared bread, onion mixture, bacon, and parsley up
   to a day ahead.
 ❧ The loaves can be formed up
   to a day ahead. Take them out
   of the refrigerator an hour
   before baking and coat them
   with the topping just before
   going into the oven.

arated by at least 1 inch of space. In a small bowl, stir
together the remaining 3 tablespoons ketchup and the
soy sauce. Spoon the mixture equally over the loaves
and spread it to coat the tops evenly.

6 Bake the meat loaves until just cooked through,
20 to 25 minutes. Transfer them to a warm platter
or plates, garnish with sprigs of parsley if you like, and
serve hot.

NOTE: To make tender loaves, it's important to mix the meat
as little as possible. Removing the ground meat from the
refrigerator about an hour ahead so it is soft when you work
with it helps to do that.

Roast Standing Rib of Beef with Potatoes and Carrots and Yorkshire Pudding

I lust for a well-marbled roast with big, beefy taste and a thin brown crust of crackling fat on top and with vegetables browning alongside, soaking up the meat's juices. Around here we're hard-pressed to decide whether we're going to have carrots and potatoes or Yorkshire Pudding, drenched in the meat's natural jus. So bets are on that we'll have both. Whichever way you go, it makes a glorious meal for a special Sunday dinner or holiday. **8 SERVINGS**

One 8-pound standing rib of beef (4 ribs)

Salt and freshly ground pepper

2¾ pounds small peeled boiling potatoes, about 2 inches in diameter, or large ones cut into 2-inch pieces

2 pounds carrots, peeled and cut into thirds on the diagonal (if large, cut the thick parts in half lengthwise first)

1 large onion, peeled and cut into eighths

10 unpeeled large garlic cloves

Bouquet garni of 4 large sprigs of fresh thyme tied with 2 large sprigs fresh rosemary, or 1 teaspoon dried thyme and ¾ teaspoon dried rosemary

2½ tablespoons olive oil

1 Remove the rib roast from the refrigerator 2 to 2½ hours before roasting.

2 Preheat the oven to 500°F with the rack in the center. Season the roast all over with a generous amount of salt and pepper, pressing it in lightly. In a large bowl, toss the potatoes, carrots, onion, garlic, and herb bundle or dried herbs with the olive oil. Season with salt and pepper.

3 Place the rib roast, bones down to act as a rack, in a large, heavy roasting pan. Distribute the vegetable mixture around it. Roast for 15 minutes. Then without opening the door, reduce the oven temperature to 350°F and roast for 45 minutes more. At the end of this time, turn the vegetables in the pan.

4 Continue to roast, turning the vegetables once or twice, until an instant-read thermometer registers 120°F for rare, about 1¾ to 2 hours total. The meat will continue to cook from its retained heat and, when served, will be medium-rare to medium.

5 Transfer the roast to a platter to rest for 30 minutes. Separate out and reserve the garlic cloves, then transfer the other vegetables to a covered dish,

Yorkshire Pudding (recipe follows)

⅔ **cup Port or Madeira wine**

1¼ **cups beef broth**

Do-Ahead Options

❧ Peel and cut the carrots, potatoes, and onion up to a day ahead.

❧ The meat can rest up to 1½ hours after roasting.

---

leaving the herb bundle in the pan. Measure out 2 tablespoons of the rendered fat in the pan for the pudding and discard the rest. Make the Yorkshire Pudding as directed on page 156 while the meat rests.

6 While the pudding bakes, set the roasting pan directly over medium heat and add the Port. Scrape up all the browned bits from the bottom of the pan and simmer for 2 to 3 minutes. Add the broth and any accumulated meat juices from the rib platter. Simmer for 3 to 5 minutes to combine all the flavors; you will have about 1¼ cups juices. Discard the herb bundle, season the *jus* with salt and pepper, and pour it into a sauceboat. Peel the garlic cloves, and scatter them over the vegetables. Carve the roast (see below) and serve the meat and vegetables with the *jus* and the Yorkshire Pudding on the side.

HOW TO CARVE A STANDING RIB ROAST

The important thing in buying a rib roast is to ask your butcher to remove the chine and feather bones, so you'll be able to slice all the way through. Although these bones are removed as a matter of course, it's still good to make sure. They're the bones on the underside of the meat that aren't the ribs. If the worst happens and the roast comes home not quite oven ready, all is not lost; you can roast it and slice it English style, as described in the third paragraph below.

To carve the meat, set a warm platter near your cutting board. Stand the roast with ribs pointing up (facing toward you or away — either works) and cut down the *outside* of the rib bone, following the bone as closely as possible, to make the outside cut (which will be one of the two most well done). Lay it on the platter. Then, cut down the *inside* of that first rib so that the slice comes off with the bone attached. Keep slicing in the same fashion, alternating on and off the bone, setting them on the platter as you go.

The traditional English method of carving, especially appropriate when the chine and feather bones have not been removed, creates a more elegant look (and can make more slices to stretch the roast). Take a thin slice off one end of the meat, then lay the roast flat side down on your cutting board to keep it from sliding. Holding the meat in place with a carving fork stuck between the ribs, make thin horizontal slices cutting toward the bone. Cut each slice off the rib and lay it on the platter as you go. Once all the meat is sliced, cut between the meaty bones and add them to the platter, for those of us who like to gnaw.

Yorkshire Pudding

1 cup all-purpose flour

1 teaspoon salt

1/4 teaspoon freshly ground pepper

2 extra-large eggs

2/3 cup milk

1/3 cup beer

2 tablespoons rendered beef roasting fat, reserved from the standing rib roast (page 154)

Do-Ahead Options

◈ The eggs, milk, and beer can be combined and held at room temperature up to 1 hour ahead. The flour and salt can be measured into the mixing bowl.

◈ The batter can sit at room temperature for up to 1½ hours.

Make this while your roast beef is resting. If you prepare your batter while the beef is still roasting, it will all come together at the right time. This pudding is more crisp than puddinglike, and as it cooks, it rises in the pan like low, rolling hills. 8 SERVINGS

1 Place the flour, salt, and pepper in a large bowl. In a medium bowl, lightly beat the eggs, then whisk in the milk and beer. Gradually add the egg mixture to the flour, stirring with a whisk until smooth; it will have the consistency of very heavy cream. Cover the bowl and let the batter sit at room temperature for at least 30 minutes, or up to 1½ hours. Preheat the oven to 450°F after 15 minutes has elapsed.

2 When the oven is hot, preheat a 9-inch square or 10-inch round ovenproof baking dish or iron skillet set on a baking sheet for 10 minutes. Add the fat to the dish and heat in the oven for 5 to 10 minutes, until it's almost smoking.

3 Pour in the batter and bake for 10 minutes. Lower the heat to 350°F without opening the oven door and bake for 15 minutes more. Bring the dish to the table, cut the pudding into squares or wedges, and serve at once.

SLOW-COOKED DISHES AND CASSEROLES

❖ Slow-Roasted Duckling with Black Currant Sauce

These ducks roast in a low oven for hours, which makes their meat practically fall off the bone when they're done. Even after all that cooking, though, they retain a satisfying chew. Serve them simply with their pan juices or get fancier with the Black Currant Sauce on page 159. Note that after the ducks are prepared for the oven, they are refrigerated for at least 6 hours and up to 3 days. **6 TO 8 SERVINGS**

2 Long Island ducklings, 5 to 6 pounds each

8 quarter-size slices of fresh ginger, lightly smashed with the side of a knife

20 sprigs of fresh thyme

2 star anise or 8 whole cloves and 10 sprigs fresh tarragon, lightly crushed with the side of a knife

½ large orange, cut in half

Salt and freshly ground pepper

About 1 cup chicken broth, if needed

Black Currant Sauce (optional; recipe follows)

1 Remove the neck and giblet packet from the ducks' cavities and discard the livers (or save for another use). Rinse the ducks inside and out and dry them, inside and out, with paper towels. Gently twist back the wing tips and tuck behind their backs.

2 Stuff each cavity with half the ginger, thyme, and star anise or cloves and tarragon. Squeeze the juice of one orange half into each cavity, then place the piece inside. Tie the legs with string and refrigerate the ducks, uncovered, for at least 6 hours or up to 3 days.

3 Preheat the oven to 500°F. Remove the ducks from the refrigerator, pat them dry again with paper towels, and set them in a large roasting pan, allowing at least 2 inches of space in between. Place the necks and giblets in the pan. Season the ducks with salt and pepper, cover loosely with foil, and place them in the oven. Roast for 15 minutes.

4 Reduce the oven temperature to 300°F and roast for 3½ hours more, occasionally pouring off the accumulated fat from the pan into a container, prefer-

continued

Do-Ahead Options

✦ The ducks can be flavored up to 3 days ahead.

✦ You can make the base for the Black Currant Sauce up to 5 days ahead. Finish it as described in the recipe.

✦ Roast the ducks up to 30 minutes ahead.

ably a heatproof glass bowl or measuring cup, which allows you to see the clear fat layer after it has risen to the top. At the end of this time, discard the foil and roast for 1 to 1½ hours more, until the ducks are browned and crisp.

5 When the ducks are done, transfer them to a platter to rest for 15 to 30 minutes. Spoon off and save the reserved duck fat for another use or discard; reserve the brown pan juices. Pour off the fat from the pan, adding the juices to those reserved during roasting. Discard the necks and giblets and set the roasting pan directly over low heat on top of the stove. Pour in the duck juices. There should be about ¾ cup; if less, make up the difference with broth. Scrape up the brown bits stuck on the bottom of the pan. Simmer the juices just long enough to slightly intensify the flavor, 1 to 2 minutes. Season with salt and pepper, transfer to a sauceboat, and keep warm.

6 Carve the ducks: snip off and discard the strings from the legs. Cut along each side of the breastbone and with your hand, peel each breast away from the carcass with its wing still attached. Cut through the skin where the leg attaches to the body. Cut through the joint and peel the leg and thigh off the body. Do the same with the other leg. Repeat the process with the second bird. Set the pieces on a warm platter and serve with the juices or Black Currant Sauce on the side.

DELICIOUS DUCK FAT

Duck fat is a wonderful thing for sautéing potatoes or sweating vegetables for a winter soup. I store it in a coffee can in the refrigerator for months (or freeze it, yikes, for years). Just be sure that you've saved only the fat, because any meat juices will turn sour over time (if not frozen).

Black Currant Sauce

1 tablespoon olive oil

1 cup unpeeled thinly sliced shallots (about 5 shallots)

1 garlic clove, crushed with the side of a knife

1 bay leaf

¼ cup balsamic vinegar

½ cup full-bodied dry red wine

1½ cups chicken broth

2½ teaspoons cornstarch mixed with 2 tablespoons cold water

⅓ cup black currant preserves

Salt and freshly ground pepper

The deep berryness of this sauce, with its foundation of red wine and balsamic vinegar, strikes a balance with the famously rich bird. If you make this sauce, do so while the roasted duck is resting. MAKES ABOUT 1½ CUPS

1 Set a heavy, medium saucepan with the olive oil over medium heat and cook the shallots, garlic, and bay leaf, stirring occasionally, until the shallots are lightly browned, 3 to 4 minutes. Add the vinegar and boil it down until about 1 tablespoon of liquid remains, 2 to 3 minutes. Add the wine and boil until reduced to 3 tablespoons, about 5 minutes. Add the broth, bring to a boil, reduce the heat to low, and simmer, uncovered, until it has good flavor, 5 to 8 minutes. Set the sauce base aside or refrigerate it for up to 5 days.

2 When the ducks are done, transfer them to a platter. Follow the basic recipe in Step 5 at left, pouring off the final fat and juices, then adding the accumulated juices back to the pan and scraping up the brown bits. Simmer until the juices have reduced to ¼ to ⅓ cup, then add the sauce base. Simmer for 1 to 2 minutes to combine the flavors, then bring to a low boil.

3 Give the cornstarch mixture a stir, then whisk it into the sauce. Cook for about 30 seconds, whisking, until the sauce turns clear and thickens slightly. Discard the necks and gizzards in the pan. Strain the sauce into a small saucepan, pressing on the solids before discarding them. Stir in the black currant preserves, season with salt and a generous amount of pepper, and serve on the side with the carved duck.

Rachel's Shepherd's Pie

Shepherd's pie was one of my daughter Rachel's favorites when she was just a little slip of a thing. Now that she's a big girl, she makes it for her husband Bob and her son — running, jumping little Max.

This traditional version is topped with simple, delicious mashed potatoes. If you feel the need to dress the pie up further, you can stir some of the roasted mushrooms (page 56) into the meat before covering it with one of the three more elaborate mashed potatoes on pages 199 to 202. **5 TO 6 SERVINGS**

---

1 cup chopped onion

2 tablespoons olive oil

2 large garlic cloves, minced

1½ pounds ground lamb

Salt and freshly ground pepper

1¾ cups tomato puree

½ cup chicken broth

1½ tablespoons fresh thyme leaves, or 1½ teaspoons dried thyme

1 small bay leaf

1½ pounds boiling potatoes, such as Yukon Gold, peeled and cut into ½-inch pieces

¾ cup milk

5 tablespoons butter

¼ cup coarsely chopped parsley, preferably flat-leaf (optional)

3 tablespoons freshly grated pecorino Romano cheese

1 Using a heavy, ovenproof 9-inch skillet (I love the look, feel, and cooking of castiron, which can go right to the table), cook the onion in the olive oil over medium-low heat, stirring frequently, until it becomes translucent and a little brown, 5 to 6 minutes.

2 Add the garlic to the skillet and cook, stirring, for about 30 seconds. Add the ground lamb, breaking it up with a wooden spoon, and cook until the exterior redness is gone, 3 to 4 minutes. Season the meat with salt and pepper and stir in the tomato puree, chicken broth, thyme, and bay leaf. Simmer, uncovered, stirring occasionally, until the mixture is thickened and very moist but not runny and the meat is tender, about 15 minutes.

3 Meanwhile, bring a large pot of salted water to a boil over high heat. Add the potatoes and cook at a medium boil (so they don't break up) until very tender but not falling apart, 15 to 20 minutes.

4 When the potatoes are almost ready, set a small saucepan with the milk and butter over low heat. When the potatoes are tender, drain them well and place them back in their cooking pot set over low heat. Dry them for about a minute, stirring. Still over very low heat, mash the potatoes while gradually adding all

- Chop the onion and garlic up to a day ahead and refrigerate them separately.

- Peel and cut the potatoes up to 2 days ahead and refrigerate them covered with cold water.

- Cook the meat up to 3 days ahead and reheat it gently before topping it with the potatoes.

the hot milk mixture. Season them generously with salt and pepper.

5 Preheat the broiler. Stir the parsley into the meat, if using it. If you don't have a skillet you want to present at the table, transfer the meat mixture to a casserole. Cover the mixture evenly with the mashed potatoes, leaving a 1-inch margin around the edge of the dish. Sprinkle the grated cheese over the potatoes and slide the pan under the broiler to brown the top lightly, 2 to 3 minutes. Bring the pie to the table and serve hot.

Lamb Shanks with Red Wine and Green Olives

In addition to the advertised wine and olives, there are dates in this dish that break up during the long cooking time and impart a subtle, mysterious sweetness. When you eat everything together — the tender lamb, astringent olives, and the date-rich wine sauce, all sprinkled with tart lemon zest, your mouth is filled with opposing yet utterly complementary flavors. 6 SERVINGS

1¾ cups full-bodied red wine, such as Cabernet Sauvignon

1 tablespoon tomato paste

6 lamb shanks, about 1 pound each

Salt and freshly ground pepper

3½ tablespoons olive oil

1½ cups sliced onions

3 large garlic cloves, crushed with the side of a knife, then peeled

6 sprigs of fresh thyme

1 sprig of fresh rosemary

1 bay leaf

⅔ cup pitted whole dates

⅓ cup coarsely chopped pitted green Mediterranean-style olives (about 12) (see page 51)

Zest from 3 large lemons

1 Preheat the oven to 325°F with a rack in the center. Boil the wine in a medium saucepan set over medium-low heat, 10 to 15 minutes, until reduced to ½ cup. Remove the pan from the heat, stir in the tomato paste and ½ cup of hot water, and set aside.

2 Dry the lamb shanks on paper towels and season with salt and pepper. Heat 2 tablespoons of the olive oil over medium-high heat in a heavy, ovenproof pot large enough to hold the shanks in no more than 1 to 1½ layers. When the oil is hot, brown the shanks in batches without crowding, removing them as they're browned, about 15 minutes total.

3 Reduce the heat to low, blot out the cooked fat with a bunched paper towel, and add the remaining 1½ tablespoons olive oil to the pot. Add the onions and garlic. Tie together the thyme and rosemary with kitchen string and add to the pot along with the bay leaf. Cook, stirring occasionally, until the onions are lightly browned, 2 to 3 minutes. Stir in the dates, return the lamb shanks to the pot, and pour the red wine mixture over the meat. Bring the liquid to a simmer and cover.

4   Transfer the pot to the oven and bake, turning and basting the shanks occasionally with the juices that form after about an hour, until they are extremely tender when pierced with a fork, 1½ to 2 hours total.

5   When the lamb shanks are done, there should be about 2¼ cups of flavorful sauce. (If there is more, transfer the shanks to a serving platter and cover to keep warm. Discard the herb bunch and bay leaf and set the pot over medium-high heat. Boil the sauce, skimming off the fat as it rises, until it's very flavorful.) Season the sauce with salt and pepper to taste. Spoon over the lamb shanks, scatter the olives over the top, sprinkle with lemon zest, and serve hot.

Sausages with White Beans and Ham Hocks

This is a smoky, meaty bean dish that's good for the soul. Ladle it steaming into stoneware soup plates right from its cooking pot set on the table. 6 SERVINGS

1¼ cups dried great northern beans

6 smoked ham hocks (about 3 pounds total)

1 medium onion, peeled and stuck with 2 cloves

3 large celery stalks, cut in half

2 bay leaves

3 tablespoons olive oil

1¼ pounds sweet or hot Italian sausage (or a mixture)**, meat removed from casings and broken into 1-inch pieces**

4 to 5 garlic cloves, chopped

¾ teaspoon dried rosemary, crumbled, or ¼ teaspoon finely chopped fresh

¾ cup drained and chopped canned plum tomatoes

Freshly ground pepper

2 tablespoons chopped parsley

Freshly grated imported Parmesan cheese

1 Rinse and pick over the beans to remove any grit. Put them in a large bowl and add enough water to cover by at least 2 inches. Soak overnight.

2 Place the ham hocks, onion, celery, and bay leaves in a 6-quart soup pot or stockpot. Drain the beans in a colander, rinse, and add them to the pot with enough cold water to cover by 3 inches. Set the pot over high heat and bring the water to a boil. Immediately reduce the heat to low, skim off any froth that comes to the surface, and simmer, partially covered, for 1¼ to 1½ hours, or until the beans are tender but intact.

3 Transfer the ham hocks to a plate. When cool enough to handle but still warm, trim off and discard the skin, fat, and bone; cut the meat into bite-size pieces. Discard the onion, celery, and bay leaves. Drain the beans, reserving 1½ cups cooking liquid (plus 1 more cup as backup if you're reheating it later).

4 Set a very large, deep skillet or flameproof casserole over medium-high heat with the olive oil. When hot, add the sausage and brown it, stirring occasionally, for 2 to 3 minutes. Stir in the meat from the ham hocks to warm through, about 1 minute. Reduce the heat to low, stir in the garlic and rosemary, and cook for 30 seconds, and stir in the tomatoes. Cook, stirring occasionally, for 1 to 2 minutes to combine the flavors. Add the beans and the reserved 1½ cups cooking liquid.

5 Simmer, uncovered, stirring occasionally, until the bean liquid is slightly thickened, about 10 minutes. Season with pepper (there should be enough salt from the hocks), stir in the parsley, and bring the dish to the table. Serve it right away, with grated cheese on the side.

Braised Beef Short Ribs with Chinese Flavor

These ribs can be simmered on top of the stove as well as in the oven, but I like to take advantage of the oven's surrounding heat, particularly since the meat is not fully covered in liquid during the braising time. As far as amount goes, I figure on two to three ribs per serving, depending on how meaty they are. 6 SERVINGS

½ cup soy sauce

½ cup fino sherry, white wine, or dry vermouth

2 tablespoons brown sugar

1⅓ cups drained and coarsely chopped canned tomatoes

4 whole star anise

6 to 6½ pounds beef short ribs on the bone, cut into 3-inch lengths

Salt and freshly ground pepper

1½ tablespoons vegetable oil

6 garlic cloves, crushed with the side of a knife and peeled

1-inch-long piece of peeled fresh ginger, about the diameter of a quarter, cut into 8 slices

6 scallions, cut into 2-inch lengths, plus 2 tablespoons thinly sliced on the diagonal

1   Preheat the oven to 325°F with a rack in the middle. Stir the soy sauce, sherry, brown sugar, and tomatoes together in a bowl. Stir in ⅔ cup water and add the star anise. Set the sauce base aside.

2   Dry the ribs with paper towels and season very lightly with salt and generously with pepper. Heat the oil over medium-high heat in a heavy, flameproof casserole large enough to hold all the ribs in no more than 2 layers. When the oil is hot, add the ribs in batches without crowding and brown them on all sides; remove them as they're browned, adding additional oil if necessary.

3   Pour off the fat and reduce the heat to low. Add the garlic, ginger, and the 2-inch-long scallions, alternately tossing and pressing them against the bottom of the pot for 1 minute to bring out their flavor. Return the ribs to the pot and pour the soy sauce mixture over them. Bring the liquid to a simmer and cover.

4   Transfer the pot to the oven and bake the ribs, turning them occasionally, until extremely tender when pierced with a fork, 2½ to 3 hours total.

- Prepare the ginger and garlic up to a day ahead.

- Refrigerate the ribs in one layer (so they are as covered as possible by the sauce) for up to 5 days or freeze them for up to 2 months. Garnish with scallions right before serving.

5 Transfer the ribs to a serving platter and cover loosely to keep warm. Discard the ginger and star anise and pour the sauce into a large, heatproof glass or measuring cup or bowl. Let stand about 5 minutes to let the fat rise to the surface, then spoon it off and discard it. Reheat the sauce, season generously with pepper, and pour it over the ribs. Sprinkle with the thinly sliced scallions and serve hot.

Veal Stew with Mushrooms and Potatoes

When I'm making certain kinds of stews, such as this one and those with lamb and pork, I like to have at least a portion of the meat be on the bone. I think the bones add flavor, and the meat that clings to them is more succulent. However, I know that some people find them a bother to eat, so for company, I'll make this stew with a mix of cuts. You could, of course, use all boneless veal, or use all on the bone and remove the cooked meat from the bones while it's still warm. Any way you make it, this old-fashioned stew has two elements that take it out of the ordinary: onions cooked until meltingly soft and golden brown so they dissolve into the gravy to deeply flavor it; and a discreet addition of vinegar, which puts the naturally sweet veal and vegetables into perfect balance. **6 SERVINGS**

¼ **cup plus 3 tablespoons olive oil**

2 **large onions, finely chopped** (2½ cups)

3 **large garlic cloves, crushed with the side of a knife, then peeled**

1½ **pounds veal riblets or other veal on the bone, in 2- to 3-inch lengths, trimmed of exterior fat**

1¾ **pounds boneless veal stew meat, cut into 2-inch chunks**

Salt and freshly ground pepper

3 **tablespoons flour**

4½ **tablespoons red or white wine vinegar**

2½ **cups chicken broth**

1 **teaspoon dried rubbed sage, or 4 large fresh sage leaves, chopped**

1 **large bay leaf**

1 Set a large, heavy stew pot over medium heat with ¼ cup of the olive oil. Stir in the onions and cook, stirring frequently, until pale gold, about 10 minutes. Reduce the heat to low, stir in the garlic, and continue cooking, stirring frequently, for 5 to 8 minutes more, or until the onions are soft and golden brown. Transfer the vegetables to a platter and wipe out any specks that remain in the pot (wash it only if it's burned because the browned surface the onions leave adds flavor to the stew). Reserve the pot.

2 Preheat the oven to 325°F with a rack in the center. Dry the veal on paper towels and season with salt and pepper. Set the pot over medium-high heat with the remaining 3 tablespoons olive oil. When it's hot, lightly brown the meat in batches without crowding, adding them to the platter as they're done, adjusting the heat if the bottom of the pot starts to get too dark (see Note).

3 Reduce the heat to low, pour off any fat, and return the meat and vegetables with any accumulated juices to the pot. Stir them together so the juices deglaze as much of the browned bottom as possible. Sprinkle with flour and cook, stirring frequently, for 1

- 1½ **pounds small boiling potatoes, 2 inches in diameter, peeled**
- 2 **teaspoons butter**
- 2 **packages** (10 ounces each) **button mushrooms, halved or quartered if large**
- 1 **tablespoon chopped dill or parsley**

Do-Ahead Options

↩ Chop the onions up to a day ahead.

↩ Prepare the stew up to 5 days ahead or freeze it for up to 2 months. Garnish it with the herbs when serving.

---

minute. Add the vinegar, continuing to scrape the bottom, then gradually add the broth to make a smooth gravy, scraping the bottom as you stir. Increase the heat to medium, bring the liquid to a simmer, and add the sage and bay leaf.

4 Cover the pot, transfer to the oven, and bake for 1 hour. Then add the potatoes, pushing them into the liquid, and cook 30 minutes more, or until both the meat and potatoes are tender.

5 Meanwhile, set a large skillet over medium heat with the butter. When it froths, add the mushrooms. Season them with salt and pepper and cook, stirring occasionally, until they are lightly browned and tender and their juices have evaporated, 5 to 8 minutes, depending on their size. Set them aside.

6 When the stew is ready, add the mushrooms with their juices, and cook, covered, 5 minutes more. Remove the stew from the oven; degrease if necessary. Season with salt and pepper to taste, and serve hot, sprinkled with the dill or parsley.

NOTE: It's important to preserve the nicely browned surface at the bottom of the pot because it's going to add important flavor to the stew. However, if you're concerned that it's getting too dark, finish browning the meat in a skillet, then deglaze the pan with some of the broth and add it to the stew pot.

HOW TO DEGREASE GRAVY

Meat on the bone often has a layer of internal fat, which renders as it cooks. To remove the fat from the stew, if there's a lot, transfer the meat and vegetables to a serving bowl with a slotted spoon and pour the gravy into a clear measuring cup or bowl. Let the gravy settle for a few minutes, then spoon off the fat that has risen to the top and pour the gravy back over the meat and vegetables.

Black Bean Tortilla Casserole with Ancho Chiles

This one-pot meatless meal (if you don't count the lard) is rich and meaty, and very satisfying. I prepare it in my well-used Mexican cazuela, *a take-it-to-the-table pottery dish that's part bowl, part casserole, and all south-of-the-border soul. When planning, don't forget to allow time for the tortillas to dry out.* 6 TO 8 SERVINGS

½ **pound dried black beans, rinsed but not soaked**

1 **small onion, quartered, plus** ⅓ **cup thinly sliced onion**

2 **tablespoons lard, or 1 tablespoon plus 2 teaspoons vegetable oil**

Salt and freshly ground pepper

4 **dried ancho chiles** (2 ounces), **seeds and stems removed**

2 **large garlic cloves, thinly sliced**

12 **corn tortillas, 6 inches in diameter, cut in half, then across into** ½**-inch-wide strips, and dried overnight on a cookie sheet at room temperature**

3 **cups shredded Monterey Jack, mild Cheddar, or Muenster cheese**

½ **cup sour cream, plus more for garnish**

1 Place the beans in a large pot with 4 cups of water, the quartered onion, and 1 tablespoon of the lard or oil. Bring the water to a boil over high heat, then reduce the heat to low so it bubbles gently. Cover the pot, leaving the lid slightly ajar, and cook the beans until they're very tender but still intact, 1½ to 2 hours. Season generously with salt, then drain and reserve ¾ cup of the cooking liquid. Set the beans and liquid both aside separately.

2 Meanwhile, lightly toast the chiles in a toaster oven or regular oven set to 350°F until they just begin to smell aromatic, 1 to 2 minutes only (they scorch easily). Transfer them to a bowl, cover with hot water, and let soak until soft and pliable, 20 to 30 minutes. Drain, discard the soaking water, and place the chiles in a blender with the garlic and 1¼ cups fresh water. Puree to a smooth sauce, 1 to 2 minutes.

3 Preheat the oven to 400°F with a rack in the middle. Set a small saucepan or medium skillet over very low heat with the remaining 1 tablespoon lard or 2 teaspoons oil. Add the ancho chile sauce and simmer gently without allowing it to reduce, stirring occasionally, for about 5 minutes. Stir in the reserved bean liquid and season generously with salt and pepper.

4 Spread 3 tablespoons of the sauce over the bottom of an 8 x 12 x 2½-inch-deep baking dish or

other casserole with a 2½- to 3-quart capacity. Top with one-third of the tortilla strips. Spread half of the beans on next, followed by half of the cheese. Continue with one-third more tortilla strips, followed by half of the remaining sauce. Stir the sour cream until smooth and drop dollops of it over the sauce; spread it slightly with the back of a spoon. Distribute the rest of the beans over next, followed by the remaining tortilla strips. Coat with the remaining sauce, spreading it as best as best you can. Finally, sprinkle the rest of the cheese over the top.

5 Cover the casserole with a lightly oiled piece of foil (to keep the cheese from sticking). Bake for 15 minutes. Uncover and bake for 15 to 20 minutes more, or until the cheese is melted and the edges are bubbling. Let the casserole stand for 5 to 10 minutes before serving.

6 Bring the casserole to the table and serve it hot, cut into squares or rectangles, or just spooned out onto warm plates. Pass a bowl of sour cream on the side.

DISHES ON THE SIDE

VEGETABLES

❖ Browned Asparagus in Buttery Lemon Sauce

It couldn't be simpler: snap and peel the spears, sauté them until golden brown and crunchy-tender in a little olive oil mixed with butter, then add another lump of butter and a good splash of lemon juice to gloss and flavor them. Or grill the spears unpeeled and moistened with olive oil. Then melt the second part of the butter in the recipe with the lemon juice in a little pan over high heat so they bubble together for a few seconds and pour it over the asparagus, which lie in wait on a platter. **6 SERVINGS**

---

2 ¼ pounds asparagus, medium to large spears

1 tablespoon olive oil

2 tablespoons butter

Salt and freshly ground pepper

2 tablespoons freshly squeezed lemon juice

Do-Ahead Options

- Snap and peel the asparagus up to a day ahead and refrigerate it rolled in damp paper towels inside a zipper-seal plastic bag.

- Prepare the asparagus up to 20 minutes ahead and serve it warm.

1 Snap off the woody ends of the asparagus. Rinse and dry the spears. Peel with a vegetable peeler, shaving off the thin, dark, outer layer of skin on the bottom two-thirds of the stalks.

2 Choose a skillet large enough to lay the spears flat in about 2 layers. Set the skillet over low heat with the olive oil and 1½ teaspoons of butter. When the butter has melted, add the spears, turning them to coat. Season with salt and pepper. Cover and cook, turning the asparagus occasionally and adjusting the heat if necessary, until they are browned all over and tender-crunchy, 10 to 15 minutes depending on their size.

3 Add the remaining 1½ tablespoons butter and the lemon juice to the skillet; it should bubble up and lightly glaze the spears within seconds. (If it doesn't, the pan is probably too small, so remove the spears, let the butter mixture bubble strongly for a few seconds until well combined, then return the spears and coat them with the sauce.)

4 Remove from the heat, transfer the asparagus to a warm platter or plates, pour any pan juices over the asparagus, and serve hot or warm.

Roasted Beets with Orange-Balsamic Butter

I'm a big fan of beets, particularly when they're roasted so their sweet flavor becomes even deeper. Here, the purple-red beauties are complemented by the fresh taste of orange and dill and drops of sweet vinegar and lemon. You can make them one of two ways: heat them in a pan with the butter as in the recipe, or grill them (lightly oiled first) just long enough to add a taste of the fire and to heat through, then toss them in a bowl with the flavored butter. **6 SERVINGS**

---

3 cups peeled roasted beets (recipe follows), **sliced about ⅜ inch thick**

3 tablespoons plus ¾ teaspoon butter, cut into pieces

2½ teaspoons balsamic vinegar

3½ teaspoons freshly squeezed lemon juice

¼ teaspoon grated orange zest

Salt and freshly ground pepper

1½ tablespoons chopped fresh dill

1 Place the sliced roasted beets in a large, heavy skillet with the butter, lemon juice, vinegar, and orange zest. Set the skillet over medium heat and cook, stirring frequently, just long enough for the butter to melt and flavor the beets, 2 to 3 minutes. Season with salt and pepper.

2 Transfer the beets to a warm serving dish or plates, sprinkle with dill, and serve hot.

Do-Ahead Options

↪ Squeeze the lemon juice and grate the zest up to a day ahead.

↪ Roast the beets up to a week ahead (see page 176).

Roasted Beets

2 bunches of beets

1½ tablespoons olive oil

1½ tablespoons mixed dried herbs, such as thyme, rosemary, savory, and oregano, or whatever you've got handy

¼ teaspoon whole black peppercorns

Roasting beets intensifies their richness, a far better method than boiling, which dilutes their flavor. You cook and refrigerate the beets with their skins still on, so when you're ready, all you have to do is trim the ends and peel off the skins, which slip off easily. And if you like cooked greens, save the leaves for another dish or mix them with chard in the Swiss Chard with Browned Onions and Feta Cheese (page 184). **6 SERVINGS**

1 Preheat the oven to 425°F with the rack in the middle. Rinse and dry the beets and place them in a heavy ovenproof skillet or other baking dish large enough to hold them in one layer.

2 Drizzle the olive oil over the beets, sprinkle with the herbs and peppercorns, and roll the whole beets in the skillet to distribute the flavorings.

3 Roast, rolling the beets occasionally in the pan, until they are tender enough for a wooden skewer to pass through with no resistance, as little as 45 minutes or as long as 1½ hours, depending on their size. Let them cool, then peel to use right away or refrigerate in their skins for another time.

❉ Slow-Sautéed Broccoli

If you're a fan of this readily available green vegetable, you won't mind hearing that this cooking method (which browns the florets as it cooks them to tenderness) brings out the essence of broccoli. It's a great method for cauliflower, too, or a mixture of both. Leftovers can be devoured straight from the fridge (they have lots of flavor even when cold), served at room temperature, or tossed into pasta with garlic and more olive oil. 6 SERVINGS

2 large heads of broccoli

¼ cup plus 3 tablespoons extra-virgin olive oil

Salt and freshly ground pepper

¼ cup freshly grated imported Parmesan cheese

Lemon wedges, for garnish

Do-Ahead Options

✤ Cut the broccoli into florets up to a day ahead.

✤ Cook the broccoli up to an hour ahead and serve it warm or at room temperature.

1 Cut off the large broccoli stems; discard them or save to make a puree (see page 178). Cut enough broccoli into 1½- to 2-inch florets, trimming the stems to about ½ inch, to measure 10½ to 11 cups, saving any extra for another use.

2 Set a large, heavy skillet with the olive oil over medium heat. When it's hot, stir in the broccoli and cook, uncovered, stirring frequently, until it turns bright green, about 2 minutes.

3 Season with salt and pepper and reduce the heat to medium-low; you should hear gentle sizzling noises as it cooks. Continue to cook, stirring occasionally, for about 30 minutes, or until the broccoli is browned in spots and tender-crunchy.

4 Transfer to a warm bowl and toss with the cheese. Serve hot, warm, or at room temperature, with wedges of lemon.

Broccoli Puree

2 bunches of broccoli stems, peeled and sliced ½ inch thick

2 tablespoons heavy cream

Salt and freshly ground white pepper

Do-Ahead Option

◇ The puree can be made up to 2 days ahead through Step 1. Finish with the cream shortly before serving.

Broccoli is one of our most popular vegetables. But think of all those big stems that go to waste. Turn those broccoli stems into something useful. Peel them with a paring knife to reach their pale, inner core. Slice and cook in salted boiling water until they are tender; then toss them in butter or olive oil. Or turn them into this delicate puree. 3 TO 4 SERVINGS

1 Cook the broccoli stems in a large pot of salted boiling water until tender; drain well. Puree to very tiny pieces in a food processor.

2 Return the puree to the cooking pot set over medium heat. Cook briefly, stirring, until it just begins to sizzle. Add the cream and cook, stirring, until the puree looks creamy and mounds nicely in a spoon, 1 to 2 minutes. Season with salt and white pepper and serve hot.

Glazed Carrots with Cardamom

When you cook carrots gently in butter with a spoonful or two of sugar, the pieces turn sweetly tender and are coated in a sheer, shiny glaze when they're done. And if you slip ground cardamom into the pot to add its warming, stimulating hint of ginger, cloves, and lemon, you'll find that it's in perfect rapport with the carrots. **6 SERVINGS**

---

8 to 9 cardamom pods or ⅜ teaspoon ground cardamom

2 tablespoons plus 1 teaspoon butter

2 pounds carrots, peeled and cut on the diagonal ¾ inch thick (6 cups)

2 tablespoons sugar

¾ teaspoon salt

1 tablespoon chopped parsley or snipped chives, for garnish

Do-Ahead Options

☙ Cut the carrots up to 2 days ahead.

☙ Cook the carrots about three-fourths of the way through up to an hour ahead, then take off the cover and remove the pan from the heat. Finish cooking and glazing them just before serving. (They may be completely done from the retained heat of the pan; if so, merely glaze them in the juices as described.)

1 If using cardamom pods, press them open with the side of a large knife, extract the seeds, and discard the pods. Finely grind enough seeds to measure ⅜ teaspoon (see page 111), or cover the seeds with plastic wrap and pulverize them by pounding with a meat mallet or heavy skillet.

2 Melt the butter in a large saucepan set over low heat. Stir in the carrots, cardamom, sugar, and salt. Cover tightly and cook, stirring occasionally, until the carrots are tender, about 15 minutes, adjusting the heat, if necessary, to keep them from browning.

3 Raise the heat to medium-high and reduce any remaining liquid in the pan, stirring, until it becomes a shiny glaze coating the carrots, 1 to 2 minutes. Transfer the carrots to a warm serving dish or plates. Sprinkle the parsley or chives on top and serve hot.

❋ Roasted Carrots with Orange

Carrots were just about the only fresh vegetable to show up in my home when I was a kid.
If I tell you that fresh green beans were wildly exotic, you'll get the picture. I loved carrots
then, and I love them now, particularly when cooked for what seems like forever in the
delicious, fatty juices surrounding a roast (see page 154 for Roast Standing Rib of Beef
with Potatoes and Carrots and Yorkshire Pudding).

But here's an equally good olive oil–roasted version, which makes browned, tender carrots
in a last-minute glaze from orange juice poured into their blistering pan. **6 SERVINGS**

---

2 ½ pounds carrots, peeled and cut into sticks 2 to 3 inches long and about ⅜ inch thick

2 ½ tablespoons olive oil

Salt and freshly ground pepper

⅔ cup freshly squeezed orange juice, at room temperature

1 tablespoon chopped fresh dill, for garnish (optional)

Do-Ahead Options

☙ Cut the carrots and chop the dill, if you're using it, up to a day ahead.

☙ Roast the carrots up to 1 ½ hours ahead and serve them warm or at room temperature. Sprinkle them with dill, if you're using it, when serving.

1 Preheat the oven to 425°F with the rack at the top. Place in the oven a heavy roasting pan or other baking dish large enough to hold the carrots in no more than 1 ½ layers. Toss the carrots in a large bowl with the olive oil and season with salt and pepper to taste.

2 When the pan and oven are hot, add the carrots, spreading them evenly over the bottom of the pan. Roast, turning the carrots a few times, until browned and tender, 30 to 35 minutes. If they brown too quickly, lower the temperature to 400°F, leave the oven door ajar for 1 or 2 minutes to cool more quickly, and continue roasting.

3 When the carrots are ready, immediately pour the juice into the pan. Gently turn the carrots in the juice with a metal spatula — most of the juice should evaporate quickly, leaving them lightly coated. If juice remains, leave the pan in the oven for less than a minute, or just until the carrots are coated.

4 Transfer the carrots to a warm serving dish or plates, garnish with the dill if you're using it, and serve hot, warm, or at room temperature. (If you're serving them later, let them cool on a platter rather than a bowl, which would trap steam and dilute their flavor. Garnish with dill when serving.)

ABOVE **Lamb Shanks with Red Wine and Green Olives** *page 162*

ABOVE **Mini Meat Loaves** *page 152*

OPPOSITE **Roast Standing Rib of Beef
with Potatoes and Carrots and Yorkshire Pudding** *page 154*

ABOVE **Avocados Stuffed with Tropical Fruit and Berries** *page 49*

OPPOSITE **High tea: scones, tea sandwiches,**
Chilled Melon Soup with Lemongrass and Mint *page 20*, **Pistachio Sugar Cookies** *page 244*

OPPOSITE (Clockwise from bottom right) **Dark Chocolate Chunk Cookies with Macadamia Nuts** *page 241*, **Pistachio Sugar Cookies** *page 244*, **Sugar Yeast Crisps** *page 239*, **Double Chocolate Cream Cheese Brownies** *page 246*

ABOVE **Buttermilk Cake with Orange Mascarpone Cream and Chocolate Glaze** *page 234*

Poached Pears with Vanilla Bean and Lemon Zest *page 260*

Cauliflower with Olives, Anchovies, and Capers

One of my favorite ways of cooking cauliflower (and broccoli; see page 177) is to slowly sauté it in olive oil to intensify its natural sweetness. Here, vigorous Mediterranean ingredients add flavors that suit the cauliflower well, and because they're chopped into small pieces, much ends up nicely lodged in the crevices of the florets. 6 SERVINGS

---

1 head of cauliflower, about 2 pounds

2 tablespoons coarsely chopped, pitted purple or black Mediterranean olives such as Alphonso, Kalamata, or Gaeta (see page 51)

2 anchovy fillets, coarsely chopped

2 teaspoons drained capers, preferably the tiny ones called nonpareil

¼ cup extra-virgin olive oil

Salt and freshly ground pepper

Pinch of crushed hot red pepper flakes

Do-Ahead Options

- Cut the cauliflower up to a day ahead and chop the olives, anchovies, and capers together up to 2 days ahead.

- Cook the cauliflower up to an hour ahead and serve it warm or at room temperature. Or cook it up to 3 days ahead and take it out of the refrigerator an hour before serving.

1 Snap off the leaves, trim out the core, and cut enough cauliflower into 1-inch florets with about ¾-inch-long stems to measure 7 cups; save any extra for another use.

2 Finely chop together the olives, anchovies, and capers.

3 In a large, heavy skillet, heat the olive oil over low heat. Add the cauliflower, season with salt and pepper, and toss to coat with the oil. Cook slowly (listening for gentle sizzling noises the entire time), stirring occasionally, until the cauliflower florets are lightly browned and tender-crunchy, 18 to 20 minutes.

4 Stir in the hot pepper and the olive mixture and cook, stirring occasionally, for about 1 minute. Transfer the cauliflower to a warm serving dish or plates and serve hot or cover loosely, then serve warm or at room temperature.

❖ Carrot, White Bean, and Eggplant Salad

Combining two of Marcella Hazan's delicious salads (or at least some of their major elements) makes a whole new thing. Eons ago I took the new combo along as part of a picnic lunch by the sea, and my husband hasn't stopped talking about it since. That day it played side dish for the stars of the meal — cold roast veal and chicken — but it ended up stealing the show. **4 SERVINGS**

---

3 tablespoons red wine vinegar

2 teaspoons minced garlic

7 tablespoons olive oil

½ teaspoon dried oregano

Salt and freshly ground pepper

3 medium carrots, peeled and cut diagonally into ¼-inch-thick slices

2 cups canned cannellini or great northern beans, drained and rinsed, or freshly cooked and drained beans

½ cup thinly sliced red onion, preferably in 1-inch lengths (see page 37)

1 medium to large eggplant (about 1 pound), rinsed and dried

Torn or coarsely chopped basil leaves, for garnish

1 Place the vinegar and garlic in a large mixing bowl, and gradually whisk in 6 tablespoons of the olive oil to make a vinaigrette. Stir in the oregano and season the vinaigrette with salt and pepper.

2 In a medium saucepan of generously salted boiling water, cook the carrots until they are tender-firm, about 5 minutes. Drain them and run under cold water to stop their cooking. Dry on paper towels. Stir the carrots into the vinaigrette. Fold in the beans and red onion.

3 Cut off and discard the stem of the eggplant, then slice it into ¾-inch-thick slices. Stack a few slices at a time and cut them into ¾-inch-wide strips. Turn the strips horizontally and cut across them at ¾-inch intervals so they fall into cubes. Cut enough of the remaining eggplant in the same fashion to measure 4 cups; save any extra for another use.

4 Set a very large nonstick skillet over high heat with the remaining 1 tablespoon olive oil. When the oil is hot, add the eggplant and season it with salt and pepper. Cook, stirring frequently, until it begins to brown nicely. Lower the heat and continue cooking until the eggplant is tender but still intact, 8 to 10 minutes total. Transfer to a plate to cool.

5 Gently fold the eggplant into the bean mixture. Season with more salt and pepper to taste. Refrigerate the salad overnight to combine the flavors, take it out an hour before serving, and garnish with basil.

Swiss Chard with Browned Onions and Feta Cheese

Chard is similar to spinach in taste, though even deeper and sweeter, and it has much bigger, meatier leaves. I often choose it over spinach when I'm cooking for four people or more because it's less hassle to clean, and there's less of it to cook. **8 SERVINGS**

---

2 large bunches Swiss chard (about 3½ pounds)**, stems and coarse center ribs removed, leaves washed and drained** (see page 40)

5 to 6 tablespoons olive oil

2 medium onions, chopped (1½ cups)

1 medium garlic clove, minced

¼ teaspoon ground allspice or freshly grated nutmeg

Salt and freshly ground pepper

¾ cup crumbled feta cheese, at room temperature

Do-Ahead Options

↪ Trim and wash the chard a day before cooking.

↪ Cook the dish up to 3 days ahead and take it out of the refrigerator 1 hour ahead. Then gently reheat it and garnish it with cheese when serving.

1 Set a very large pot of salted water over high heat to come to a boil. Add several handfuls of chard, pushing it into the water. As the leaves wilt, add another batch and push it in. Continue in the same fashion until all the leaves are in the pot and simmer until tender, 5 to 8 minutes.

2 Drain into a colander. Rinse the chard under cold running water to stop its cooking. Let drain, then squeeze the water out of the chard a handful at a time. Chop into roughly ¾-inch pieces and put in a medium bowl.

3 Set a medium skillet with 5 tablespoons olive oil over low heat. When it's hot, add the onions and cook, stirring occasionally, until soft and browned, 7 to 10 minutes. Stir in the garlic and cook 1 minute more, stirring occasionally.

4 Add the chard and remove from the heat. Toss with two forks to mix. Toss again with the allspice or nutmeg and add up to 1 more tablespoon oil if the vegetable seems dry. Season with salt and pepper and toss again. Serve warm, with the feta cheese sprinkled on top.

❊ Tender Green Beans with Olive Oil and Thyme

I like to make these mellow green beans at least a day before I want to serve them so their seasonings can penetrate. They really are a do-all side dish, ready to go when I want them to be and suitable for lots of menus. **6 TO 8 SERVINGS**

¼ cup olive oil

2 medium onions, thinly sliced (1½ cups)

1 medium garlic clove, finely sliced

1¾ pounds green beans, ends trimmed, rinsed and drained well

Salt and freshly ground pepper

⅓ cup chicken or vegetable broth

¾ teaspoon dried thyme

2 tablespoons freshly squeezed lemon juice

⅛ teaspoon nutmeg, preferably freshly grated

Do-Ahead Options

- Snap the ends off the beans and slice the onion and garlic up to 1 day ahead.
- Cook the beans up to 4 days ahead and take them out of the refrigerator 1 hour before serving.

1 Set a large, deep skillet with the olive oil over high heat. When it's hot, add the onions and garlic and cook for 1 to 2 minutes, stirring several times, to take away some of their rawness. Stir in the beans to coat with oil and season with salt and pepper.

2 Pour the broth over the beans, reduce the heat to low, cover the skillet, and cook for 8 to 12 minutes, or until the beans are tender with a slight crispness.

3 Remove the lid, stir in the thyme, and cook for another 30 seconds. Increase the heat to high, stir in the lemon juice, and cook until the juices are lightly syrupy, about 1 minute. Stir in the nutmeg and season generously with salt and pepper.

4 Transfer the beans to a dish and let their flavors mingle for at least 2 hours before serving (or refrigerate them for up to 4 days). Stir them before serving and add more salt, pepper, thyme, or lemon juice, if you like.

❈ Sautéed Corn and Summer Squash in Tomato Butter with Basil

If you're like me, you eagerly await the arrival of white and yellow corn (particularly the young ones with small, crisp kernels) and August tomatoes, plump and red and ready to burst with juice. And how further blessed are we that these late-summer classics have a perfect affinity! One of my favorite ways of cooking them is to chunk up some zucchini and cook them all in a pan just until the tomatoes seem to melt into the butter, surrounding the vegetables in delicate pink sauce. **6 SERVINGS**

---

5 to 6 ears of fresh corn, husked, stems snapped off and trimmed

3½ tablespoons butter

3 to 4 medium zucchini (3½ cups), well scrubbed and cut into ¾-inch chunks

1½ tablespoons very thinly sliced garlic

2 medium fresh tomatoes (1½ cups), peeled, seeded, and coarsely chopped (see page 187)

Salt and freshly ground pepper

6 or 7 large basil leaves, torn into bite-size pieces

1 One at a time, stand the ears of corn on end and cut down the cob in sections to release the kernels, then scrape down the cobs with the back of the knife to release the remaining pulp and milk (about 2½ cups in total).

2 Melt the butter in a very large skillet set over high heat. Add the squash and garlic, and sauté, stirring frequently, until the squash starts to become tender, 3 to 4 minutes; reduce the heat if the garlic starts to brown.

3 Add the tomatoes and cook, stirring occasionally, until the juices begin to flow, about 1 minute, then stir in the corn-pulp mixture. Cook, stirring, for 1 to 3 minutes more, until the zucchini and corn are crisp-tender.

4 If the vegetables have thrown off a lot of liquid, transfer them all with a slotted spoon to a colander set inside a larger bowl and boil down the juices in the pan, adding the juices from the bowl, until nicely thickened and rich, then recombine with the vegetables. Season to taste with salt and pepper.

Do-Ahead Options

❧ Cut the corn kernels and scrape the pulp, cut the squash, and slice the garlic up to a day ahead.

❧ Peel and seed the tomatoes up to a day ahead and chop them up to 2 hours ahead, draining off their accumulated water before using.

❧ The dish can be made up to an hour ahead and garnished with basil when serving. It's also good when gently reheated, though the green color of the zucchini won't be quite as fresh.

5 Transfer the vegetables to a warm serving dish or plates and serve hot, warm, or at room temperature. Sprinkle the basil over the dish just before serving.

HOW TO PEEL AND SEED TOMATOES

First put a pot of water on to boil that's big enough to hold one or two tomatoes at a time. Then cut out the core of the tomatoes and cut an X through the skin at the opposite end. When the water's boiling, lower one (or two) into the water for 10 seconds and immediately remove it with a slotted spoon. To see if it's ready, try pulling a little of the skin away from the X — it should come off easily. If not, put the tomato back in the water for one or two more seconds or until it does peel. Then peel it and discard the skin, cut it in half, gently squeeze out the seeds, and chop or dice the pulp any way you want.

Roasted Eggplant with Garlic and Mint

From swan to ugly duckling is the fate of eggplant roasted in a hot oven (or over low coals). Collapsed go its voluptuous curves into flattened furrows weeping liquid; gone is its proud sheen of skin turned dark and dull. But wait! Cut open, this shriveled package reveals wonderful soft, rich eggplant, waiting to be seasoned with onions and garlic cooked to sweetness in fruity olive oil. Served spread almost flat on a handsome plate and "painted" with curving lines of yogurt, then sprinkled with shreds of fresh mint, this duckling has an allure of its own. **6 SERVINGS**

---

2 ½ **pounds eggplant**
(2 medium to large)

2 **tablespoons olive oil**

1 **medium to large onion, very thinly sliced** (1 cup)

3 **medium to large garlic cloves, crushed with the side of a knife**

Salt and freshly ground pepper

2 **tablespoons freshly squeezed lime juice**

2 **tablespoons plain yogurt**

2 **tablespoons finely shredded mint leaves**

Do-Ahead Options

❧ Roast or grill and chop the eggplant up to 2 days ahead. Drain the liquid that accumulates in the bowl before finishing the cooking.

❧ Prepare the finished dish up to 3 days ahead and take it out of the refrigerator about 30 minutes before serving.

1 Preheat the oven to 450°F. Pierce the eggplants with a sharp fork 5 or 6 times. Set them on a baking sheet and roast, turning once, until completely soft when pressed and almost collapsing, 35 to 40 minutes. Let cool.

2 Meanwhile, heat the olive oil in a heavy, medium skillet set over very low heat. Stir in the onion and garlic and season lightly with salt and pepper. Cook, stirring occasionally, until the onion is light gold in color, very tender, and translucent, about 30 minutes. Remove the skillet from the heat and reserve.

3 Slice off and discard the stem ends of the eggplants. Cut each in half lengthwise, scrape out the flesh with a spoon, discard the skins, and chop the eggplant into roughly ½-inch pieces (you should have about 3½ cups); discard any excess liquid.

4 Return the skillet to medium-low heat and stir in the eggplant. Cook the vegetables together, stirring occasionally, for about 5 minutes, until the flavors are well combined and no liquid remains. Stir in the lime juice and season generously with salt and pepper.

5 Serve the eggplant somewhat cool, but not cold, drizzled with yogurt and sprinkled with mint.

Baked Acorn Squash with Rosemary-Garlic Butter

I love the mundane things of life, like the aromatic steam that pours forth when you cut a baked winter squash in half, scrape out its seeds and strings, then drop butter into the cavity and watch it melt into the tender flesh. All in all, it's a simple enough way to get the squash on the table. For entertaining, though, you can easily dress up this humble vegetable by scooping out the squash, mashing it with a flavored butter, and serving it in a dish as a puree. **6 SERVINGS**

---

3 acorn squash or other individual winter squash, each about 1¼ pounds

3 tablespoons butter, slightly softened

1½ teaspoons minced garlic

¾ teaspoon minced fresh rosemary

Salt and freshly ground pepper

Do Ahead Options

❧ Refrigerate the butter for up to 2 weeks and take it out to soften slightly before serving. Or freeze it for up to 2 months.

❧ Bake the squash up to 2 days ahead and scoop out the flesh when it's warm. Reheat it on top of the stove before serving, and stir in the softened butter.

1 Preheat the oven to 425°F with the rack in the middle. Pierce the squash in several places with a sharp kitchen fork or metal skewer, place on a baking sheet, and roast until the sides feel tender when lightly squeezed or until they are easily penetrated with a fork, about 45 minutes.

2 Meanwhile, thoroughly combine the butter in a small bowl with the garlic and rosemary, then season with salt and pepper. Set the flavored butter aside.

3 When the squash are tender, transfer them to a cutting board. Protecting your hand from the heat with a towel, cut each in half lengthwise; scrape out and discard the seeds and stringy parts. Scoop out the squash into a mixing bowl. Mash with a fork (or puree in a food processor if you prefer a smoother texture). Add the flavored butter and blend well. Season with more salt and pepper to taste.

Turnip Puree with Caraway Seeds, Scallions, and Bacon

Turnips are a sweet vegetable with a faintly bitter edge, which when pureed become soft, buttery, and light. Their delicate creaminess is made even more apparent when sprinkled with the crunch of caraway, the mild oniony freshness of scallion, and the smoky flavor of bacon. But you could also stick with vegetables and garnish it with the deeply caramelized onions from Chewy Red Onions on page 34. **6 SERVINGS**

---

3 pounds white turnips, peeled and cut into 1-inch chunks

1 teaspoon caraway seeds (see Note)

4½ tablespoons butter, slightly softened

Salt and freshly ground pepper, preferably white

3 tablespoons very thinly sliced scallion

3 strips of bacon, cooked until crisp, then crumbled

1 In a large saucepan of boiling salted water, cook the turnips over moderately high heat until they're very tender when pierced with the tip of a knife, 10 to 15 minutes.

2 Meanwhile, very lightly toast the caraway seeds in a small, dry skillet set over very low heat, shaking the pan frequently, until you can smell its fragrance, about 1 minute. Set aside.

3 When the turnips are tender, drain them in a colander. Puree in a food processor until smooth, 1 to 2 minutes, scraping down the sides at least once. Return the puree to the saucepan set over medium-high heat and evaporate the excess moisture for 1 to 2 minutes, stirring frequently. (If the puree has been made ahead and refrigerated, warm it gently before increasing the heat.)

4 Gradually stir in the butter one small lump at a time (see Note) and cook, stirring frequently, until the puree pulls away from the sides of the pan and mounds nicely in the spoon. Season with salt and pepper. Transfer to a warm serving dish and sprinkle the toasted caraway seeds, scallion, and bacon on top. Serve hot.

NOTE: If caraway is not your favorite flavor, cumin seeds or black sesame seeds can be substituted. Gradually stirring slightly softened butter (instead of melted or cold butter) into the puree allows the butter to absorb better and creates a silken texture.

AN ELEGY FOR SILVER PLATTERS

When my Restaurant Leslie was on the map, we served a mélange of fresh vegetables with most main courses, such as broccoli, snow peas, carrots, and cauliflower. The silver platters we used were often worn or even a little bent, but I loved their great old character. In fact, much of the tableware from cutlery to plates was a mismatch of pre-owned restaurant and hotel stuff, and even if I'd had more money back then, I wouldn't have forsaken these pieces; they were a real link with New York food history.

I had my favorites, of course. There were the smallest platters, for two or three servings, or in a stretch, for four. Each was oval with its middle drawn in, which gave it something of an hourglass shape, beautified further by a narrow raised scroll running around its perimeter, inviting you to see, if you didn't already, its lovely sinuousness.

During dinner service, a heap of pungent, freshly grated ginger mingled with a mound of creamy sweet butter, suffusing and filling it with spice. The two held together in a semimolten state, accurately reflecting the kitchen's temperature and atmosphere. Over and over we plunged orders of the multicolored vegetables into a boiling water bath, then drained them and set them on one of the unique silver platters I had hunted down in restaurant supply houses. We glossed the vegetables with the ginger butter and sent them out steaming to the dining room.

Vegetables with Ginger Butter from Restaurant Leslie

For not much effort, this mixture of broccoli, snow peas, cauliflower, and carrots is a nice variety of easy-to-find vegetables that make a show of color on the plate. But you can serve the butter just as well with a single vegetable like asparagus, Brussels sprouts, artichokes, steamed potatoes, the Roasted Beets on page 176, or over any grilled vegetable you choose. **6 SERVINGS**

4½ tablespoons butter, preferably unsalted

4 teaspoons grated fresh ginger (see page 139)

Salt and freshly ground pepper

7½ to 8 cups mixed vegetables, such as:

Broccoli and/or cauliflower, cut into 1½-inch florets

Carrots, peeled and cut diagonally about ⅜-inch thick

Snow or snap peas, strings removed (see page 193)

1 Melt the butter with the ginger in a small skillet set over low heat. Season generously with salt and pepper and set aside.

2 In a large pot of boiling salted water, cook all the vegetables except the peas for 1 minute. Add the peas and boil for 1 minute more, or until the peas are bright green and crisp and the other vegetables crisp-tender. Immediately drain them well in a colander to get rid of the excess water.

3 Set the skillet with the ginger butter back over low heat to warm. Transfer the vegetables to a warm platter, drizzle with the ginger butter, and serve steaming hot.

HOW TO CHOOSE AND STRING SNOW PEAS

Superficial beauty is everything here because we choose snow peas for their pods, not their peas, which should be so undeveloped they don't even make bumps. The peas inside sugar snap peas, on the other hand, are more developed, but you still shouldn't be able to feel them through their plump pods.

Really fresh snow peas are deep green in color and show no sign of wrinkling. The ones I like best are young, no more than 2 inches long, and feel firm and smooth. Sometimes, perfectly good ones are flabby, though they meet all the other requirements, so I buy them anyway, knowing that after a good soak in cold water they'll be rejuvenated.

To remove the strings from the peas, pinch a tiny piece of the stem end, snap it back, and pull it down the edge that looks like a seam — it will pull the string along with it. Sometimes there's a string on the other edge too, so snap off the tip of the other end and pull it down to check.

Grilled Vegetables with Lemon-Basil Oil

Grilled vegetables are popular for good reasons — they're easy, all the cooking is done outside, and they're right for practically every occasion. Well, that covers it for the cook! But for all of us, they simply taste good. When you make these, think about cooking extra so you have some ready to go for the Grilled Vegetables in Asian Vinaigrette on page 198. And for more vegetables that are good for grilling in addition to those in the recipe, see the Note on page 195. **6 SERVINGS**

Assorted vegetables (or choose one kind) **such as:**

3 portobello mushrooms

3 small Japanese or 1 medium Italian eggplant

1 large unpeeled Vidalia, Maui, or red onion

1 to 2 red or green bell peppers, stemmed, seeded, and quartered

3 yellow or green summer squash, scrubbed, dried, and cut in half lengthways

3 ripe tomatoes, cut in half horizontally

⅔ cup olive oil, plus more for grilling

4½ tablespoons freshly squeezed lemon juice

¾ cup lightly packed basil leaves

Salt and freshly ground pepper

1 Prepare a medium fire in the grill. About 10 minutes before cooking, set the grate 4 to 6 inches above the coals (see page 147).

2 Snap off the stems of the portobellos, saving them for another use, briefly rinse the tops of the caps, pat them dry with paper towels, and cut them in half. If using Japanese eggplant, rinse, dry, and cut it in half lengthwise. If using regular eggplant, rinse, dry, trim, and discard the stem end, and cut it crosswise into ¾-inch-thick slices. Cut the onion lengthwise through the skin and root end (to hold the layers together) into 1-inch-thick wedges measured at the widest part.

3 Place the vegetables on a cookie sheet, then lightly rub the tops of the portobellos and skin of the peppers with olive oil. Rub all the surfaces of the squash, eggplant, and onion wedges with oil, and drizzle the flat side of the tomatoes with oil, lightly rubbing it in all around.

4 Place the ⅔ cup oil, the lemon juice, and basil in a blender (or a food processor, but it won't get as smooth), and puree until it is very smooth, 2 to 3 minutes, scraping the jar down several times. Season generously with salt and pepper and set it aside. (It will be

◆ Clean and cut the vegetables, except for the tomatoes, up to a day ahead.

◆ Make the lemon-basil oil up to 2 hours ahead and serve it at room temperature.

◆ Grill the vegetables up to an hour ahead and serve them either warm or at room temperature.

bright green at first but will turn slightly khaki soon after — it tastes fine either way.)

5 Season the vegetables generously with salt and pepper and put the squash, eggplant, and onions on the grill, cut sides down. Place the peppers skin side down and the mushrooms rounded side down. (If there's not enough space, cook them in batches, one or two kinds at a time.)

6 Grill the vegetables, turning once, for a total of 8 to 15 minutes (depending on your grill and the vegetables), until brown and tender but still holding together well (to check, pierce them at least halfway through with a wooden skewer), moving any that are browning too quickly to a cooler part of the grill. At about the halfway point, add the tomatoes cut side down and cook until their edges brown. Turn them and continue cooking until their juices begin to bubble, 4 to 6 minutes total.

7 Transfer the vegetables to a platter, drizzle them with some of the lemon-basil oil, and serve them right away. Or serve them warm or at room temperature with the rest of the oil on the side.

NOTE: Other great vegetables to grill are asparagus (rinsing them and snapping off their woody ends first but not peeling them), slices of fennel and turnip, and fat lengths of carrot, all first blanched briefly in simmering water (even a day ahead); or try corn on the cob, and roasted beets (see page 176 for how to roast them). And potatoes, too, which can turn these grilled vegetables into a nice, light supper. Lightly oil and season the vegetables before grilling.

Roast Zucchini with Herbes de Provence

Reminiscent of ratatouille but taking a different route, the zucchini here is first roasted in a hot oven (with a tomato alongside), then tossed with herbs, cumin, garlic, lemon, and its already disclosed ovenmate, now chopped. The result is lively and rich, but tempered by the subdued personality of the zucchini itself. It's good served at any temperature, except ice cold. **6 SERVINGS**

2½ pounds medium zucchini or yellow summer squash, scrubbed and dried, cut on a slight diagonal into ¾-inch-thick slices

3 tablespoons extra-virgin olive oil

1 teaspoon ground cumin, preferably freshly ground (see 111)

Salt and freshly ground pepper

1 large ripe tomato, cored and cut in half

2¼ teaspoons dried *herbes de Provence* or mixed dried herbs such as thyme, tarragon, rosemary, fennel seed, lavender, and oregano

1 teaspoon minced garlic

1 to 1½ tablespoons freshly squeezed lemon juice

1½ tablespoons chopped parsley, preferably flat-leaf

1 Preheat the oven to 450°F with the rack at the top. About 5 minutes before cooking, heat a roasting pan large enough to hold the zucchini in one layer with space around each piece, or a baking sheet, for about 3 minutes.

2 Toss the zucchini in a large bowl with the olive oil and cumin and season generously with pepper only (salting). When the pan is hot, distribute the zucchini over the bottom, reserving their bowl. Place the tomato halves cut side down in the pan as well.

3 Roast until the zucchini is golden brown on one side and tender but not mushy, 10 to 15 minutes, and the tomato halves feel squishy when pressed. (If either the zucchini or tomato halves are done first, remove them and let the others finish cooking.)

4 Return the zucchini to their bowl and transfer the tomatoes to a cutting board. Mix the zucchini with the herbs, garlic, and 1 tablespoon lemon juice, tossing gently with a rubber spatula. Pull off and discard the tomato skin, chop the pulp, and add it to the mixture. Season with salt and more pepper or lemon juice to taste.

5 Mix half of the parsley into the vegetables and serve them hot, warm, slightly cool, or at room temperature, sprinkled just before serving with the rest of the parsley.

✤ Grilled Vegetables in Asian Vinaigrette

If you have leftover grilled vegetables, you can put this together in a flash. And if not, grill some as for the Grilled Vegetables with Lemon-Basil Oil recipe on page 194. Either way, the vinaigrette is a born flavor enhancer. It goes about unobtrusively mixing with the vegetable juices, marrying all their flavors, and turning this dish into a stylish accessory for all sorts of summer get-togethers. **6 SERVINGS**

---

4 teaspoons white wine or other vinegar

1 teaspoon tamari or soy sauce

1 teaspoon mirin

1½ teaspoons Dijon mustard, preferably French

1½ teaspoons minced garlic

¼ cup plus 2 tablespoons extra-virgin olive oil

Salt and freshly ground pepper

5½ cups grilled vegetables, sliced about ¼ inch thick after cooking, such as yellow or green summer squash, portobello mushrooms, red or green bell peppers, sweet onions, asparagus, tomatoes, eggplant

⅓ cup torn basil leaves

1 Whisk the vinegar, tamari, mirin, mustard, and garlic together in a large bowl. Gradually whisk in the olive oil to make a lightly thickened vinaigrette. Season generously with salt and pepper.

2 Fold the vegetables into the vinaigrette with a rubber spatula, taste a piece, and add more salt, pepper, vinegar, or tamari, if you like.

3 Transfer the vegetables to a serving dish or plates, scatter the basil on top, and serve. Or refrigerate for up to 4 days and serve lightly chilled or at room temperature.

Do-Ahead Options

✤ Make the vinaigrette up to 5 days ahead; return to room temperature before using.

✤ Make the finished dish up to 4 days ahead and serve it slightly chilled or at room temperature.

POTATOES, RICE, COUSCOUS, AND ROLLS

❋ Mashed Potatoes with Basil Oil

Green mashed potatoes are unexpected, of course, but when you taste them it's even more surprising to get an elusive essence of vegetable, like asparagus or peas. And yes, they do taste like basil, but somehow the marriage of potatoes with basil and olive oil creates a little alchemy. **6 SERVINGS**

Salt and freshly ground pepper

2 ¾ pounds boiling potatoes, preferably Yukon Golds or Yellow Finns, peeled and cut into 1- to 1½-inch pieces

¾ cup loosely packed basil leaves

¾ cup olive oil, plus 2 to 3 tablespoons, if needed

1½ tablespoons freshly squeezed lemon juice

Do-Ahead Option

◇ Make the potatoes up to 3 days ahead and reheat them in a covered, shallow ovenproof casserole in a moderate oven.

1 Bring a large pot of salted water to a boil over high heat. Add the potatoes and cook at a medium boil (so they don't break up) until very tender but not falling apart, about 20 minutes.

2 Meanwhile, put the basil in a blender, followed by ¾ cup olive oil and the lemon juice. Puree until they become a smooth green liquid, about 2 minutes, scraping down the jar with a rubber spatula once or twice. Season with salt and pepper. Set the basil oil aside.

3 Drain the potatoes in a colander and return them to their cooking pot set over low heat; dry for about a minute, stirring. Still over low heat, mash them with a potato masher, gradually adding the basil oil until it has been fully absorbed and the potatoes are a pale but vibrant green. (If the potatoes seem a little dry, add up to 3 tablespoons more oil, 1 tablespoon at a time.) Season with salt and pepper.

4 Transfer the potatoes to a warm serving dish or plates and serve steaming hot.

✤ Cheese Mashed Potatoes

There are two ways to go with these: mash 'em, cheese 'em, and eat 'em right away;
or give them a second incarnation as a baked gratin with a golden crust — a perfect
party potato. 8 SERVINGS

2 pounds boiling potatoes, such as Yukon Golds, peeled and cut into 1½-inch pieces

1 cup plus 2 tablespoons milk

5 tablespoons butter, cut into 5 pieces

1 medium garlic clove, minced

Salt and freshly ground pepper

1 cup lightly packed shredded Swiss or Emmentaler cheese

½ cup freshly grated imported Parmesan cheese, or ¼ cup Parmesan plus ¼ cup pecorino Romano cheese

1 In a large saucepan of salted boiling water, cook the potatoes at a medium boil (so they don't break up) until very tender but not falling apart, 15 to 20 minutes.

2 Meanwhile, put the milk, butter, and garlic in a small saucepan. Season with salt and pepper. Warm over low heat until the milk is hot and the butter melts. Remove from the heat and cover to keep warm.

3 When the potatoes are very tender, drain them in a colander and return to their cooking pot set over very low heat. Cook, stirring frequently, for about 1 minute to dry them out. Still over low heat, mash the potatoes with a potato masher, gradually adding the hot milk mixture until it has been fully absorbed. (The potatoes will be very light but shouldn't be soupy — the cheese will firm them up somewhat.)

4 Stir in both the Swiss and Parmesan cheeses and season with more salt and pepper, if you like. Serve the potatoes very hot.

5 Alternatively, transfer the mashed potatoes to a lightly buttered, shallow 8- or 9-inch baking dish. Press a piece of plastic wrap directly over the surface to keep a skin from forming and let cool; cover and refrigerate.

6 Remove the potatoes from the refrigerator 1 hour before baking and place them, uncovered, on the

top rack of a preheated 425°F oven until golden, 35 to 40 minutes (see Note).

NOTE: I've used baking dishes of two different materials: heavy ceramic and tin-lined copper. The potatoes turn golden-crusted on the top, bottom, and sides in the ceramic dish, while in the copper pan only the top crusted. Either way, they were delicious.

HOW TO HOLD OVER MASHED POTATOES

Mashed potatoes can be held over for about an hour in a very low oven or set in a water bath on top of the stove. The trick is to pour 2 to 3 extra tablespoons of hot milk on top, cover them, and keep them warm using whichever method you choose. When you're ready, stir in the milk and serve.

Mashed Potatoes with Caramelized Onions

I devised these beauties as part of my cooking audition for the job of head chef at The Inn at Pound Ridge (I got the job). The basic mash is particularly good to begin with because it's made with buttery Yukon Golds, and when you stir in deeply browned, tender onions, it becomes even better. **6 SERVINGS**

7½ tablespoons butter

3 medium onions, thinly sliced (3 cups)

Salt and freshly ground pepper

2¼ pounds Yukon Gold or Yellow Finn potatoes, peeled and cut into 1½-inch pieces

1 cup plus 2 tablespoons milk

Do-Ahead Options

◈ Cook the onions up to 4 days ahead and reheat them over very low heat, stirring frequently, before adding them to the potatoes.

◈ Make the finished mashed potatoes up to an hour ahead. For how to hold them, see page 201.

1 In a large, heavy skillet, melt 1½ tablespoons of the butter over medium-high heat. Add the onions and cook, stirring, until lightly browned and slightly limp, about 1 minute. Reduce the heat to low and cook, stirring frequently, until they are golden brown and very tender, about 15 minutes. Stir in 3 tablespoons water to dissolve the brown bits stuck on the bottom of the skillet (the water will evaporate, leaving the onions rich and moist). Remove the pan from the heat and season the onions with salt and pepper.

2 Meanwhile, bring a large a pot of salted water to a boil over high heat. Add the potatoes and cook at a medium boil (so they don't break up) until they're very tender but not falling apart, 15 to 20 minutes. When they're almost ready, set a saucepan with the milk and remaining 6 tablespoons butter over low heat.

3 Drain the potatoes in a colander, then return them to their cooking pot set over low heat and dry them for about a minute, stirring constantly. Still over low heat, mash them with a potato masher, gradually adding the hot milk mixture until it has been fully absorbed. Stir in the caramelized onions, season generously with salt and pepper, and serve piping hot.

❋ Minty New Potatoes with Summer Herbs

When you boil new potatoes with lots of mint, the herb penetrates in a refreshing, breathy sort of way. Finished with a roll in sweet butter with basil, thyme, and chives, the potatoes couldn't be simpler or more charming. And if you cut them into quarters after they're cooked and toss them with olive oil instead of butter (with lemon juice or vinegar and the herbs), they become a delicate potato salad, good served at just about any temperature. **6 SERVINGS**

---

3 cups packed mint sprigs cut into 3- to 4-inch lengths, plus 3 tablespoons chopped leaves

2¼ pounds small new potatoes (red or white), preferably 1½ to 2 inches in diameter, scrubbed halved

2½ tablespoons butter, slightly softened

1½ tablespoons mixed chopped fresh herbs, such as thyme, chives, tarragon, and basil

Salt and freshly ground pepper

1 Set a large pot of water over high heat to come to a boil with the mint sprigs. Salt it generously and cook the potatoes at a medium boil, partially covered, for 15 to 20 minutes or until tender but firm when pierced with a wooden skewer.

2 Remove the pot from the heat and pick out and discard the clumps of mint with tongs (it isn't as annoying as it sounds). Drain the potatoes in a colander, and if any leaves still cling to them, gently rinse them off under hot running water and drain well.

3 Return the potatoes to their cooking pot along with the butter, chopped mint, and mixed fresh herbs. Toss them together gently with a rubber spatula, season with salt and pepper to taste, and serve hot.

Do-Ahead Option

❧ Scrub the potatoes and prepare the mint sprigs up to a day ahead.

Potatoes Fried in Olive Oil with Fresh Garlic Salt and Pepper

On a trip to Greece, I ate delicious potatoes simply fried in olive oil, and that was enough for me (see Great Home Cooking, page 4). But at home more seemed called for, so I tossed them in a mix of garlic with coarse salt, a pinch of cayenne, and lots of black pepper to highlight their crisp simplicity. They make an irresistible side dish, but you can also think of them as an hors d'oeuvre, with a bowl of olive oil mayonnaise alongside for dipping. **4 SERVINGS**

¾ **teaspoon kosher or coarse sea salt**

⅛ **teaspoon cayenne**

Freshly ground black pepper

Olive oil

2 pounds boiling or baking potatoes (the cooked texture of the former is somewhat creamy, while the latter is more dry and fluffy), **peeled, cut lengthwise, then across into ½-inch-thick slices**

2 teaspoons minced garlic

Sweet or medium hot Spanish paprika, *pimentón dulce* or *agridulce,* **to taste** (optional)

Olive Oil Mayonnaise (optional; see page 205)

1 Preheat the oven to 350°F with a rack in the middle. Mix the salt, cayenne, and a generous amount of pepper together in a small bowl and set aside.

2 Fill an electric deep-fryer to the manufacturer's recommended level with olive oil (or if you are comfortable with frying, use a very large, shallow pan with ¾ to 1 inch of oil). Slowly begin heating it to 365° to 370°F, and set a baking sheet, double-lined with paper towels, next to the fryer.

3 When the oil has reached the proper temperature, fry one batch of potatoes at a time without crowding (see Note), turning them occasionally, until golden brown on the outside and tender on the inside, 5 to 8 minutes. As they're done, spread them in a single layer on the prepared cookie sheet and keep them in the oven while you continue frying (letting the oil return to proper temperature between batches).

4 When all the potatoes are fried, transfer them to a large warm bowl, toss with garlic, sprinkle with the salt mixture and *pimentón* to taste, if you're using it, then toss again and serve right away with mayonnaise on the side, if you like.

NOTE: It's important not to crowd the potatoes as they fry to keep the temperature of the oil as consistent as possible. Should it drop dramatically from adding too many pieces at once, the potatoes will absorb the oil and turn greasy. And be sure to save the frying oil — it can be strained and used once or twice again if it isn't dark.

Olive Oil Mayonnaise

1 large egg yolk, at room temperature

1½ tablespoons freshly squeezed lemon juice

½ cup olive oil

Salt and freshly ground white pepper

You can whip up this easy mayonnaise in a food processor in practically seconds, and, if you want, make it up to a week ahead. Just be sure to remove it from the refrigerator at least 30 minutes before serving. MAKES ABOUT ¾ CUP

1 Place the yolk and lemon juice in the bowl of a food processor and pulse several times to incorporate (or mix by hand in a large bowl with a wire whisk). With the machine running, begin adding the oil in a slow, steady stream — the yolk will begin to absorb the oil and start to thicken.

2 Continue adding the remaining oil in a slow stream until it's all incorporated and has created a thick sauce. Season it generously with salt and white pepper.

Mashed Sweet Potatoes with Maple Syrup

These mashed sweets, oh-so-discreetly enhanced by a little maple syrup and an almost imperceptible tang of buttermilk, aren't flashy at all — they're just, well, good. They reheat nicely, too, making them terrific for times when it helps to get as much cooking done ahead as is humanly possible. And you can double or triple the recipe if you want. **4 TO 6 SERVINGS**

1½ pounds sweet potatoes (see page 209), **peeled and cut into 1½-inch pieces**

⅓ cup buttermilk, milk, or light cream, at room temperature

6 tablespoons butter, slightly softened

2 tablespoons maple syrup, or to taste

Salt and freshly ground pepper

1 Set a large pot of salted water over high heat to come to a boil. Add the potatoes, and cook them at a medium boil (so they don't break up) until very tender, about 15 minutes.

2 When they're done, drain them in a colander, then return them to their cooking pot set over low heat and dry them for about 1 minute, stirring frequently. With a potato masher, mash them as coarsely or smoothly as you like, gradually adding the buttermilk, then the butter, several pieces at a time. Stir in the syrup, season with salt and pepper, and stir for about 30 seconds more to dry them slightly and ensure that they're hot (they will have a slightly loose consistency).

3 Spoon them into a warm serving dish and serve piping hot.

Do-Ahead Option

◆ Make the potatoes up to 4 days ahead and reheat them, covered, in a moderate oven until steaming hot.

NOTE: If you'd rather, you can bake the whole, unpeeled potatoes until tender, scrape out the flesh, and pick up the recipe after the boiled ones have been dried in the pot. The mash will be slightly less loose than the boiled version.

POTATOES IN CRETE

One late afternoon in Crete, I pushed open a high gate, not knowing what lay behind and found myself on a path enclosed by rough white stucco walls taller than my head, draped with the brilliant papery blooms of bougainvillea. I followed the path as it ascended by gentle turns, content to let its beauty draw me onward. Within minutes my amble was greeted by green herbs and crimson flowers flourishing in large rectangular vessels used in Greece for packing olive oil.

A few steps later the path widened, and I was at the top. In front of me appeared a small outdoor living space furnished with a square wooden table and chairs, the table covered by a cloth with a bowl of roasted nuts set on it. The wall dropped to chest height on one side of this open-air room and hastening to it, I gasped at the panorama of whitewashed houses terracing the hillside before me and coming to rest at the lapping waters of the Mediterranean below.

When I turned back to the patio, I saw an oil barrel fashioned into a cooking grill with a makeshift rack and a thin, old black pan perched on top. The grill was fueled by flames from olive wood cuttings, I found out later, and a modest pile of their angular branches lay in a jumble next to it.

Thick slices of potatoes were browning in bubbling olive oil, attended to by what was clearly the woman of the house. I watched her go about her tasks — poking this, prodding that, adding sticks to the fire, and now and then peering into the pots that were simmering on a second cookstove in a corner of the terrace (this one fueled by gas), all the while working in that seemingly effortless way that comes from a lifetime of experience. Her sense of ease and authority was all the more clear to me because she never spoke a word.

Those crisp potatoes were only one of many dishes she made and brought to the table for us that night. There were bowls and platters of rabbit stew, marvelous snails, wild mountain greens, rusks moistened with tomato and milky feta, and sweet spoon fruit made of cherries, all foraged or trapped or grown on the Cretan hills. It was by far more of a banquet than an evening's meal, but take away even half and you're still left with one sure thing: this woman's heart beat in her cooking, and she lived to nourish her family's bodies and souls.

✤ White and Sweet Potato Salad

This surprisingly light, flavorful potato salad is from my days at the restaurant One Fifth Avenue in Manhattan, where we served it alongside brunch dishes such as frittatas and my take on eggs Benedict: poached eggs with smoked sable hollandaise (the fish, not the fur). The potato salad was an unexpected but welcome accompaniment, looking cheerfully decked out in its orange, white, red, and green colors. It's the kind of thing that's good to have in the fridge, a ready companion for lunches and food off the grill. **8 SERVINGS**

1½ pounds unpeeled sweet potatoes

2 pounds small unpeeled boiling potatoes

Salt

2 teaspoons whole-grain (Pommery) or Dijon mustard, preferably French

¼ cup plus 2 tablespoons red wine vinegar or other vinegar (but not balsamic)

¾ cup olive oil

1 medium green bell pepper, cut into ½-inch dice

1 medium red bell pepper, cut into ½-inch dice

Freshly ground pepper

1½ tablespoons chopped parsley

1 Set a large pot of water over high heat to come to a boil for the potatoes. If the potatoes are very large, cut them in halves or quarters, keeping them in a bowl of cold water as you cut the rest.

2 Salt the boiling water generously, add the sweet and boiling potatoes, and cook them at a medium boil (to keep them from breaking up) until tender-firm, about 20 minutes depending on their size. As they cook, check the smallest ones first for tenderness by piercing them with a wooden skewer and removing them as done.

3 Meanwhile, place the mustard in a very large bowl, whisk in the vinegar, and gradually whisk in the olive oil to make a lightly thickened vinaigrette. Stir in the green and red peppers and season generously with salt and pepper.

4 When the potatoes are done, drain in a colander, and let them cool for 10 to 15 minutes. When they're cool enough to handle but still warm, peel and scrape off their skins with a paring knife and cut them into ⅓-inch-thick slices. Fold them into the vinaigrette gently but thoroughly and season with more salt and pepper, if you like.

5 The salad can be served warm, chilled, or at room temperature. To serve it warm, fold in 1 teaspoon of parsley, sprinkle the rest over the top, and serve right away.

SWEET POTATO OR YAM?

So, is it a yam or a sweet potato you are buying? The chances are great that they're sweet potatoes, no matter what they're called or whether their flesh is bright orange or yellow. When they're dubbed "yams," smile knowingly because American-grown sweet potatoes aren't true yams at all.

True yams are, in fact, a huge and important crop grown in tropical and subtropical climes. And to quote Elizabeth Schneider's invaluable book *Uncommon Fruits & Vegetables*: "Although there are 600 species of yam, what we are most likely to encounter in the United States is a brown, black-brown, or rusty-tan shaggy-coated tuber that may be shaped like a log, an elongated sweet potato, a distorted mitten, or a rhinoceros foot. The raw flesh is crisp, slippery, mucilaginous; either white, ivory, or yellow. A cooked yam's taste will be more potato-like than any of the other tropical starches, but the texture is looser, coarser, and drier, the flavor blander."

You do find yams in ethnic markets in the United States, but when traditional stores call a sweet potato a yam, they are merely marketing them.

❋ Aromatic Yellow Rice

This buttery rice is daffodil-yellow from turmeric and full of flavor from onion, ginger, and coconut milk. Sometimes it sticks to the bottom of the pot when it cooks (depending on the pot), so welcome it when it does and let everyone know that the crunchy crust is the golden prize. Rice in general, and this one in particular, reheats well, so if it suits your purpose, divide the batch and serve some or all of it later. **8 SERVINGS**

¾ cup canned unsweetened coconut milk

¾ teaspoon ground turmeric

2½ tablespoons vegetable oil

1½ tablespoons butter

½ cup finely chopped onion

1¾ teaspoons grated fresh ginger (see page 139)

1½ tablespoons seeded, finely chopped jalapeño pepper or a pinch of cayenne

1½ cups long-grain white rice (not converted style)

Salt and freshly ground pepper

1 Stir the coconut milk, 1¾ cups plus 2 tablespoons warm water, and the turmeric in a bowl and set it near the stovetop. Set a large, heavy saucepan over medium heat with the oil and butter. When the butter is melted, cook the onion, ginger, and jalapeño, if using it, until they begin to soften, stirring frequently, 2 to 3 minutes. Add the rice, stir to coat each grain with fat, and cook, stirring, 1 minute.

2 Stir in the coconut milk mixture, season with salt and pepper, and bring to a boil, stirring frequently. Cover the pan tightly and simmer over very low heat for 18 minutes.

3 Remove from the heat and, without removing the cover, let the rice steam for at least 10, or up to 30 minutes. Separate and fluff the rice grains with a fork and serve hot.

Do-Ahead Options

☙ The cooked rice can sit, covered, in its pot for up to 30 minutes.

☙ Make the rice up to 4 days ahead and refrigerate it wrapped in foil or freeze it for up to 2 months. Reheat the packet in a moderate oven until steaming (defrosting it first in the refrigerator overnight, if it's frozen).

Lemon Rice Pilaf with Dill

We're a rice pilaf kind of house, whether it's the classic one of rice and onions simmered in broth, or the same done up for company, all lemon-scented and pleasingly tart. 6 SERVINGS

3 tablespoons butter

1 medium-large red onion, chopped (1 generous cup)

1 bay leaf

1½ cups long-grain white rice (not converted style)

2⅔ cups chicken broth

Salt and freshly ground pepper

1½ teaspoons grated lemon zest

3 tablespoons chopped fresh dill

1 Melt the butter in a large saucepan set over medium-low heat. Add the red onion and bay leaf and cook, stirring occasionally, until the onion begins to turn translucent, 3 to 5 minutes.

2 Stir in the rice and cook together for about 2 minutes, stirring frequently. Stir in the broth (careful, it may spit), bring to a boil, and season with salt and pepper. Tightly cover the pan and cook over low heat until the rice is tender and all the broth is absorbed, 15 to 18 minutes.

3 Remove the saucepan from the heat and transfer the rice with a rubber spatula to a warm serving bowl, gently breaking up any clumps, if necessary. Fold in the lemon zest and dill and serve hot.

Do-Ahead Options

◈ Chop the onion and grate the zest up to a day ahead and refrigerate them separately.

◈ The cooked rice can sit, covered, in its pot for up to 30 minutes.

◈ Make the rice up to 4 days ahead and refrigerate it wrapped in foil or freeze it for up to 2 months. Reheat the packet in a moderate oven until it's steaming (defrosting it first in the refrigerator overnight, if it's frozen).

Arborio Rice Pilaf with Mushrooms

Arborio is a short-grain rice from Italy, one of the varieties of risotto-type rices that are used for making — no surprise here — risotto, the rice dish that gets naturally creamy from the thickening action of its starch with gradual additions of hot broth. When properly cooked, the individual grains retain their integrity and chewy texture. However, if you rinse the rice well before cooking, sauté it with onions and mushrooms (for example), and add all the broth in one fell swoop, it becomes a pilaf with a slightly different character. The grains remain a little sticky but separate easily with the nudge of a fork. And as you eat, there's the lovely suggestion of creaminess that the grains still retain, the degree dependent upon which risotto-type rice you use (see page 213). **6 SERVINGS**

---

1 cup plus 2 tablespoons risotto-type rice, such as Carnaroli, Arborio, Vialone Nano, or Baldo

3 tablespoons butter

1 medium onion, chopped

1½ cups finely chopped white or cremini mushrooms (4 to 5 ounces), by hand or in a food processor

1 bay leaf

½ teaspoon dried thyme

Salt and freshly ground pepper

1¾ cups plus 2 tablespoons chicken or vegetable broth, heated

1 Preheat the oven to 350°F with the rack in the middle. Rinse the rice in a large strainer held under cold running water until the water begins to look clear. Let the rice drain.

2 Meanwhile, melt the butter in a large, heavy saucepan over medium heat. Stir in the onion, mushrooms, bay leaf, and thyme. Season lightly with salt and pepper (you will be seasoning the dish again later) and cook, stirring frequently, until the onion starts to turn translucent and the mushrooms look cooked, 5 to 8 minutes.

3 Give the strainer a final shake to get rid of any excess water, stir the rice into the vegetables, and cook them together for 1 to 2 minutes, stirring frequently. Add the broth all at once, stirring. Season with salt and pepper and bring to a boil. Cover the pan tightly and immediately transfer to the oven. Bake the rice until the grains are tender-firm and all the liquid has evaporated, 15 to 20 minutes.

4 Remove the pan from the oven and fluff the rice gently with a fork. Transfer the rice to a warm serving dish or plates and serve hot.

ABOUT ARBORIO RICE

Arborio is used in the United States as a generic term for any variety of short-grain Italian rice (designated *superfino*) meant for making risotto, although it is, in fact, its own variety. There are three others that I know of: Carnaroli, Vialone Nano, and Baldo (they're rice varieties, not brands). They can be used interchangeably, although they differ somewhat in the length and shape of the grain, starch content, and final chewiness. This, of course, means that your finished pilaf or risotto will be more or less creamy or more or less chewy depending on which you use. If you can find a selection, try a few to see which you like the best. I prefer Carnaroli for risotto because its grains remain firm with no hard, chalklike center when it has reached just the right stage of doneness. I also like its balance of creaminess to chew.

Basmati Rice with Olives, Lemon, and Nutmeg

If cooking rice makes you nervous, try basmati — it's a snap to cook. This Indian and Pakistani rice, beyond its ease in cooking, has a fragrance and taste that might remind you of popcorn. It makes a lovely saladlike dish when seasoned with spices, lemon, olives, and sun-dried tomatoes, served warm or at room temperature. It's best served the day it's made, but if there are leftovers, don't eat them cold — chilling turns the rice chalky and unpleasant. 8 SERVINGS

1½ cups basmati rice

1 teaspoon cumin seeds

3½ tablespoons extra-virgin olive oil

Salt

½ teaspoon grated nutmeg, preferably freshly grated

⅓ cup coarsely chopped pitted green or black Mediterranean olives, such as Atalanti (green) or Kalamata (black), or a mixture

2 tablespoons finely chopped sun-dried tomatoes

2½ teaspoons drained capers, preferably the small ones called nonpareil

2 teaspoons grated lemon zest

4 or 5 fresh basil leaves, torn into bite-size pieces, or 2 tablespoons coarsely chopped flat-leaf parsley, for garnish

1 Soak the rice in cold water to cover by at least 2 inches for a minimum of 15 or up to 30 minutes, stirring occasionally to loosen the starch.

2 Meanwhile, toast the cumin seeds in a small, dry skillet set over very low heat, moving the pan back and forth frequently, just until they smell fragrant, 2 to 3 minutes (if cooked too long, the taste is harsh). Transfer to a small dish and let cool.

3 Drain the rice and rinse it 2 or 3 times under cold, running water; drain well. Put 2¼ cups of cold water in a medium, heavy saucepan. Stir in the rice along with 1½ tablespoons of the olive oil and salt to taste. Bring to a boil over high heat, stirring several times. As soon as the water boils, stop stirring and let it continue to boil, uncovered, until the water level reaches just below the rice and holes appear on the surface, about 5 minutes.

4 Immediately reduce the heat to very low (set the pan over a heat diffuser if you have one), cover the pan tightly, and cook for 10 minutes more. Remove from the heat and let stand, covered, for 10 more minutes without removing the lid.

◈ Grate the lemon zest up to a
day ahead and chop the olives
and sun-dried tomatoes up to
2 days ahead.

◈ The finished salad can be made
up to 2 hours ahead and served
at room temperature (if it's a hot
day, only up to 1 hour ahead
because it can't be refrigerated).

5 Fluff the rice with a fork, transfer it to a large bowl, drizzle with the remaining 2 tablespoons olive oil, and tossing with 2 forks, mix in the cumin and nutmeg, followed by the olives, sun-dried tomatoes, capers, and lemon zest. Season the rice generously with salt and pepper, tossing, and serve it warm or at room temperature sprinkled with basil or parsley, if you like.

Saffron Couscous with Dried Cranberries, Pistachios, and Fresh Herbs

Inspired by the hauntingly delicate yet vivid Persian flavors that I experienced in an evening of dishes that Najmieh Batmanglij cooked from her book New Food of Life, *I fooled around with a few of their basic elements to make a quick and festive couscous. I infused it with the strange and alluring mineral taste of saffron and punctuated it with a clear, but not overly sweet, note of fruit. Lots of pistachios and a handful of bright, fresh herbs completed the play of tastes and textures. Sound like a lot of work? It's not.* **6 SERVINGS**

---

3 tablespoons olive oil

¾ teaspoon saffron threads

1½ cups chicken broth diluted with ⅓ cup water

1½ teaspoons grated lemon zest

Salt and freshly ground pepper

1½ cups quick-cooking couscous

¼ teaspoon Tabasco sauce

¼ cup plus 2 tablespoons dried cranberries

¼ cup coarsely chopped salted green pistachios

¾ cup torn basil, mint, and cilantro leaves

Do-Ahead Options

- Grate the zest and chop the pistachios up to a day ahead.
- Cook the couscous up to an hour ahead and serve it warm or at room temperature.

1 Set a large, heavy saucepan over low heat with the olive oil and saffron. Lightly toast the saffron, stirring, for about 1 minute. Add the diluted broth and lemon zest, season with salt and pepper, increase the heat to high, and bring the liquid to a boil.

2 Stir in the couscous, tightly cover the pan, and remove from the heat. Let the couscous stand, covered, for 5 minutes. Fluff the grains with a fork, then stir in the Tabasco, cranberries, and more salt and pepper, if you like. Transfer the couscous to a warm serving dish, sprinkle with the pistachios followed by the herbs, and serve right away. Or serve warm or at room temperature, garnishing it when serving.

Israeli Couscous with Red Peppers and Shallots

Most of us know couscous as a tiny, quick-cooking Moroccan-style pasta, but Israeli couscous (also called pearl couscous) hasn't become quite as familiar yet. Both begin as semolina, a type of wheat, precooked and dried before we buy it. In the case of the Israeli style, a steaming process puffs it up into somewhat large, round, white grains resembling small pearls; hence, one of its names. And when cooked, it continues to look strikingly different from the couscous we know, becoming almost translucent and creamy, though both have a mild, nutty taste. 6 SERVINGS

3 tablespoons olive oil

1 medium red bell pepper cut into strips, about 1/4 inch x 1 inch

4 large shallots, thinly sliced (3/4 cup)

1 1/2 cups Israeli couscous

2/3 cup well-drained chopped canned tomatoes

1/8 teaspoon ground cloves

1 bay leaf

1 3/4 cups vegetable or chicken broth

Salt and freshly ground pepper

3 tablespoons chopped fresh dill or a mixture of parsley, chives, and tarragon

Do-Ahead Options

➣ Cut the peppers and shallots up to a day ahead and chop the tomatoes anytime.

➣ Make the couscous up to 2 days ahead and reheat it in a covered pan in a moderate oven.

1 Set a large, heavy, saucepan with the olive oil over medium-low. When the oil is hot, stir in the peppers, shallots, and couscous. Cook, stirring frequently, until the grains are light gold in color and the vegetables are beginning to wilt or even starting to brown, about 5 minutes. Stir in the tomatoes and cook about 1 minute more. (If the tomatoes remain very wet, increase the heat slightly to evaporate some of their liquid for another minute, stirring frequently.)

2 Add the cloves, bay leaf, broth, and 2 tablespoons water, stirring. Bring the broth to a boil, then immediately lower the heat so it simmers slowly. Stir once, cover the pan tightly, and cook until the grains are translucent, chewy-tender, and only a slight moistening remains, 8 to 10 minutes. Season with salt and pepper to taste and stir in the dill or other herbs.

3 Transfer the couscous to a warm serving dish or plates and serve hot.

❖ Buttermilk Biscuits

In some ways I'm just an old-fashioned southern girl . . . from the north side of Chicago. I hanker for warm homemade biscuits dripping with honey alongside such food greats as skillet-fried chicken or spareribs. But these little gems are just as happy to play their part in a simple chicken dinner or when the call comes, grace the Thanksgiving table.

MAKES 8 LARGE (2- X 3-INCH) BISCUITS OR 16 SMALLER ONES

---

2 cups sifted all-purpose flour, plus more for dusting

2 ½ teaspoons baking powder

½ teaspoon salt

¼ teaspoon baking soda

6 tablespoons cold unsalted butter, cut into small pieces

¾ cup cold buttermilk, plus 1 tablespoon more, if necessary

1 Preheat the oven to 425°F with the rack in the middle. Place the flour, salt, baking powder, and baking soda in a large bowl and combine with a whisk. Scatter the butter over the top, and with a wire pastry cutter (like one used for making pie doughs), cut the butter in until it's well distributed and the mixture is the size of large peas. Gradually pour ¾ cup of the buttermilk over the surface, tossing and mixing with a fork at the same time, just long enough to moisten the mixture. Add up to 1 tablespoon more buttermilk if the dough seems dry.

2 Lightly dust the rolling surface with flour. With floured hands, gather the dough into a rough ball and turn it out of the bowl. Gently knead the soft, slightly sticky dough 6 or 7 times (handling the dough minimally keeps the biscuits tender). It will become more cohesive but remain soft.

3 Scrape the surface clean with a dough cutter (see page 265) or metal spatula and dust lightly with flour. With floured hands or a rolling pin, pat or gently roll the dough into a rectangle 8 x 5 x ¾ to 1 inch thick. Pierce the dough about 20 times with the floured tines of a fork. Cut the rectangle in half lengthwise without twisting or sawing. Wiping the blade clean between each cut and reflouring it, cut across the middle to form 4 quarters. Cut across each quarter to make 8 rectangular biscuits (and if you like, cut each in half again to make 16 smaller ones).

Do-Ahead Options

⟐ Mix the dry ingredients together anytime.

⟐ Wrap and freeze the biscuits for up to 2 months. Defrost them overnight (wrapped) at room temperature and reheat them, unwrapped, in a moderate oven.

⅓ cup dried apricots, raisins, or other dried fruit

2 tablespoons plus 2 teaspoons sugar

⅓ cup hazelnuts, almonds, or walnuts, toasted and coarsely chopped

4 Using the dough cutter or spatula to lift one biscuit at a time, transfer them to an ungreased cookie sheet and put 1 inch apart for crisp sides (for soft sides, place about ½ inch from one another); bake until the tops are light gold, 13 to 16 minutes. Serve hot.

Scones

Buttermilk biscuits become buttermilk scones when you add a little sugar and some dried fruit and/or nuts. Cut and bake them just like the biscuits.

1 Set a small saucepan of water over high heat to come to a boil. Add the fruit, remove from the heat, and let it sit for 5 minutes. Drain, and if large, cut into narrow strips. Either way, dry the fruit well with paper towels.

2 Mix 2 tablespoons of sugar into the biscuits' dry ingredients and cut in the butter according to the recipe. Stir in the fruit and nuts, then stir in the buttermilk. Cut the dough into rectangles or rounds and sprinkle with 2 teaspoons of sugar before baking.

───────── ❖ ─────────

WHAT TO DO WITH LEFTOVER BUTTERMILK

If you've bought a quart of buttermilk for a recipe and you don't drink it, you've probably got a lot sitting in the refrigerator not getting any younger. Here are a few recipes in the book to help use it up:

Mashed Sweet Potatoes with Maple Syrup (page 206)

Buttermilk Cake with Orange Mascarpone Cream and Chocolate Glaze (page 234)

Buttermilk Biscuits (page 218)

Scones (page 219)

Raspberry Shortcakes (page 264)

Mom's Potato Rolls

When you think of homey, comforting rolls, these fit right in. They're pillowy on the inside and ever-so-slightly crusty-chewy on the outside. And because the cooked potato makes it a soft, voluptuous dough, your hands and kneading surface should be floured, but just enough to keep it from sticking — too much makes them less moist and light. MAKES 1 DOZEN 3-INCH ROLLS

---

1 medium boiling potato (6 ounces), **scrubbed and cut in half**

¾ cup milk

2 tablespoons unsalted butter

1 teaspoon sugar

1 teaspoon active dry yeast (not rapid-rise)

2 cups all-purpose flour, plus more for dusting

1¼ teaspoons salt

Vegetable oil

1 Cook the potato in a saucepan of unsalted boiling water until tender, about 15 minutes. Peel and coarsely mash enough of it to measure ⅔ cup (saving the rest, if any, for something else). Set a small saucepan over low heat with the milk, butter, and sugar and heat until tiny bubbles appear around the edges, stirring once or twice to help dissolve the sugar. Remove the pan from the heat and let the milk cool until tepid.

2 Sprinkle the yeast over the milk and let it dissolve for 3 to 5 minutes. Meanwhile, mix the flour and salt together in the bowl of a stand mixer (or in a large bowl if kneading by hand).

3 When the yeast is dissolved, stir in the potato. Stir the milk-potato mixture into the flour to combine. Knead with a dough hook (or floured hands on a lightly floured counter — a bench scraper is helpful here; see page 265) for about 10 minutes, or until it becomes less stringy and more cohesive. The dough should be soft and somewhat sticky — if it's wet, add more flour 1 tablespoon at a time. (If kneading by machine, transfer the dough to a floured surface and knead it 2 or 3 times by hand.)

4 Place the dough in a large, lightly oiled bowl, turning to coat it on all sides. Let it rise, covered, in a warm place (such as near a pilot light) until dou-

Do-Ahead Options

- Let the dough make its first rise in the refrigerator overnight. If it hasn't doubled in volume by the morning, let it sit at room temperature until it does.

- Wrap and freeze the rolls for up to 2 months. The recipe can be doubled without increasing the yeast.

bled in volume, about 1 1/2 hours. (Or overnight in the refrigerator.)

5 With a floured hand, scoop the dough out onto a lightly floured surface and knead it 3 or 4 times. The dough will be soft and supple and still slightly sticky. Return the dough to the bowl, cover, and let it rise again until doubled, 45 to 60 minutes.

6 With a floured hand, scoop out the dough and knead it 2 or 3 times on a lightly floured surface. With a floured knife or bench scraper, divide it into 12 equal pieces (each about 1 3/4 ounces).

7 One at a time, slightly flatten each piece with your fingers to form a small, rough circle. Bring the edges up to meet in the center and pinch together. Shape into a smooth round ball by rolling it between floured hands.

8 Set the balls 3 inches apart on a lightly floured cookie sheet and cover with a large roasting pan (or something that won't touch them as they rise). Let them rise until they almost double in size and feel springy when gently squeezed on the sides, 30 to 40 minutes. Meanwhile, preheat the oven to 425°F with a rack in the middle.

9 Lightly sprinkle the tops of the dough with flour and make a 1-inch-deep snip in the center of each with floured scissors. Bake the rolls until golden, 16 to 20 minutes. Serve warm.

✤ Corn Muffins

These muffins have slightly craggy tops touched with gold, delicately crunchy exteriors and buttery-crumbly insides. They're good just as they are, but during blackberry season, who could resist tossing a handful of those black beauties into the batter? Or for a savory touch anytime, add chopped scallion. **MAKES 6 MUFFINS**

---

1 cup whole-grain yellow cornmeal

¼ cup plus 1½ teaspoons all-purpose flour

½ teaspoon baking soda

1 tablespoon sugar

½ teaspoon salt

4½ tablespoons chilled unsalted butter, cut into small pieces

1 extra-large egg yolk

⅔ cup plain low-fat yogurt

⅔ cup fresh blackberries or 1 tablespoon finely chopped scallion, both white and green parts (optional)

Do-Ahead Options

❧ Mix the dry ingredients days or even weeks ahead.

❧ Freeze the muffins for up to 2 months, still wrapped. Defrost them overnight and serve warm.

1 Preheat the oven to 450°F with a rack in the middle.

2 Stir the cornmeal, flour, sugar, baking soda, and salt together in a large mixing bowl. Cut the butter into the dry ingredients with a wire pastry cutter (like one used for making pie dough) until it is well distributed and the mixture is the size of small peas. In a small bowl, lightly beat the egg yolk and yogurt together. Pour it over the ingredients in the bowl and mix with a fork to just combine; if using blackberries or scallions, fold them in now. The batter will be somewhat soft but not liquid.

3 Spoon the batter into 6 nonstick muffin cups 2¾ inches in diameter, filling them. Bake for 10 to 13 minutes, or until a toothpick inserted in the middle of one comes out with a few moist, but not wet, crumbs. Let the muffins sit in the tin for 2 to 3 minutes to firm up slightly, then remove them and serve while still warm.

DESSERTS

CAKES

✤ Rich Chocolate Gateau

I invented this dark and rich, fine little number when I was the chef at the Inn at Pound Ridge. There it was dubbed "Baked Chocolate" in honor of what it is: chocolate baked with sugar and butter in cakelike form. Each wedge of this confection was crowned by a delicately thin sheet of edible silver, a corner of which was attached to the cake by a dab of cream, leaving the rest free to flutter and shimmer its way to the table. These sheets are called vark, and you can buy them at a store that sells Indian groceries, but the only adornment this cake really needs is a soft, billowing spoonful of freshly whipped cream. **12 SERVINGS**

½ **pound semisweet chocolate, chopped**

½ **pound (2 sticks) unsalted butter, cut into 1-inch pieces, slightly softened**

½ **cup plus 3 tablespoons granulated sugar**

5 eggs, at room temperature

¾ **cup heavy cream**

Confectioners' sugar

1 Preheat the oven to 325°F with a rack set in the center. Set a baking pan large enough to comfortably hold a 9-inch round cake pan 2 inches deep on the rack and add enough hot water to reach halfway up its sides. Grease the cake pan and line the bottom with a round of waxed or parchment paper cut to fit. Grease the paper and set the pan aside.

2 Melt the chocolate in a double boiler set over low heat (see page 229), and stir it with a wooden spoon (or a whisk if small lumps remain) until completely smooth. Stir in the butter 3 or 4 pieces at a time until it's all incorporated and the mixture is smooth and glossy; it will be somewhat liquid. Remove the chocolate from the heat, scrape it into a large bowl, and set aside to cool slightly, but don't let it get cold.

3 Place the sugar in a shallow ovenproof dish (a pie pan is good) and set the dish in the oven for 5 minutes, or until the sugar is very warm to the touch. Meanwhile, break the eggs into the bowl of an electric mixer. When the sugar is ready, pour it over the eggs all at once and whip them on high speed until pale in color, thick, and tripled in volume (it will look like softly whipped cream that doesn't hold its shape), 3 to 4 minutes.

◇ Chop the chocolate even
    weeks ahead.

◇ Bake and refrigerate the cake in
    its pan up to a week ahead.
    Unmold it, then let it sit at
    room temperature for at least
    30 minutes or up to 1 hour
    before serving.

4   Stir half of the whipped eggs into the melted chocolate until no streaks remain. Carefully but thoroughly fold in the remaining beaten eggs. Pour the batter into the prepared pan (it will fill by a generous three-quarters). Set it in the water bath and bake for 1½ hours, or until a wooden skewer inserted in the center comes out with moist but not wet crumbs.

5   Remove the pan from the oven, run a thin knife around the edge to release the sides, and let the cake cool in the pan on a rack for 1 hour. Then set the cake, still in the pan, in the refrigerator to chill for at least 5 hours or overnight.

6   Meanwhile, whip the cream to soft peaks and refrigerate it.

7   To remove the cake from the pan, set the pan directly over very low heat and slide it around briefly (so the bottom of the cake becomes slightly softened to allow its release). Place a large plate or cake rack over the pan and turn them together so that the cake drops onto the plate or rack. (If the cake sticks, return the pan to the heat for a few more seconds.) Remove and discard the paper liner. Place a serving plate over the bottom of the cake, sandwiching it with the first plate or rack, and turn them together so the top of the cake is right side up again.

8   Lightly dust the top of the cake with confectioners' sugar. Cut it into wedges with a long, thin, sharp knife, wiping the blade clean with a paper towel between each cut. (It's a very moist cake and a little messy to cut, so I slice it in the kitchen before bringing it out, and you can be sure I eat the parts that get stuck on the knife.) Garnish each slice with whipped cream and serve.

Little Chocolate Spice Cakes with Strawberries and Warm Mocha Sauce

These are strawberry shortcakes made with delicate chocolate cakes instead of biscuits and a dress-up drizzle of coffee-spiked chocolate sauce. Each one is complete unto itself, a sweet little gift to set in front of friends. **8 SERVINGS**

¼ cup sifted all-purpose flour

¼ teaspoon ground cinnamon

A large pinch each ground ginger, ground cloves, and grated nutmeg

⅛ teaspoon salt

6 ounces semisweet chocolate, chopped

3 tablespoons unsalted butter

2 egg whites, at room temperature

½ cup plus 2 tablespoons sugar

⅓ cup milk

½ teaspoon instant espresso powder

1 teaspoon vanilla extract

½ cup heavy cream

1 pint strawberries, hulled and sliced

1 Preheat the oven to 375°F with a rack in the center. Have ready 8 nonstick muffin cups 2¾ inches in diameter. Thoroughly mix the flour with the spices and salt in a small bowl and set the spiced flour aside.

2 Melt 2 ounces of the chocolate with the butter in a double boiler set over hot but not boiling water (see page 229). When it has melted, stir with a whisk until it's smooth and glossy, then remove it from the heat.

3 Whip the egg whites in the bowl of an electric mixer set on medium speed until they form soft peaks, about 1 minute. Increase the speed to high, gradually add 6 tablespoons of the sugar, and continue whipping until very stiff and glossy, 2 to 3 minutes. Reduce the speed to low, gradually sprinkle the spiced flour over the top, and stir together just long enough to combine, scraping down the sides of the bowl once. Gradually mix in the chocolate mixture just until the batter becomes a solid color, scraping down the sides of the bowl once.

4 Fill the muffin cups by about half. Bake until the tops of the cakes are flat, smooth, and slightly shiny and a toothpick just comes out clean, 13 to 15 minutes; do not overbake. Remove from the oven and let the cakes cool in the pan on a rack for 5 minutes,

then remove them from their pans and let cool completely on the rack.

5 Meanwhile, heat the milk with the remaining ¼ cup sugar, the espresso powder, and the vanilla in a small saucepan set over low heat, stirring occasionally, until the sugar dissolves, about 3 minutes. Remove the pan from the heat and add the remaining 4 ounces chocolate (if the milk has boiled, let it cool to warm before adding the chocolate). Allow the chocolate to melt for 1 to 2 minutes, then stir it with a whisk to make a smooth and glossy mocha sauce.

6 Whip the cream to soft but distinct peaks and refrigerate it.

7 Gently reheat the mocha sauce, if necessary, and keep it warm. Split each cake horizontally and place the bottom halves on plates. Spoon a dollop of whipped cream on each, followed by some of the berries, then set the tops on the filling. Coat each cake with a spoonful of sauce, top with more whipped cream, spoon the remaining berries all around, and serve right away.

DOUBLE BOILERS

I own a fancy double boiler only because I found one in a moving sale. Until that discovery I happily used my tried-and-true setup: a small saucepan set inside a larger one so that the smaller one partially sits in the water (or a stainless steel bowl sitting on top of a saucepan half filled with water). I found that as long as the water was merely hot, the chocolate wouldn't scorch. But if you're looking for a great excuse to go buy a French copper beauty, here it is.

❋ Pecan-Apricot Roulade

The roulade is a slender sheet of feather-light pecan cake rolled around an airy filling of tangy, pureed apricots mixed with freshly whipped cream. The cake's delicate texture is due in large part to grating the nuts in a handheld rotary grater (like a Mouli or Swiss Zyliss) so they turn into dry little wisps full of nutty flavor. 8 SERVINGS

Generous ⅓ cup packed dried apricots (3 ounces)

5½ tablespoons granulated sugar

24 segments of clementine or tangerine, for garnish

2 tablespoons Grand Marnier or other orange liqueur

⅓ cup pecan pieces, plus 8 halves for garnish, all lightly toasted

½ cup sifted all-purpose flour

⅛ teaspoon salt

6 eggs, at room temperature

¼ cup packed light brown sugar

2 teaspoons grated clementine, tangerine, or orange zest

1 teaspoon vanilla extract

3 tablespoons confectioners' sugar

1 cup heavy cream

1 Preheat the oven to 450°F with a rack in the center. Grease the bottom and sides of an 11- x 15-inch jelly-roll pan, line it with waxed or parchment paper cut to fit the bottom with 1 to 2 inches of overhanging ends. Grease the paper and set the pan aside.

2 Simmer the apricots with ½ cup water and 1½ tablespoons of the granulated sugar in a small saucepan set over low heat, covered, until very tender, 10 to 15 minutes.

3 When the apricots are tender, stir in 1 tablespoon of the Grand Marnier and puree the mixture in a blender or food processor until it's in very small pieces, adding a little more water if it's too thick to move in the machine. You should have a very generous ⅓ cup of thick puree. Set aside in a large bowl.

4 Grate enough of the pecan pieces with a rotary-style grater (do not chop them in a food processor) to measure ¼ cup; put them in a medium bowl. Coarsely chop the remaining pieces (to add texture to the cake) and add them to the same bowl. Add the flour and salt, stir together well, and set aside.

5 Separate the eggs, reserving only 3 of the whites. Place the yolks in the bowl of an electric mixer with the brown sugar, zest, and vanilla. Whip the yolk mixture on high speed until it is thick and light in color and the whip leaves tracks that quickly dissolve, about 4 minutes. Set aside (or transfer to another bowl if you have only one mixer bowl).

Do-Ahead Options

- Prepare the fruit segments up to 4 hours ahead stored in their juice. Take them out of the refrigerator an hour before serving.

- Make the apricot puree up to 7 days ahead and take it out of the refrigerator to come to room temperature before using.

- Assemble the cake up to 2 days ahead.

6 Place the 3 egg whites in the clean bowl of an electric mixer and whip them on medium speed until they form soft peaks, about 1 minute. Increase the speed to high and gradually add the remaining ¼ cup granulated sugar in a steady stream, scraping down the sides of the bowl after all the sugar has been added. Continue whipping until the whites are stiff and glossy, about 2 minutes.

7 Pour the yolk mixture over the whites, sprinkle with one-third of the flour-nut mixture, and partially fold them together. Sprinkle with more flour-nut mixture and partially fold again. Sprinkle the remainder over the top and fold it in thoroughly. Spoon large dollops of batter onto the prepared pan and spread it with a long, thin metal spatula or rubber spatula to cover the bottom as evenly as possible.

8 Bake the cake until the center springs back when lightly pressed, 7 to 9 minutes. Meanwhile, spread a large, clean towel (not terry cloth) on a countertop and sift the confectioners' sugar over it.

9 When the cake is done, flip it upside down onto the sugared towel, holding the pan and the long ends of the paper liner together. Lift off the pan, then carefully peel off and discard the paper. Immediately roll the cake, starting from the long side closest to you, with the towel rolled inside the cake and let it cool on a rack for 10 to 15 minutes.

10 Whip the cream to soft peaks. Stir about one-third of the cream into the apricot puree to lighten it, then fold in the rest of the whipped cream along with the remaining 1 tablespoon Grand Marnier.

11 Unroll the cake with one of its long sides facing you and remove the towel. With a long, narrow icing-type spatula, spread the filling evenly over the

continued

cake, leaving ½ inch along the edge of the opposite long side. Reroll the cake to enclose the filling. Trim about ½ inch off each end with slightly diagonal, parallel cuts. Transfer the roulade to a cookie sheet seam side down, cover, and refrigerate it.

12 To serve, cut the roulade into 8 slightly diagonal pieces, cutting parallel with the ends; place each piece flat side down on a dessert plate. (To cut the cake equally, it's easiest if you cut or score it in half first, then in quarters, and finally into eighths.) Decorate the center of each with a pecan half and nestle 3 citrus segments next to each slice. Serve right away.

NOTE: Remove as many of the strings from the tangerine segments as possible, slice off the straight, fibrous edge, and remove their seeds before serving.

HOW TO PREPARE CITRUS SEGMENTS

To prepare perfect, glistening orange, lemon, grapefruit, or lime segments, first slice off just enough of the top and bottom of the fruit to expose the flesh. Standing it on a flat end, place your knife at the top just behind the white section of the peel. Cut down with a slight sawing motion, following its rounded shape, to remove a vertical section.

Repeat this process all around the fruit until the insides are completely exposed. Remove the segments by cutting between their thin white membranes. Pick out any seeds with a paring knife, and if the segments are large and meant to be a garnish, cut each one in half on the diagonal. You can prepare and refrigerate the segments several hours ahead in the juice from their "skeletons," or simply squeeze the juice into a glass and down it right then and there.

❖ End of the Summer Upside-Down Plum and Blueberry Cake

To make this cake, pour the basic batter from the Buttermilk Cake recipe (page 234) into a pan strewn with sliced Italian plums and scatter blueberries on top before baking it. When the cake comes out of the oven, most of the blueberries have drifted to the bottom to join the purple plums, and when you flip the cake over, the bottom becomes a glistening, old-fashioned fruit-covered top. **8 SERVINGS**

---

6 small ripe but firm purple Italian prune plums, rinsed, dried, and cut into ½-inch-thick slices

Ingredients for Buttermilk Cake batter (page 234)

1 teaspoon grated lemon zest

1 cup blueberries, rinsed and dried well with paper towels

1 teaspoon flour

1 Preheat the oven to 350°F with a rack in the center. Oil a 9-inch springform pan and dust it with sugar; tap out the excess. Arrange the plums in a single layer on the bottom of the pan.

2 Prepare the batter as in the original Buttermilk Cake recipe (see page 234), but add the lemon zest when you add the lemon juice in Step 3. Pour the batter into the pan over the plums. Place the blueberries in a medium bowl, toss them gently but thoroughly with the flour, and scatter them over the batter. Bake the cake for 45 to 50 minutes, or until a toothpick inserted in the middle comes out clean.

3 Cool the cake in the pan on a rack for 10 minutes, then remove the ring. Cool 5 minutes more, and invert onto another rack. Inch by inch, slowly lift off the pan base, nudging loose any resisting fruit with a metal spatula or knife. Let the cake cool completely before serving.

Buttermilk Cake with Orange Mascarpone Cream and Chocolate Glaze

There's far too much to tell you about this cake. The layers are light and delicate, with a texture halfway between angel food and butter cake. While I drew you in (I think) by calling it a buttermilk cake, one of its big secrets is olive oil in the batter, which makes the crumb moist without imparting any flavor of its own.

The cake's combination of elements makes for an elegant sweet that is both luscious and refined. But the cake itself is so versatile, you can finish it in lots of other ways. I have made it into the End of the Summer Upside-Down Plum and Blueberry Cake (page 233), turned two layers into an impromptu birthday cake filled with raspberry jam and whipped cream covered with a thick chocolate frosting, and also made it into delicious strawberry shortcake. I've also used apricot and strawberry preserves and lemon marmalade instead of orange for the filling. **8 SERVINGS**

---

1 ¼ cups cake flour (not self-rising)

½ teaspoon baking soda

¼ teaspoon salt

1 cup plus 1 tablespoon sugar

½ cup buttermilk, at room temperature

¼ cup pure or light olive oil (not extra-virgin)

1 teaspoon vanilla extract

3 extra-large eggs, at room temperature, separated

1 tablespoon freshly squeezed lemon juice

¾ cup mascarpone (see Note on page 236)

¼ cup heavy cream

1 Preheat the oven to 350°F with a rack in the center. Grease a 9- x 2-inch round cake pan with olive oil. Insert a waxed or parchment paper round cut to fit the bottom. Oil the paper, dust with flour, tap out the excess, and set it aside.

2 Place the flour, baking soda, salt, and ¾ cup of the sugar in the bowl of an electric mixer and combine well. Pour the buttermilk into a 2-cup liquid measuring cup followed by the ¼ cup olive oil and the vanilla. Add the egg yolks to the measuring cup and lightly combine the mixture with a fork.

3 With the machine on low speed, gradually add the liquid ingredients to the dry and mix until smooth, 1 to 2 minutes, or beat them by hand in a large bowl. Stir in the lemon juice, scraping down the sides of the bowl at least once, and if any lumps remain, increase the speed to medium for about 30 seconds.

¼ cup plus 2 tablespoons sweet orange marmalade or other preserves, at room temperature

Chocolate Glaze (recipe follows)

Do-Ahead Options

☙ Chop the chocolate even weeks ahead. Make the glaze up to a day ahead and store it at room temperature. Or refrigerate it for up to 2 weeks. Either way, reheat it over hot water, stirring occasionally, just until it's pourable again.

☙ Make the mascarpone filling up to 1 day ahead and take it out of the refrigerator about 30 minutes before using it, or just long enough for it to become spreadable.

☙ Bake the cake layer up to 1 day ahead, wrapping it well and storing it at room temperature. Or freeze it for up to 2 months.

☙ Make the finished cake up to 1 day ahead and take it out of the refrigerator to return to room temperature before serving.

Set the cake batter aside (or transfer to another bowl if you have only one mixer bowl).

4 Whip the egg whites in the clean, dry bowl of an electric mixer on medium speed until they form soft peaks, about 2 minutes. Increase the speed to high, and gradually add 3 tablespoons of the sugar in a steady stream, scraping down the sides of the bowl. After all the sugar has been added, continue to whip until the egg whites are stiff, about 2 minutes. Remove the bowl from the machine.

5 Transfer half of the cake batter to the top of the whites and, by hand, combine it with a whisk (I use the whip from the machine). Pour the remaining batter over the whites and gently fold and stir it in until no white streaks can be seen. Turn the batter into the prepared pan and bake for 28 to 30 minutes, or until a toothpick inserted in the middle comes out dry. Transfer the cake to a cooling rack, run a knife around the inside edge to loosen the sides, and let it cool for 10 minutes. Invert to unmold onto the rack. Peel off and discard the paper and let the cake cool completely bottom side up.

6 Meanwhile, prepare the filling. Blend the mascarpone with the cream and the remaining 2 tablespoons sugar using an electric mixer on the lowest speed or by hand with a wooden spoon until very smooth, 30 to 60 seconds. (If necessary, beat briefly on high speed to eliminate any lumps.) Cover and refrigerate the mascarpone cream until firm but spreadable, 1 to 2 hours.

7 Slice the cake in half horizontally with a serrated knife and separate the halves. Slide a cardboard cake round under the bottom half for support (or a removable metal base from a tart pan) and place

continued

it on the cooling rack set over a cookie sheet or large piece of waxed paper. Using a long, narrow spatula, spread the marmalade evenly over the bottom half, leaving a 1/2-inch margin around the edge. Spoon the mascarpone cream on top of the marmalade and spread it as evenly as possible up to 1/2 inch from the edge. Set the top half over the filling, cut side down, and press gently to adhere; the filling should not ooze out.

8 Pour the Chocolate Glaze over the top of the cake and with a clean spatula, spread it over the entire top as evenly and smoothly as possible so it begins to flow over the sides. Coat the sides evenly with the overflow, using any drips that have fallen onto the sheet. Transfer the cake to a plate and refrigerate it for about 15 minutes to set the glaze, or up to 24 hours, taking it out to return to room temperature before serving. Cut the cake into wedges with a sharp knife dipped in hot water and wiped clean between each cut. Place the wedges on plates and serve right away.

NOTE: In place of mascarpone, you can substitute 6 ounces cream cheese, at room temperature, blended with 2½ tablespoons heavy cream and 2 tablespoons sugar.

Chocolate Glaze

MAKES ABOUT 1⅔ CUPS

6 ounces high-quality semisweet chocolate, finely chopped

½ cup heavy cream

1 Place the chocolate in a heatproof medium bowl. Bring the cream to a boil in a small saucepan set over medium heat. Immediately pour all the cream over the chocolate.

2 Let the chocolate melt for a minute or 2, then whisk it slowly to make a smooth, glossy glaze. Cover the bowl and set it aside.

Black Skillet Banana Cake with Rich Chocolate Sauce

When I serve this cake for brunch, I bake it in one of my trusty old black cast-iron pans and bring it to the table, still warm, to cut into wedges. For tea, it gets baked in a square pan and cut into squares in the kitchen. For dessert, I put it to bake in a round pan and when it's done, set pieces on plates and dress them up with a drizzle of rich chocolate sauce (and sometimes a spoonful of whipped cream). No matter the time of day it makes its entrance or the shape it takes, the cake is light and moist with lovely banana flavor. **8 TO 10 SERVINGS**

1 teaspoon vanilla extract

½ cup mashed banana

1½ cups all-purpose flour

½ teaspoon ground cinnamon

⅛ teaspoon ground ginger

¼ teaspoon salt

1 teaspoon baking soda

1 cup sugar

½ cup unsalted butter, slightly softened

2 extra-large eggs, lightly beaten, at room temperature

½ cup sour cream, at room temperature

⅓ cup pecans, very coarsely chopped

Brown Sugar Chocolate Sauce (recipe follows)

2 cups unsweetened whipped cream (optional)

1 Preheat the oven to 350°F with a rack in the center. Grease a 9-inch cast-iron skillet, 9- x 2-inch round cake pan, or 8- x 2-inch square cake pan. (Grease more generously if unmolding the cake from either cake pan.)

2 Stir the vanilla into the mashed banana. In a medium bowl, mix the flour, baking soda, cinnamon, ginger, and salt.

3 Reserve 1 tablespoon of the sugar and cream the butter and remaining sugar in the bowl of an electric mixer set on medium speed until it becomes pale in color and somewhat fluffy, about 2 minutes, scraping down the sides of the bowl once. Gradually add the eggs and beat until well combined, scraping down the sides of the bowl once, 1 to 2 minutes. Reduce the speed to low and stir in the sour cream followed by the mashed banana, scraping down the sides of the bowl once, about 1 minute. (The mixture may look slightly curdled at this point.) Gradually stir in the dry ingredients and mix until just incorporated, 1 to 2 minutes, scraping down the sides of the bowl once.

continued

Do-Ahead Options

- Mix all the dry ingredients together except the sugar even weeks ahead.

- Make the chocolate sauce up to a month ahead. Serve it at room temperature or reheat it just a bit to take the chill off.

- The cake can be baked up to 2 days ahead, wrapped in foil, and warmed in a low oven.

4 Transfer the batter to the prepared pan, spreading it evenly. Scatter the pecans over the batter. Sprinkle the reserved 1 tablespoon sugar on top. Bake 30 to 35 minutes, or until the top is golden and shiny and a toothpick inserted in the middle comes out dry. Meanwhile, prepare the chocolate sauce, if using it.

5 When the cake is done, transfer it to a rack and let cool for 20 minutes (if unmolding, turn it out after this cooling period). Cut the cake into wedges or squares depending on the shape of the pan and serve them warm, drizzled with chocolate sauce and garnished, if you like, with a dollop of whipped cream.

Brown Sugar Chocolate Sauce

MAKES ABOUT ¾ CUP

3 tablespoons brown sugar

½ cup heavy cream

2½ ounces semisweet chocolate, finely chopped

1 Stir the brown sugar and heavy cream together in a small saucepan set over low heat and simmer until the sugar dissolves, about 2 minutes, stirring once or twice.

2 Increase the heat to medium-high, bring the mixture to a quick boil, and remove the pan from the heat. Add the chocolate and let it melt for 1 to 2 minutes without stirring, then stir it slowly with a whisk until smooth and glossy.

3 Set the chocolate sauce aside to serve warm or at room temperature.

COOKIES

❊ Sugar Yeast Crisps

Christmas isn't Christmas in our family without these big sugar cookies. Thin and crisp, with a slight chewiness and yeasty flavor, their name doesn't do them justice. The yeast in the dough doesn't raise it so much as create a few flaky layers with a top and bottom of caramelized sugar. It's a recipe from my daughter's Grandma M, who passed it on to me, but where she got it no one knows. **MAKES ABOUT 3 DOZEN COOKIES**

---

1 ounce active dry yeast
(four 1/4-ounce packets),
not rapid-rise

1 cup (2 sticks) **unsalted butter, softened**

2 cups all-purpose flour

1/8 teaspoon salt

Granulated sugar

Do-Ahead Options

- Measure the flour anytime.
- Refrigerate the dough up to 5 days ahead.
- Bake the cookies up to a week ahead and store them in an airtight container.

1 Dissolve the yeast in 1/3 cup lukewarm water until creamy, 2 to 3 minutes. Cream the butter in the bowl of an electric mixer set on medium speed for about 30 seconds, scraping down the sides of the bowl once. Reduce the speed to low, stir in the yeast, and mix until well blended, about 1 minute. Stir in the flour and salt until smooth. Wrap the dough in plastic wrap and refrigerate it until it's firm and can be easily handled, 1 to 2 hours or overnight. (If it has gotten very hard, let it sit out for a short while but don't let it get soft.)

2 Preheat the oven to 375°F with a rack in the center. Place a plate with sugar 1/4 to 1/2 inch deep near your work area. Shape the dough into small walnut-size balls. One at a time, press them into the sugar until flat and about 1/16 inch thick, turning them 3 or 4 times in the sugar as you press (and replenishing the sugar whenever necessary). Place them, about 1 inch apart, on ungreased cookie sheets.

3 Bake the crisps until golden and caramelized on the bottom with golden spots on top, 8 to 12 minutes. Watch carefully because these can burn quickly. Transfer them to racks (they'll be a little fragile for about a minute) and let them cool completely.

✤ Pine Nut Cookies

Fresh and spicy tastes of lemon, ginger, cloves, and cinnamon embrace the buttery pine nuts in these crunchy-crumbly cookies. And I think they get even better after a day. MAKES ABOUT 2 DOZEN COOKIES

---

1 cup all-purpose flour

¼ teaspoon salt

⅜ teaspoon ground cinnamon

¼ teaspoon ground ginger

¼ teaspoon ground cloves

½ cup (1 stick) **unsalted butter, slightly softened**

½ teaspoon grated lemon zest

½ cup plus 2 tablespoons sugar

1 egg yolk

1 tablespoon freshly squeezed lemon juice

½ teaspoon vanilla extract

1 cup pine nuts

Do-Ahead Options

☙ Grate the lemon zest up to a day ahead. Combine the flour, salt, and spices up to 3 days ahead.

☙ Bake the cookies up to a week ahead and store them in an airtight container. If they soften in humid weather, crisp in a low oven for several minutes and cool them on a rack.

1 Preheat the oven to 350°F with a rack in the center. Sift the flour, then mix it thoroughly with the salt, cinnamon, ginger, and cloves in a small bowl. Set the spiced flour aside.

2 Cream the butter and lemon zest in the bowl of an electric mixer set on medium speed for about 30 seconds, scraping down the sides of the bowl once (or by hand in a large bowl). Gradually add the sugar and beat the mixture until it's fluffy and light, 1 to 2 minutes, scraping down the sides of the bowl once. Mix in the egg yolk, lemon juice, and vanilla until well blended, about 1 minute.

3 Reduce the speed to low and gradually mix in the flour mixture just until it forms a dough, about 1 minute, scraping down the sides of the bowl once. Stir in the pine nuts until just combined.

4 Using a 1-tablespoon measuring spoon, drop somewhat level spoonfuls of dough about 1½ inches apart on nonstick cookie sheets (or greased regular sheets). Bake them (switching the upper and lower trays midway through baking) for 12 to 15 minutes, or until their edges and bottoms are golden brown but the tops have barely colored.

5 When the cookies are done, transfer them carefully to cooling racks (they're a little fragile at this point) and let them cool completely before serving.

Dark Chocolate Chunk Cookies with Macadamia Nuts

With intense hunks of chocolate, big crunches of macadamias and walnuts, and just enough coconut to add richness, this clumpy cookie has got "for grown-up kids" written all over it. Treat yourself to one while the chocolate is still warm and oozy. (And if you're not a fan of coconut, just leave it out.) **MAKES ABOUT 2 DOZEN COOKIES**

---

4 ounces bittersweet chocolate, chopped into ½-inch pieces (about ⅔ cup)

1 cup salted dry-roasted macadamia nuts, split in half

½ cup walnuts, broken or cut into ½-inch pieces

⅓ cup lightly packed sweetened shredded coconut

5 ounces (1 stick plus 2 tablespoons) **unsalted butter, slightly softened**

⅔ cup plus 1 tablespoon packed dark brown sugar

1 egg, lightly beaten, at room temperature

2 teaspoons vanilla extract

1 cup plus 2 tablespoons all-purpose flour

¼ teaspoon salt

Do-Ahead Options

- Measure the flour anytime and chop and mix the chocolate and nuts up to 3 days ahead. Add the coconut to the chocolate-nut mixture just before starting the dough.

- Store the cookies in an airtight container for up to a week.

1 Preheat the oven to 350°F with 2 racks in the center section. Mix the chocolate, macadamias, walnuts, and coconut in a medium bowl; set aside.

2 Cream the butter and brown sugar in the bowl of an electric mixer on medium-high speed for 2 to 3 minutes, scraping down the sides of the bowl once. Gradually add the egg, followed by the vanilla, and beat until the mixture is beige in color and looks like fluffy frosting, 2 to 3 minutes, scraping down the sides of the bowl once or twice.

3 Reduce the speed to low and gradually stir in the flour and salt until smooth, scraping down the sides of the bowl once, about 1 minute. Stir in the chocolate-nut mixture to just combine, about 10 seconds. Remove the bowl from the machine and briefly mix the dough with a rubber spatula to incorporate the chunks as evenly as possible. Drop heaping tablespoons of dough about 2 inches apart on nonstick cookie sheets.

4 Bake the cookies until their bottoms and edges turn golden brown and the tops feel slightly soft when lightly pressed, 18 to 20 minutes, switching the top sheet with the bottom midway through baking. Transfer the cookies to a rack to cool completely.

❋ Chocolate Shortbread

A glass of cold milk or a cup of hot tea is perfect with these crumbly chocolate cookies. You might fall in love with their faintly sweet, buttery denseness. MAKES 16 SMALL WEDGES

---

1 cup plus 2 tablespoons all-purpose flour

⅓ cup sugar

2 tablespoons Dutch-process cocoa

¼ teaspoon salt

⅓ cup finely chopped pecans or other nuts

½ cup (1 stick) unsalted butter, slightly softened but still cool

1 teaspoon vanilla extract

1 Preheat the oven to 325°F with a rack in the center. Mix the flour, sugar, cocoa, salt, and pecans in a small bowl; set the dry ingredients aside. Place a cookie sheet near your work surface.

2 Mix the butter and vanilla in the bowl of an electric mixer set at low speed (or in a bowl by hand) until combined and the butter is smooth but not at all fluffy; the cookie's texture is the result of keeping the butter cool and not aerated and handling the dough minimally. Gradually add the dry ingredients and mix just until the butter is evenly distributed in small pieces throughout and looks like coarse meal, 1 to 2 minutes.

3 Gather the mixture in your hands and transfer it to a sheet of waxed paper set on your work surface. Press it together to form a rough ball (it will be very crumbly; as you press, the warmth of your hands will make it more cohesive, but don't knead it). Shape the dough into a disk about 5 inches in diameter, pinching the edges together with your fingers and pressing them back into the circle to make them as smooth as possible. (If the dough is still very crumbly, let it sit for a few minutes to allow the butter to soften further and then form it. As you work with the dough it becomes much more cohesive.) Place another large sheet of waxed paper on top and gently roll the dough to about a 7-inch diameter, pinching and pressing the split edges back into place. Continue to roll the dough until it's an 8-inch disk about ⅜ inch thick.

◆ Mix the flour, sugar, cocoa, and salt anytime, but chop and stir in the pecans before starting the dough.

◆ Store the cookies in an airtight container for up to a week.

4 Remove and discard the top sheet of paper, place the cookie sheet on top of the dough (using the underside of the sheet if it's one with sides), slipping your hand under the bottom paper to support the dough, and flip them over together so the dough now rests on the cookie sheet. Peel off and discard the paper and give the edges a clean finish by pressing them into the circle with a metal spatula or table knife. Prick the dough 25 to 30 times with a sharp fork.

5 Deeply score the circle in half with a large knife. Score it in quarters, then each quarter into fourths so that you have 16 scored wedges still in the shape of a circle (if you've cut all the way through, leave them in place, and it will still work fine).

6 Bake the shortbread 25 to 27 minutes, or until it looks somewhat dry and feels somewhat firm when lightly pressed. Remove the cookie sheet from the oven and immediately cut all the way through the scored lines without moving the cookies (they're fragile at this point). Let them cool for 5 minutes, then transfer to a rack to cool completely.

Pistachio Sugar Cookies

The distinctive, though elusive, flavor of pistachios is captured in these tender, old-fashioned sugar cookies. There's a nice amount of nuts in the dough, and the cookies are sprinkled with more pistachios and sugar as soon as they come out of the oven.

MAKES ABOUT 2 DOZEN COOKIES

½ cup plus 2 tablespoons **shelled salted pistachios**

¼ cup plus 2 tablespoons **sugar**

½ cup (1 stick) **unsalted butter, somewhat soft but still cool**

1 **egg, lightly beaten**

½ teaspoon **vanilla extract**

1 cup plus 2 tablespoons **all-purpose flour**

¼ teaspoon **grated nutmeg, preferably freshly grated**

Pinch of salt

1 Preheat the oven to 400°F with 2 racks in the center section. Chop ½ cup of the pistachios with the sugar in a food processor as finely as possible, 1 to 2 minutes. Reserve 2 generous tablespoons to sprinkle over the cookies when they come out of the oven. Set aside the rest to go into the dough.

2 Chop the remaining 2 tablespoons pistachios into small pieces with a large knife (the processor does a poor job of this) and set them aside to go into the dough for added texture.

3 Cream the butter in the bowl of an electric mixer set on low speed for about 30 seconds, scraping down the sides of the bowl with a rubber spatula once. Increase the speed to medium and gradually add the reserved larger amount of pistachio-sugar just to combine. Scrape down the sides of the bowl, increase the speed to high, add the egg and vanilla, and beat just until well incorporated, less than 30 seconds, scraping down the sides of the bowl once.

4 Reduce the speed to low and gradually add the flour, nutmeg, and salt, and mix just until a soft dough is formed, about 1 minute. Scrape down the sides of the bowl and stir in the 2 tablespoons hand-chopped pistachios.

5 Form level tablespoons of dough into balls and set them about 2 inches apart on nonstick cookie sheets. Press the balls with the bottom of a moistened

glass to about ⅜-inch thickness. Bake the cookies until the bottoms are light gold but the tops are still pale, 9 to 12 minutes, switching the upper tray with the lower midway through baking (the center of a cookie will look slightly underdone if it is broken in half).

6 Remove the cookies from the oven and immediately sprinkle them with the reserved 2 tablespoons pistachio-sugar. Transfer the cookies to racks set over other cookie sheets or large pieces of waxed paper and sprinkle them again with the pistachio-sugar from the sheets. Let the cookies cool completely.

Double Chocolate Cream Cheese Brownies

These brownies are on the fudgey side, shot through with a rich vein of cream cheese and, if you want, raspberry jam, too. While I like them cut into large squares, you can also serve them in smaller pieces. MAKES 9 LARGE BROWNIES

½ cup walnuts

6 ounces cream cheese, slightly softened

1 extra-large egg yolk, plus 2 whole extra-large eggs, at room temperature

¾ cup plus 2 tablespoons sugar

1½ teaspoons vanilla extract

2 teaspoons freshly squeezed lemon juice

6 tablespoons unsalted butter, melted and cooled

¼ cup plus 2 tablespoons Dutch-process cocoa

⅓ cup all-purpose flour

¼ teaspoon salt

2 tablespoons semisweet chocolate chips

¼ cup seedless raspberry jam, melted (optional)

1 Preheat the oven to 350°F with a rack in the center. Grease an 8-inch square baking pan. Fold a 16-inch-long piece of foil so it measures 8 x 16 inches. Line the pan with the foil so it covers the bottom and two of its sides with an equal amount of overhang (to lift out the baked brownies). Grease the bottom and sides of the foil (but not the overhang) and set the pan aside.

2 Toast the walnuts on a pan in the oven until golden, 8 to 10 minutes. Let them cool, then chop them coarsely and set aside.

3 Beat the cream cheese, egg yolk, 2 tablespoons of the sugar, ½ teaspoon of the vanilla, and the lemon juice in the bowl of an electric mixer (or in a bowl by hand) until smooth, about 1 minute, scraping down the sides of the bowl once. (If the cheese was too soft to start, the mixture may be somewhat runny. If so, set the bowl in the refrigerator for 5 to 10 minutes, until the cheese firms up but is still spreadable.)

4 In a medium mixing bowl, lightly beat the whole eggs. Stir in the butter and remaining 1 teaspoon of vanilla. Sift the cocoa on top and stir them together until smooth (some tiny cocoa lumps may still remain). Stir in the remaining ¾ cup sugar until it's incorporated. Blend in the flour and salt. Stir in the nuts and chocolate chips.

5 With a rubber spatula or angled narrow metal one, spread half of the brownie batter over the bottom of the prepared pan as even as possible. Drop large dollops of the cream cheese mixture over the batter, spreading it to cover as even as possible. If using the jam, drizzle it over the cheese (rewarming it first, if necessary, but don't use it hot). Drop the remaining batter in large dollops on top and spread it to cover as even as possible. Drag a knife or metal spatula through the layers 2 or 3 times to slightly marbleize them. Bake the brownies for 35 to 40 minutes, or until a toothpick inserted in the middle comes out with a few moist, but not wet, crumbs.

6 Let the brownies cool in the pan on a rack for 15 minutes. Lift out the square and set it on the rack. With the aid of a second rack, flip it over, peel off and discard the foil, and turn it top side up. Let it cool completely. Cut the square into 3 equal strips, wiping the blade clean between each cut, then cut across in the same fashion to make nine brownies.

FRUIT DESSERTS

❋ Glazed Berries with Orange, Lemon, and Lime

The refreshing charm of these citrus-flavored berries comes from tossing them in their glaze, then serving them immediately. If the berries are prepped and the juices squeezed, dessert can be ready in minutes. **6 SERVINGS**

---

3 tablespoons freshly squeezed lime juice

3 tablespoons freshly squeezed orange juice

3 tablespoons freshly squeezed lemon juice

3 tablespoons sugar

3 cups mixed berries, such as strawberries, halved if large; blueberries; blackberries; raspberries

Do-Ahead Options

❧ Squeeze all the juices and combine them with the sugar up to 6 hours ahead in a nonreactive container.

❧ Have the glaze ingredients in the saucepan and the berries in the bowl waiting to be finished up to an hour ahead.

1 Stir the 3 citrus juices and the sugar together in a small nonreactive saucepan set over medium heat until the sugar dissolves, about 1 minute, stirring once or twice. Simmer until the liquid becomes syrupy and reduced to about 6 tablespoons, 2 to 4 minutes.

2 Place the berries in a large bowl. When the glaze is ready, immediately pour it over the berries and gently toss with a rubber spatula. Spoon the berries into stemmed glasses or bowls and serve right away.

❋ Warm Apple-Walnut Crumble

Chunks of apples are simmered with spices and sweet butter until they're just about ready to give up the ghost, then served warm with cream and a smattering of crunchy topping. It has the same wonderful homey quality as a traditional crumble or crisp baked in the oven, but this one is done on top of the stove. **6 SERVINGS**

---

1 lemon

4 to 5 large Granny Smith apples, peeled, cored, and cut into 1½-inch chunks (6 cups)

½ cup granulated sugar

½ teaspoon ground cinnamon

½ teaspoon grated fresh ginger (see page 139)

¼ teaspoon freshly grated nutmeg

4½ tablespoons slightly softened unsalted butter

2 tablespoons dry bread crumbs

¼ cup plus 2 tablespoons walnuts, lightly toasted and coarsely chopped

1½ tablespoons light brown sugar

¼ cup plus 2 tablespoons heavy cream

2 tablespoons sour cream

2½ teaspoons dried currants

Do-Ahead Options

☙ Make the nut crumble up to 3 days ahead. Take it out of the refrigerator to come to room temperature before using it.

☙ Cook the applesauce up to 3 days ahead.

1 Grate enough lemon zest without any bitter white pith to measure ½ teaspoon. Squeeze enough juice to measure 1½ tablespoons.

2 Place the apples in a large saucepan set over medium heat. Add the lemon juice, granulated sugar, cinnamon, ginger, nutmeg, and 6 tablespoons water. Cover the pan and cook, stirring occasionally and adjusting the heat to keep the liquid from boiling over, until the apples are very tender but not falling apart, about 10 minutes.

3 Meanwhile, melt 1½ tablespoons of the butter in a small skillet set over low heat. Add the bread crumbs and toast them, stirring frequently, until light gold, 1 to 2 minutes. Stir in the walnuts, brown sugar, and lemon zest (mashing the zest with the back of the spoon to break it up, if necessary). Immediately remove the skillet from the heat. Transfer the crumble to a small bowl and set it aside.

4 Whip the heavy cream and sour cream together to soft peaks and refrigerate it, whipping it again slightly before serving, if necessary.

5 When the apples are ready, stir briskly and mash them with the back of the spoon, keeping some pieces coarser to add texture. Stir in the currants and the remaining 3 tablespoons of slightly softened butter and remove the pan from the heat. Let cool slightly, then spoon into stemmed glasses or bowls. Top with a dollop of cream, sprinkle with the crumble, and serve warm.

Brown Sugar Bananas in Phyllo

As good as this flaky banana pastry drizzled with lime-rum butter is, with even less effort you can do as my daughter suggests: warm the bananas in the butter and spoon them over scoops of ice cream. Whichever way you serve them, the bananas are soft and sweet, intensely banana, and have a hint of the Caribbean about them. For other ideas for serving them and how they become a sundae, see page 252. **6 SERVINGS**

---

1 stick (4 ounces) plus 3 tablespoons unsalted butter

¼ cup plus 2 tablespoons packed dark brown sugar

⅛ teaspoon ground cinnamon

2 to 2½ tablespoons golden rum

3 ripe but firm bananas (yellow but without spots), each about 6 inches long

3 tablespoons freshly squeezed lime juice

1 package phyllo dough, thawed in the refrigerator overnight

½ cup heavy cream

1 Preheat the oven to 375°F with a rack in the center if baking the pastries right away. Make the flavoring butter. Thoroughly blend 6 tablespoons of the butter with the brown sugar, cinnamon, and 1 tablespoon of the rum in a food processor (or in a bowl with a spoon) and refrigerate it. (It's easier to handle when firm and melts more slowly inside the pastries during baking, which is good.)

2 Partially melt the remaining 5 tablespoons butter in a small saucepan set over low heat (see Note). Thoroughly dampen 1 or 2 kitchen towels, wring them out well, and set them aside. Peel the bananas, and cut them in half crosswise and then lengthwise to make 12 pieces total, each about 3 inches long. Transfer them to a platter and roll them in 1½ tablespoons of the lime juice.

3 Remove the phyllo dough from the refrigerator, carefully unroll it, and place about 12 sheets on a cookie sheet so they lie flat, covering them immediately with the towel(s). Return the remaining phyllo to the refrigerator.

4 Stir the partially melted butter to amalgamate it. Carefully peel off one phyllo sheet and lay it on the counter with the long side facing you, and immediately cover the remaining sheets with the towel(s). Lightly but completely brush the sheet with a thin coat of butter, starting from the edges and working toward

---
Do-Ahead Options

⬦ Refrigerate the flavored butter
up to 3 days ahead or freeze it.

⬦ Form and refrigerate the pastries up to 2 days ahead.

---

the center (the edges dry out more quickly). Carefully peel off a second sheet, lay it on top of the first, and butter it in the same fashion.

5 Assemble the pastries: Cut the sheets crosswise to make 5-inch-wide strips of dough. Forming one at a time, place a banana 2 inches from the long end of a strip with a 1-inch border of dough on each side. Place about 1 teaspoon of the chilled butter on the banana; fold over both sides of the dough strips to enclose the ends of the banana and create a fold along each length. Lightly brush the folds with butter.

6 Bring the end of the strip up over the banana and butter to cover them, then roll them together somewhat loosely to form a closed cylinder. Lightly brush the pastry all over with butter and place it seam side down, if possible, on an ungreased cookie sheet. Wrap the remaining bananas in the same fashion, using as many sheets of phyllo as necessary, and placing them at least 1 inch apart on the cookie sheet as they're done. Reserve the remaining flavored butter and refrigerate any extra phyllo dough for another use. (At this point the pastries can be refrigerated for up to 2 days.)

7 Bake the pastries until golden, turning them once, 10 to 15 minutes. About 2 minutes before they're done, melt the reserved flavored butter in a small skillet set over low heat and stir in the remaining 1½ tablespoons lime juice and remaining 1 to 1½ tablespoons rum. Place 2 pastries per person on warm plates, drizzle with a little of the melted butter, and spoon the rest around them. Drizzle the plates with a little cream and serve right away.

NOTE: Brushing the phyllo dough with soft butter makes for a somewhat flakier result but is slightly more difficult to do. If you'd rather, you can melt the butter completely instead.

Brown Sugar Banana Sundaes and Other Ideas

3 tablespoons unsalted butter, slightly softened

3 tablespoons packed dark brown sugar

1/8 teaspoon ground cinnamon

3 firm, ripe bananas

1 1/2 tablespoons freshly squeezed lime juice

1 tablespoon golden rum

Strawberry or vanilla ice cream, chocolate sorbet, or frozen yogurt

Try "plain" brown sugar bananas simply accompanied by Chocolate Shortbread (page 242); roll them inside crêpes; use them as the fruit for a shortcake; top pancakes, waffles, or French toast with them; or serve them over ice cream. Here is the basic recipe to serve 6 fortunate souls Brown Sugar Banana Sundaes. (Double the amounts if you're serving the bananas alone.)

1 Cream the butter, brown sugar, and cinnamon together in a small bowl. Peel the bananas and cut them in half crosswise. Cut each half lengthwise to make 12 pieces.

2 Melt the flavored butter in a large skillet set over low heat and warm the bananas through for about a minute, then add the lime juice and rum. Remove the skillet from the heat, spoon the bananas over scoops of ice cream, and serve right away

❖ Strawberries in Raspberry-Balsamic Glaze

Our everyday balsamic vinegar is put to quick and elegant use when it's simmered with raspberry jam and red wine to make an ever-so-slightly piquant, glossy coat for strawberries. Once the berries have been tossed in the warm glaze, they need to be eaten right then and there, but the ingredients can be readied even hours ahead so the last-minute cooking is easily done. **6 SERVINGS**

---

3 tablespoons seedless raspberry jam

1½ tablespoons balsamic vinegar

1½ tablespoons red wine

3 cups strawberries, halved or quartered if large

⅓ cup mascarpone or unsweetened whipped cream (optional)

Do-Ahead Option

❖ The syrup ingredients can go in the saucepan up to 4 hours ahead.

---

1 Whisk the jam, vinegar, and red wine together in a small, heavy saucepan set over low heat until smooth. Simmer, stirring occasionally, until the glaze is reduced by about half and has a syrupy consistency, 3 to 5 minutes.

2 Place the strawberries in a large bowl, pour the warm glaze over them, and gently fold together with a rubber spatula until they're just coated.

3 Spoon the berries into stemmed glasses or bowls, garnish with a small dollop of mascarpone or whipped cream, and serve right away.

ENCHANTED

It's probably no accident that I adore dessert. My father was the quality control manager of a large baking operation in Chicago, and that's where I got my first taste.

When I was a little girl, Dad would take me to his work at the bakery and for an hour or two I had the run of it, or at least it seemed to me then. I must have been about six the first time I went, and we started to develop something of a routine.

We'd make a stop in his office where he'd spend time with the papers on his desk while I propelled myself around the room in his swivel chair on wheels. Then, hand in hand, we'd "start the rounds."

The pulled-sugar room came first, a smallish rectangular space, which, when contrasted with the open spaces of the rest of the bakery, made it seem like the inner sanctum it no doubt was. The moment we walked in, we were surrounded by the sweet smell of sugar, and my eyes scanned the room to try and take in all the glistening objects that covered the shelves.

Nils, the pulled sugar chef, was there. Seated at his workbench, his hands lit beneath the lamp that kept the sugar malleable, formed ribbons for Easter baskets he'd made and filled with colored eggs. Or he'd be forming elves and little animals of all kinds to decorate the top of some lucky kid's birthday cake. Silken sugar flowers were everywhere: roses and tulips, daffodils and lilies. There were bows of every size in wonderful carnival-colored stripes of orange and green, purple and yellow, red and blue.

The bakery was a few steps away through double swinging doors, and when we entered the immense room, the voices and movement of the bakers and the whirring of the machinery was electric after the peace of the sugar room.

Mountains of bread dough rose in huge troughs. Carts with rows of racks filled with just-baked cookies were being rolled through the room, and massive refrigerators held cookies waiting to be baked. Bakers dropped ridged swirls of moist dough into a huge metal vat filled with hot oil. I watched the rings swell and puff, sputtering in the fat, turning golden. They were French doughnuts getting ready for their sugar glaze.

Christmas was gingerbread house time, and I was allowed to help (along with my older brother, who sometimes deigned to join us). We glued together the walls and set on the roofs, then passed the roughed-in little houses to the bakers, who drew windows and doors and snow on the roofs in white icing and made smoke come from the chimneys with cotton. And there was the fruitcake room, where what seemed like hundreds of small, dense loaves, smelling darkly of dried fruit and alcohol, sat on long tables. One by one, each was set on a square of shiny cellophane, then wrapped and sealed with the quick sizzle of a hot metal wand.

The air in the bakery was always warm and moist and sweet. The fragrance of just-baked cookies and cakes hung in the atmosphere and mixed with the subtle tang of yeast and the room's low din. It was a strange and happy symphony, which cast a spell to last a lifetime.

I never did learn to make sugar flowers, nor have I made a gingerbread house since then. But few days go by when I don't pull out the pans and tins and set to work filling my house with the aroma of baking. I hunger for the smell of breads and pies just pulled from the oven, the promise of crunchy cookies and tender muffins. I am bewitched by chocolate cake in any form. Ever in the thrall of baking, I'm just as happy to make old favorites as to come up with new.

Blueberry Crisp

I'm crazy for fruit crisps, simpler than a pie but with the same innocent perfection. I like when the fruit practically jumps out of the pan with flavor and their juices run pure and sweet. Make this dessert when the fruit is at its height of goodness and begging to be bought. This crisp is intensely blueberry and topped with classic crumbly, buttery streusel, its ideal partner. (Which, incidentally, freezes beautifully and one batch is enough for two crisps or to sprinkle over two pies.) **6 SERVINGS**

1¼ cups all-purpose flour

⅓ cup packed light or dark brown sugar

¾ teaspoon ground cinnamon

1 cup coarsely chopped pecans, walnuts, almonds, or other nuts

½ cup (1 stick) cold unsalted butter, cut into small pieces, plus 1 teaspoon softened butter

4 cups blueberries, stemmed, rinsed, and dried (see page 257)

2 teaspoons freshly squeezed lemon juice

¾ cup granulated sugar

Unsweetened whipped cream, ice cream, or mascarpone, as accompaniment

1 Preheat the oven to 425°F with the rack at the top. Pulse 1 cup of the flour, the brown sugar, and ¼ teaspoon of the cinnamon in the bowl of a food processor for several seconds, just until well combined. Add the nuts and pulse once or twice to mix. Drop in the pieces of cold butter and pulse just until chopped into small, granular pieces, about 30 seconds, being careful not to let the mixture become a dough. Refrigerate half of the streusel to use here; wrap and freeze the other half for up to 3 months.

2 Place the blueberries in a large bowl and with a rubber spatula gently toss them with the lemon juice, remaining ½ teaspoon cinnamon, and the granulated sugar. Sprinkle the mixture with the remaining ¼ cup flour and toss again to combine well.

3 Butter the bottom and sides of a 9- or 10-inch baking dish about 1 inch deep with the 1 teaspoon softened butter. Transfer the berries to the dish, and distribute the streusel evenly over the top.

❧ Make the streusel up to 3 days
ahead (and freeze half of it for
up to 3 months).

❧ Make the crisp up to 2 hours
ahead and rewarm it slightly
before serving.

4 Bake the crisp until the streusel is golden brown and the blueberry juices are bubbling, 25 to 30 minutes. Bring the crisp to the table while it's still warm and serve it on warm plates topped with whipped cream, ice cream, or mascarpone.

CHOOSING THE FRESHEST BLUEBERRIES

Fresh blueberries are plump and firm and silver-white frosted. And the fresher they are, the more frosted they look. But blueberries that are past their prime turn soft, lose their sheer silvery beauty, and look blue.

Peaches Sautéed with Butter and Cinnamon Sugar

There's not much to match the experience of biting into a peach dripping with juice; they're orbs of sunshine with an aroma from heaven. When you peel, slice, and sauté these marvels in butter, sugar, and cinnamon for mere seconds, you add a simple, saucy dimension. Eat them warm right out of the pan with a dollop of whipped cream, spoon them over ice cream or frozen yogurt, or turn them into peach shortcake with slices of cake from the Buttermilk Cake on page 234. 6 DESSERT SERVINGS OR 10 TO 12 SERVINGS AS A TOPPING

- **6 large, ripe but firm peaches**
- **¼ cup plus 2 tablespoons sugar**
- **1½ teaspoons ground cinnamon**
- **1 tablespoon freshly squeezed lemon juice if holding over peaches** (optional)
- **6 tablespoons unsalted butter**

1 Bring a medium pot of water to a boil over high heat and set a slotted spoon and large bowl next to the stovetop. Cut a shallow x through the skin opposite the stem end of each peach. Stir the sugar and cinnamon together in a small bowl and set it aside. When the water reaches a boil, drop in 1 or 2 peaches for 10 seconds. Immediately remove them with the spoon and place them in the bowl. Let the water return to a boil and repeat the process with the remaining peaches.

2 Peeling from the x with a paring knife, remove and discard the skin — it will come right off; if not, drop the peach back into the boiling water for 1 to 2 seconds (unripe peaches will not peel). Holding each peach over the bowl, cut it into ½- to ¾-inch-wide wedges, letting the wedges fall into the bowl.

3 Melt the butter in a very large skillet, so the peaches are in no more than 1½ layers (or use 2 pans, dividing the butter between them) set over high heat. Add the peaches (dividing them between the 2 skillets, if using), tossing or stirring them to warm for about 1 minute. Sprinkle with the cinnamon sugar, and stir them gently until the sugar has dissolved and formed a sauce that looks like thin butterscotch, about

Do-Ahead Options

◆ Mix the cinnamon sugar anytime.

◆ Peel the peaches and leave them whole or cut them into wedges, moisten with lemon juice, and refrigerate for up to 1½ hours. They will discolor slightly, but their taste will be fine.

1 minute. Immediately remove the skillet(s) from the heat; the peaches should still be firm and intact. (If they've broken up, tell everyone it's a chunky peach sauce.)

4 Transfer the peaches and their sauce to a warm serving bowl or bowls and serve them right away.

Poached Pears with Vanilla Bean and Lemon Zest

These pears emerge from their poaching bath as exquisite, translucent objects that look lit from within, the color of palest yellow buttercream. Tiny specks of vanilla bean seeds freckle their sides, and they are served in a shallow pool of lemon-scented syrup. When shaving off the strips of lemon peel, be sure to pick up only the bright yellow zest, leaving the bitter white pith behind. **6 SERVINGS**

¾ cup sugar

9 strips of lemon zest, about 2 x ½ inches each

One 6-inch-long piece vanilla bean, cut lengthwise in half

6 medium to large ripe but firm Bartlett or Anjou pears, preferably with stems

2 or 3 lemons cut in half for moistening pears, plus 4½ tablespoons strained lemon juice

1 Preheat the oven to 325°F with a rack in the center. Place the sugar, 3 cups of water, the lemon zest, and split vanilla bean in a large ovenproof casserole or deep skillet large enough to hold the pears comfortably lying down (or use 2 pans, dividing the ingredients). Set the pan(s) over low heat and simmer the liquid, stirring occasionally, until the sugar has dissolved and the flavorings have begun to infuse the syrup, 5 to 8 minutes.

2 Meanwhile, core the pears through their bottoms with the smaller end of a melon baller, then peel them with a vegetable peeler, moistening each with squeezes of lemon juice from the lemon halves to prevent darkening (do not rub their surface, however, because it will damage the fruit). Finally, slice a thin section from the base of each pear so it can stand upright.

3 Stir 3 tablespoons of the strained lemon juice into the syrup, add the pears, and roll them gently in the syrup with a rubber spatula (they won't be covered by the syrup). Cover the pan(s) and place in the oven.

4 Poach the pears until they're just tender but firm, about 15 minutes, turning them gently with a rubber spatula once during this period. To check for doneness, insert a wooden skewer into the cored middle and

deeply pierce the upper, solid section of the pear (without going all the way through, if you can avoid it). If the skewer meets with more than a little resistance, continue cooking a few minutes longer.

5 Transfer the lemon strips and pears, supporting them with a rubber spatula as you lift them by their stem, if there is one, to a platter (see Note). Loosely cover with plastic wrap and let the pears stand until cool, then refrigerate them.

6 With a teaspoon, scrape out the tiny black seeds from the center of the vanilla beans into the syrup; save or discard the pods (see page 277). Transfer the syrup to a small saucepan (there should be about 3 cups). Bring the syrup to a boil over medium-high heat and reduce it until lightly thickened and about 1 cup in volume, stirring occasionally, about 15 minutes, scraping down the sides of the pan from time to time to loosen any vanilla seeds. Stir in the remaining 1½ tablespoons lemon juice, or to taste. Let the syrup cool and refrigerate it until lightly chilled.

7 Stand the chilled pears in shallow soup plates or bowls, stir the syrup to reincorporate the vanilla seeds, spoon it over the pears, slip 1 lemon strip into each bowl, and serve.

NOTE: The pears retain the nicest shape if allowed to cool standing up.

Roasted Pineapple with Rum Cream

I've been making this dish since I was the chef at the restaurant One Fifth Avenue, and I showed it on my segment of the "Master Chefs of New York" PBS television series, where I presented it with thin slices of raw pineapple. Here, boat-shaped wedges of fruit get roasted in a hot oven (or grilled over coals) just long enough to lightly caramelize their outsides. Then they're served with a lightly chilled, thick and luscious rum sauce. The contrasts of warm and cool, buttery and juicy make this a dish to remember. The sauce is perfect for fresh berries, too, such as raspberries, strawberries, blueberries, or blackberries. **6 SERVINGS**

---

3 egg yolks

3 tablespoons sugar

4½ tablespoons cold unsalted butter, cut into small pieces

1½ tablespoons dark or golden rum or other liqueur

1 ripe medium pineapple

3 tablespoons heavy cream

1 Whisk the yolks and sugar together in the top of a double boiler set over simmering water. Continue to whisk slowly until warm to the touch, 1 to 3 minutes.

2 Whisk in the cold butter several pieces at a time. When it has all been incorporated, continue whisking slowly until the sauce is creamy, smooth, and thickened enough to coat the back of a wooden spoon lightly, 3 to 5 minutes. Remove the sauce from the heat, stir in the rum, and let it cool with a piece of plastic wrap pressed directly against its surface to keep a skin from forming. When cool, cover the sauce and refrigerate for up to 5 days.

3 Slice off the top and bottom of the pineapple, saving some of the prettiest leaves for garnish, if you like; discard the rest. Standing the pineapple on end, remove the skin by cutting from top to bottom in sections, then removing the remaining eyes with a swivel-bladed vegetable peeler.

4 Cut the pineapple in half, then cut lengthwise into 12 wedges, trimming them so that each is 1 to 1¼

inches thick and about 4 inches long; save any extra for another use. Trim and discard the cores.

5 Whip the cream to soft peaks, fold it into the chilled sauce base, and refrigerate it for up to 2 days. Remove from the refrigerator 20 minutes before serving.

6 Preheat the oven to 450°F with the rack at the top. Oil a cookie sheet, low-sided baking pan, or 2 cast-iron skillets (any large enough to hold the pineapple with about 2 inches of space between each piece; see Note). About 10 minutes before roasting, preheat the pan(s) in the oven.

7 Place the pineapple wedges on the cookie sheet or pan and roast until their bottoms turn golden brown, 5 to 8 minutes (check early to be safe, or if they're not browning but are still firm, leave them up to 5 minutes longer). Turn them and roast 3 to 5 minutes more, or until the second side is light brown (taking them out any time they start to get soft).

8 Spoon about 2 tablespoons of sauce on the bottom of each plate and arrange 2 wedges of pineapple, prettiest side up, on top. Decorate the plate with a pineapple leaf or 2, if you like, and serve right away.

NOTE: The pineapple will brown well, and somewhat quickly, in dark pans such as cast iron. Lightweight metal pans, on the other hand, don't always do as good a job. If your pineapple emerges nearly as yellow as when it started, simply spoon the sauce over the top and carry the plates to the table with a smile.

Raspberry Shortcakes

*Imagine juicy raspberries mashed with sugar on warm, buttered biscuits with dollops
of cool cream and a handful of whole, perfect berries spilling over all. Happily for
us, shortcakes make one of the great party desserts (who doesn't love them?) and
they're truly easy to prepare, particularly if you've got biscuits stashed in the freezer.
No raspberries? Then make these shortcakes with the Peaches Sautéed with Butter
and Cinnamon Sugar (page 258), or blackberries, blueberries, or strawberries — or
a spectacular mixture of whatever's in season.* **8 SERVINGS**

**4 containers 6 ounces each,
red or black raspberries,
at room temperature**

⅓ cup sugar

1 cup heavy cream

Buttermilk Dessert Biscuits
(recipe follows)

**8 teaspoons unsalted butter,
softened**

**½ cup sour cream or crème
fraîche**

1 Preheat the oven to 375°F. Empty 2 containers of raspberries into a bowl, sprinkle them with the sugar, mash with a fork, cover, and set aside to give off their juice for about 15 minutes.

2 Meanwhile, whip the cream to soft peaks. Cover and refrigerate briefly.

3 Split the biscuits in half, spread the softened butter over their bottoms, and place them on a cookie sheet. Set the top halves on the same sheet, but cut side down, and heat them in the oven for about 5 minutes, or until they are very warm and lightly recrisped.

4 Place the bottoms on plates, spoon an equal amount of mashed berries over each, then top each with a tablespoon of sour cream. Divide one of the remaining 2 containers of raspberries over the sour cream, then set the biscuit tops on the filling. Spoon big dollops of whipped cream on top of each serving and garnish with the berries from the last container, letting some of them spill onto the plate. Serve right away.

ABOUT DOUGH CUTTERS

A dough cutter — or, in professional parlance, a bench scraper — is a terrifically useful and inexpensive tool. It's an almost-square 5-inch sheet of stainless steel with a somewhat sharp edge and a bar-shaped handle that runs along the top, usually made of wood, plastic, or rolled steel. It's great for scraping and cleaning surfaces, supporting and moving cookies or biscuits, and chopping up doughs, to name a few of its many uses. Look for it in kitchenware shops, mail order catalogs, some hardware stores, and in any professional kitchen supply store.

Buttermilk Dessert Biscuits

3 tablespoons sugar

¼ teaspoon ground cinnamon

1½ cups sifted all-purpose flour, plus more for dusting

½ cup sifted cake flour (not self-rising)

2½ teaspoons baking powder

¼ teaspoon baking soda

½ teaspoon salt

6 tablespoons cold unsalted butter, cut into small pieces

¾ cup cold buttermilk, plus 2 to 3 teaspoons at room temperature

1 Preheat the oven to 425°F with a rack in the center. Mix 1 tablespoon of the sugar with the cinnamon in a small bowl. Thoroughly combine the all-purpose and cake flours, baking powder, baking soda, salt, and remaining 2 tablespoons sugar in a large bowl. Scatter the 6 tablespoons of cold butter over the top and cut it in with a wire pastry cutter (like one used for making pie dough) until it's well distributed and the mixture is the size of large peas. Drizzle the ¾ cup cold buttermilk over the top to moisten the dry ingredients, tossing with a fork the entire time.

2 Dust the rolling surface with flour, gather the dough into a rough ball, and turn it out of the bowl onto the floured surface, letting any remaining unmoistened particles fall on top of the dough. With floured hands, give the soft, slightly sticky dough a light knead by gently folding the top half over the bottom 6 or 7 times, giving it a quarter-turn between each fold (handling the dough minimally keeps the biscuits tender). After this short knead, the dough will be more cohesive but still soft.

3 Scrape the area clean of any dough with a dough cutter or metal spatula, and reflour the surface. With your floured hands or a rolling pin, pat or gently roll out the dough to form a 5- x 8-inch rectangle ¾ to 1 inch thick. Pierce the dough about 15 times with the floured tines of a fork. Cut the rectangle in half lengthwise with the floured dough cutter or a large, sharp knife, making clean cuts without twisting or sawing. Wipe the blade, reflour it, and cut across the middle of the rectangle to form 4 quarters, wiping and flouring

the blade between each cut. Cut each quarter in half to make 8 rectangular biscuits.

4 Using your dough cutter or spatula, carefully transfer 1 biscuit at a time to an ungreased cookie sheet, separating them by at least 1 inch. Lightly brush the tops with the remaining 2 to 3 teaspoons room-temperature buttermilk, not allowing it to drip down the sides (and keeping them from rising). Sprinkle the cinnamon sugar over the biscuits and bake until the tops are light gold, 12 to 15 minutes. Serve warm or let cool. (Well wrapped, the biscuits can be frozen for up to 3 months.)

❋ Strawberry Sauté

When I was the chef for Driscoll's Berries, this recipe was the first one I came up with, and it's still a favorite. The strawberries are tossed in a pan with butter, nuts, sugar, and chocolate. Just brief contact with heat brings out the berry flavor to the utmost without cooking them at all. The chocolate, added last, melts in a flash and surrounds the berries in an irresistible pool. It's a heavenly combination on its own and a show-stopper topping for ice cream, frozen yogurt, or cheesecake. And while it has to be cooked at the last minute, all the elements can be prepped ahead so it can be ready to serve in about 5 minutes. 4 SERVINGS AS A DESSERT OR 8 SERVINGS AS A TOPPING

---

3 tablespoons unsalted butter

¼ cup coarsely chopped walnuts

3 tablespoons dark brown sugar

2 cups strawberries, cut in half, or quartered if large

3 tablespoons finely chopped semisweet chocolate

Do-Ahead Options

◈ Chop the walnuts and chocolate and measure the sugar anytime.

◈ Prepare the strawberries up to 2 hours ahead.

1 Melt the butter in a medium skillet set over low heat. Add the walnuts and cook, stirring, until they begin to brown and smell toasty, 1 to 2 minutes. Sprinkle the brown sugar over the nuts and stir, mashing any lumps with the back of the spoon; heat for less than 30 seconds.

2 Remove the skillet from the heat, stir in the strawberries, and immediately add the chocolate. Gently but quickly, combine the mixture until the berries are coated with melted chocolate.

3 Divide the berries into stemmed glasses or bowls and serve right away.

PUDDINGS AND A MOUSSE

❋ Milk Chocolate Parfait with Strawberries

This graceful duet of sweet strawberries and milk chocolate pudding is ridiculously easy to make: Melt the chocolate in coconut milk, stir, and chill. When the parfait is all dressed up with berries, cream, macadamia nuts, and toasted coconut, no one could ever guess how quick it was. **8 SERVINGS**

---

12 ounces milk chocolate, chopped

1¼ cups canned unsweetened coconut milk (see page 119)

½ cup heavy cream

2 pints strawberries

¼ cup plus 2 tablespoons coarsely chopped salted, dry-roasted macadamia nuts or other toasted nuts

¼ cup shredded coconut, lightly toasted

Do-Ahead Options

↬ Chop the chocolate anytime.

↬ Make the pudding up to 3 days ahead and refrigerate it in its glasses (or in a bowl).

1 Place the chocolate and coconut milk in a double boiler set over hot — but not boiling — water. When the chocolate is melted, stir with a whisk until smooth and lustrous, making sure to reach any chocolate stuck in the corners.

2 Spoon the pudding into 8 stemmed glasses or a serving bowl, cover, and refrigerate until firm, about 1 hour.

3 Meanwhile, whip the cream to soft peaks and refrigerate it, rewhipping it slightly before serving, if necessary.

4 Rinse, hull, dry, and slice the strawberries and divide them among the parfaits. Top each with a dollop of whipped cream, sprinkle with nuts and coconut, and serve right away.

Dark Chocolate Crème Caramels

When these crème caramels are baked, some of their chocolate drifts out of the mix and floats to the top of the cups. And when they're turned out onto plates after chilling, the chocolate becomes a thin, firm layer on the bottom and a bittersweet foil for the silken custards. This recipe makes individual custards, but if you'd like to make one large custard, see page 272 for instructions. **8 SERVINGS**

1¾ cups sugar

4 whole eggs, at room temperature

4 egg yolks, at room temperature

3 ounces chopped bittersweet chocolate

2½ cups milk

1 teaspoon vanilla extract

1½ tablespoons Grand Marnier, Cointreau, or other orange liqueur

1 Preheat the oven to 325°F with the rack in the middle. Place in a heavy roasting pan or other ovenproof pan large enough to contain eight 4-ounce custard or coffee cups, each separated by about 1 inch, if possible. Place a folded kitchen towel on the bottom of the pan (to help moderate the heat for a smooth custard) and fill the pan with hot water by about one-third. Set the custard cups near the stovetop.

2 Make the caramel: Stir 1 cup of the sugar into 3 tablespoons hot water in a medium, preferably light-colored (to better see the sugar change color) skillet or small saucepan set over medium heat. Cook, stirring frequently, until the sugar dissolves and the water starts to boil around the edges, 2 to 3 minutes. Tightly cover the pan and boil the syrup undisturbed for 2 minutes — the steam will wash down any sugar crystals clinging to the sides. (Or you can wash down the sides with a brush dipped in water instead of covering the pan, if you'd rather.)

3 Remove the cover and continue to boil without stirring until the sugar begins to turn light gold, about 2 minutes, swirling the pan by the handle to equalize the color. Continue cooking and swirling, without stirring, until the syrup is a deep gold. Immediately remove the pan from the heat, and pour

the caramel into the bottom of the cups, dividing it as equally as possible (do *not* touch the caramel; it burns badly). Swirl the cups to coat as much of the sides with caramel as is easily done and let them cool (see Note).

4 Whisk the whole eggs and egg yolks together in a large bowl with the remaining ¾ cup sugar to combine well without aerating it; set aside.

5 Place the chocolate in a medium ovenproof bowl or saucepan and set it in the water bath to melt (or melt it in a water bath on top of the stove). Place the milk in a medium saucepan set over low heat until it's warm to the touch, then remove it from the heat (if the milk is hot, let it cool to warm before using it). Once the chocolate is melted, very gradually whisk or stir in ½ cup of the milk to make a smooth mixture. Gradually whisk in the remaining milk. Whisk the chocolate milk into the egg-sugar mixture without aerating it, then whisk in the vanilla and liqueur. Skim off any froth on the surface.

6 Fill the caramel-lined cups with custard by about three-fourths and set them in the water bath. The water should reach halfway up the sides of the cups; if it doesn't, add more very hot water. Bake the custards until a knife inserted in the center of one comes out clean, 25 to 35 minutes.

7 Remove the cups by grabbing the top of each with a towel-wrapped hand and slipping a metal spatula underneath. Cool them on a rack, then cover and refrigerate them.

8 To serve, run a paring knife around the inside of each cup about ½ inch deep. Place a plate over the top, flip the cup and plate together, and together, give them several vigorous shakes back and forth.

continued

Slowly lift the cup, and the custard will drop onto the plate. Unmold the remaining crème caramels in the same fashion. Serve them chilled.

NOTE: The caramel that's stuck in the pan, and in the cups once the custard has been unmolded, can be cleaned by filling the pan and cups with hot or boiling water and letting them soak. It can take a few hours, but it will dissolve eventually.

ONE LARGE DARK CHOCOLATE CRÈME CARAMEL

For a dessert party or a buffet, serving one big custard in its pool of caramel is a good choice instead of a slew of small ones. It cuts down on preparation and helps limit the number of items that have to go on the table.

For one large custard, you need a 5- to 6-cup baking dish that's 2½ to 3 inches deep. Line the dish with caramel as you do for the individual ones, pour in the custard, and bake it for 1 to 1¼ hours, depending on the dish. Check if it's done with a knife inserted in the center, just as you do for the small ones.

Lemon Cloud Pudding with Blueberries

This pudding, which manages to be both homey and sophisticated at the same time, is full of lemon flavor, soft and creamy-rich, whether you serve it as soon as it's made or give it an overnight stay in the refrigerator. Raspberries or blackberries make a tart-sweet replacement for the blueberries (studding the top with them before serving) or simply spoon on some lightly sugared strawberries. **6 TO 8 SERVINGS**

2¼ cups milk

1 cup sugar

3 tablespoons cornstarch

1 tablespoon grated lemon zest

6 extra-large egg yolks

¾ cup heavy cream

2¼ cups blueberries, picked through, rinsed, and dried well (see page 257)

Do-Ahead Options

❧ Make the pudding with blueberries up to a day ahead.

❧ Make the pudding without berries up to 2 days ahead. Garnish it with berries right before serving.

1 Heat the milk in a small heavy saucepan set over low heat until tiny bubbles form around the edges, 2 to 3 minutes. Remove the pan from the heat .

2 Mix the sugar, cornstarch, and lemon zest in a medium to large, heavy nonreactive saucepan. Stir in the egg yolks until very well mixed. Strain the milk if a skin has formed and gradually stir the milk into the sugar mixture.

3 Set the saucepan over medium-low heat and cook, stirring slowly with a whisk, until the mixture begins to thicken. Whisk more vigorously to keep it smooth and continue whisking until it bubbles and becomes very thick, 4 to 5 minutes. Remove the pan from the heat and continue to whisk until the pudding is very smooth, about 30 seconds.

4 Transfer the pudding to a bowl and press a piece of plastic wrap directly against the surface to prevent a skin from forming. Set it in a larger bowl of water with ice to cool completely.

5 Meanwhile, whip the cream to soft but distinct peaks and refrigerate it until cool. Fold in the cream (rewhipping it slightly first, if it needs it), followed by the blueberries. Spoon the pudding into stemmed glasses or a serving bowl and serve right away.

Chocolate Mousse

It might be safe to call chocolate mousse old-fashioned, and by that I mean no disrespect — just that it hasn't been in fashion's eye for quite a while. Old-fashioned or not, it's an irresistible dessert with elegance and panache. And it's all done ahead!

8 SERVINGS

---

8 ounces semisweet chocolate, chopped

½ cup (1 stick) unsalted butter, softened

2 teaspoons vanilla extract

4 extra-large eggs, separated, at room temperature

Pinch of salt

½ cup superfine sugar (see page 275)

½ cup heavy cream, whipped

3 tablespoons bittersweet chocolate shavings made with a vegetable peeler, cocoa nibs (available by mail order), or 8 pieces dark chocolate–covered orange peel, for garnish

1 Melt the chocolate in the top of a double boiler set over hot, but not boiling, water. Check to see if the chocolate is melted by pressing on it with a rubber spatula without stirring — it will collapse under the pressure.

2 When it has melted, remove from the heat and stir until smooth. Stir half of the butter. The chocolate may stiffen at first, but when the rest is added it will smooth out. Add the remaining butter in 3 batches, stirring each time until smooth. Stir in the vanilla, followed by the yolks, adding them one at a time. Set the mixture aside but don't let it get cold.

3 Whip the egg whites and salt in the bowl of an electric mixer on medium speed until they form soft peaks, 1 to 2 minutes. Increase the speed to high and gradually add the sugar in a steady stream, scraping down the sides of the bowl once when all the sugar has been added. Continue whipping until very stiff, 2 to 3 minutes.

4 Stir half of the chocolate into the beaten egg whites to combine. Push the mixture to one side of the bowl, then pour the remaining chocolate into the empty side. With a rubber spatula, set the already mixed chocolate whites on top of the chocolate and fold them together until no white streaks remain. (Or pour the second half of the chocolate into a large bowl, top with the chocolate whites, and fold together.)

◈ Chop the chocolate anytime.

◈ Prepare the mousse up to a day ahead and take it out of the refrigerator 30 to 45 minutes before serving.

5 Spoon the mousse into stemmed glasses or a large serving bowl, cover, and refrigerate until well chilled and set, 3 to 4 hours, or up to 24 hours.

6 Remove the mousse from the refrigerator 30 to 45 minutes before serving. Garnish with dollops of whipped cream and sprinkle with chocolate shavings or cocoa nibs, or insert a piece of orange peel part way into the cream on a slight angle.

HOW TO MAKE SUPERFINE SUGAR

No superfine sugar in the house? No problem. Whir granulated sugar in a food processor until it's very fine, then measure the amount called for in the recipe and store any leftover in the pantry.

Raspberries with Vanilla Bean Custard

The custard here provides a little bed of airy pudding for raspberries to rest on, and the combination of tart-sweet berries and seductive vanilla is a heavenly match — even more so when served in pretty stemmed glasses. Quick to make, this dessert just requires some chilling time before folding in stiffly beaten egg whites to finish. **8 SERVINGS**

---

2 cups milk

1 vanilla bean, split length-wise, or 4 teaspoons vanilla extract

4 eggs, separated, at room temperature

½ cup sugar

3 tablespoons cornstarch

4 packages (6 ounces each) **fresh red or golden raspberries**

3 tablespoons coarsely chopped pistachios

1 Heat 1½ cups of the milk with the vanilla bean in a large, heavy saucepan set over low heat until tiny bubbles form around the edge. (If using vanilla extract, add it now.) Turn off the heat, cover the pan, and set it aside for the vanilla to flavor the milk.

2 Meanwhile, whisk the egg yolks, ¼ cup of the sugar, and the cornstarch together in a medium bowl. Gradually add the remaining ½ cup milk, continuing to whisk slowly until the mixture is smooth. Set aside.

3 Remove the vanilla bean from the hot milk, scrape out the seeds from the center of the bean with a teaspoon, and add them to the milk. Reserve the bean for vanilla sugar if you like (see page 277).

4 Increase the heat to medium under the milk and gradually whisk in the egg yolk mixture. Cook, whisking vigorously until very thick and shiny, 1 to 3 minutes. Transfer the custard base to a bowl, scraping out the pan with a rubber spatula, and press a piece of plastic wrap directly against its surface to keep a skin from forming. Set the bowl in a larger bowl of ice water to cool completely.

5 When it's cool, whip the egg whites in an electric mixer on medium speed until soft peaks form.

Do-Ahead Options

- Measure the dry ingredients anytime.
- Make the puddings up to 6 hours ahead and garnish them with berries right before serving.

Increase the speed to high, gradually add the remaining ¼ cup sugar, and beat until stiff and glossy, 2 to 3 minutes, scraping down the sides of the bowl once after all the sugar has been added.

6 Stir one-fourth of the beaten whites into the cool custard base to lighten it, then fold in the rest. Spoon the pudding into stemmed glasses or bowls to serve now, or cover and refrigerate for up to 6 hours. Divide the raspberries over the custards, sprinkle with pistachios, and serve right away.

HOW TO MAKE VANILLA SUGAR

Vanilla beans are the seed pods of a climbing orchid, which grows in Madagascar, Indonesia, Mexico, and Tahiti. The beans start out on the vine as green pods, and only after curing do they become the fragrant flavoring we all love. Once you've used the seeds, you can make vanilla sugar from the leftover pod. Vanilla sugar is perfect for sprinkling on top of muffins or pies before baking, to replace regular sugar in cakes and tarts, to sprinkle over fresh berries, and to eat with hot or cold cereal. These are only a few of the possibilities, and it's truly easy to make. Here's how.

Rinse the used, split vanilla pods and let them dry completely on a paper towel. Place them in a jar, cover them with granulated sugar (roughly 1 cup sugar to 2 halves of a vanilla bean), cover the jar tightly, and let it sit for at least 2 weeks, until the vanilla permeates the sugar (taste it to check). I replenish the jar with another vanilla bean whenever I've got one and add more sugar whenever the level starts to get low.

ICE CREAM SUNDAES AND CHOCOLATE TRUFFLES

✻ Rachel's Ice Cream Sundaes with Caramel Sauce and Toasted Hazelnuts

This sundae tastes great even without chocolate truffles. And if that's the way you choose to go, double the caramel sauce for the right amount of lusciousness.

8 SERVINGS OR 1 CUP OF SAUCE

⅔ cup granulated sugar

⅔ cup heavy cream, at room temperature, plus 1 cup chilled

⅔ cup hazelnuts

24 Chocolate Truffles (page 281)

Ice cream or frozen yogurt

1 To make the caramel, stir the sugar into ⅓ cup of water in a small to medium, preferably light-colored (to better see the sugar change color) skillet or saucepan, and cook over medium heat, stirring, until the sugar dissolves and the water starts to boil around the edges, 2 to 3 minutes. Tightly cover the pan and boil the syrup undisturbed for 2 minutes so the steam washes down any sugar crystals clinging to the sides (or wash down the sides with a brush dipped in water).

2 Remove the cover and continue boiling without stirring until it begins to turn light gold, 1 to 2 minutes, swirling the pan by the handle to equalize the color. Continue cooking and swirling until the syrup is deep gold (see Note at right), 5 to 8 minutes. Immediately remove the pan from the heat and carefully pour in the ⅔ cup room temperature cream; stand back — the caramel will boil up and may spit. Stir with a wooden spoon until all the caramel (which will have formed a candylike mass) is completely dis-

solved, 1 to 2 minutes. If there are still a few lumps, set the pan back over very low heat until all the caramel is incorporated, stirring the whole time. Transfer the sauce (it will be somewhat thin) to a bowl, cover it with plastic wrap and poke holes in the top to let the steam escape, and set it aside to cool or refrigerate it for up to 2 weeks.

3 Preheat the oven to 350°F with a rack in the center to toast the nuts, or use a toaster oven. Toast the hazelnuts until light gold, 8 to 10 minutes (their insides will be darker than their outsides), wrap them in a towel while still warm, and roll them on the counter or between your hands to remove as much of their skins as possible and let them cool; if you have blanched nuts, only the toasting is necessary. When cool, press on them firmly with the side of a large knife or chop them to break nuts into coarse pieces.

4 Whip the remaining 1 cup chilled cream to soft peaks. Cover and refrigerate until ready to serve. Rewhip slightly before serving, if necessary.

5 Take the truffles out of the refrigerator just before you begin to assemble the sundaes; if they're frozen, take them out about 5 minutes earlier. Scoop the ice cream into chilled, stemmed glasses or bowls, coat each with about 2 tablespoons of the caramel sauce. Top with whipped cream, garnish with 3 truffles each, scatter the hazelnuts over the top, and serve right away.

NOTE: The deeper the gold, the more intense the caramel flavor — to a point: when it's brown, it's burned.

❋ Rachel's Chocolate Truffle Ice Cream Sundaes with Raspberry Sauce

My daughter Rachel told me she wanted chocolate truffles for her wedding weekend as treats for the family, and she had searched high and low in her West Coast city for this dreamy confection. What she found, apparently, were not quite the dream she had in mind: "Each piece weighed in at about a ton," she said, "and was the size of a small Spaldeen," explaining her dilemma over the phone.

Needless to say, Rachel got her truffles. And thinking I'd use them as a garnish for a sundae for the book, I asked what kind of sauce she'd like: "Berry," she said, "and how about caramel with hazelnuts for good measure?" **6 SERVINGS**

---

3 containers of fresh raspberries (6 ounces each)**, or about 3 cups frozen and defrosted whole raspberries**

¼ cup plus 2 tablespoons superfine sugar (see page 275)

1 to 2 tablespoons Grand Marnier (optional)

¾ cup heavy cream

18 Chocolate Truffles (recipe follows)

Ice cream or frozen yogurt

Frosted almonds (recipe follows; optional)

Do-Ahead Option

⬦ Make the raspberry sauce up to 5 days ahead or freeze it for up to 1 month.

1 Puree the raspberries in a food processor until just liquefied, about 1 minute (or pass them through the fine disk of a food mill). Transfer the puree to a strainer set over a bowl and press the pulp through the strainer with a rubber spatula, adding the puree that accumulates on the underside of the strainer. Discard the seeds. Stir ¼ cup of the sugar into the sauce and add the Grand Marnier, if using it. Taste and add up to 2 more tablespoons sugar to suit your level of sweetness. Cover and refrigerate.

2 Whip the cream to soft peaks. Cover and refrigerate it, rewhipping it slightly before serving, if necessary.

3 Remove the truffles from the refrigerator just before you begin to assemble the sundaes; if they're frozen, take them out about 5 minutes earlier. Scoop the ice cream into chilled, stemmed glasses or bowls and generously cover with the sauce. Top with whipped cream, garnish with three truffles each, scatter on the nuts, if using them, and serve right away.

CHOCOLATE TRUFFLES

MAKES 2 DOZEN ¾-INCH PIECES

1/4 cup heavy cream

1 tablespoon superfine sugar
(see page 275)

3 ounces semisweet
chocolate, finely chopped,
or 1/2 cup semisweet
chocolate chips

1 extra-large egg yolk

2 tablespoons unsalted
butter, cut into small
pieces and softened

1 1/2 teaspoons Grand
Marnier, dark rum,
Cognac, or other liqueur

3 tablespoons unsweetened
cocoa powder

Do-Ahead Options

❧ Refrigerate the truffle mix up
to 2 weeks ahead.

❧ Refrigerate the finished truffles
up to 3 days ahead or freeze
them for up to 2 months.

1 Put the cream and sugar in a small, heavy saucepan and set over low heat. Cook, stirring frequently, 1 to 2 minutes, to dissolve the sugar.

2 Place the chocolate in a medium bowl. Bring the cream to a boil, pour it over the chocolate all at once, and stir until it's smooth, thick, and glossy. Stir in the egg yolk, followed by the butter, adding 2 or 3 pieces at a time until it's smoothly blended. Stir in the liqueur. Transfer the mixture to a bowl and cover and refrigerate it for 2 to 3 hours, or until firm.

3 To form the truffles, place the cocoa on a plate. Have ready 2 more large plates. Have ready a glass of hot water and a melon baller or teaspoon for scooping. Scoop out rough balls of chocolate about ¾ inch in diameter with the baller or teaspoon (dipping it into the water first and shaking off all the water before scooping each piece) and tap them out onto one of the waiting plates (or coax them out with a finger) Refrigerate the mixture if it gets too soft to handle at any point.

4 Doing 1 or 2 truffles at a time (see Note), roll them in the cocoa by sliding the plate back and forth, touching them as little as possible and adding additional cocoa, if necessary. Transfer them to the second plate as they're finished. Cover and refrigerate them until chilled before serving.

NOTE: I find that given their softness, the process of rolling the truffles in cocoa gives them a final shaping. However, if they seem particularly misshapen (remembering that true truffles are naturally irregular), gently compress each one between your thumb and index finger to form a more controlled, but interesting truffle shape.

Frosted Almonds

Sprinkle these crisp, shiny nuts over ice cream or frozen yogurt or press them around the sides of an iced cake. 6 SERVINGS

¼ **cup plus 2 tablespoons sliced almonds**

1½ **teaspoons sugar**

Do-Ahead Option

↪ Make the almonds up to 1 week ahead and store them on a plate at room temperature.

1 Preheat the oven to 350°F with a rack in the center. Place the almonds in a small bowl, sprinkle with water (a plant mister works well), and toss them to be sure each is moistened. Sprinkle the sugar over the nuts and toss again to coat them as evenly as possible.

2 Place the almonds in a shallow baking pan in a single layer and toast in the oven until they're golden and shiny, stirring once or twice, 12 to 15 minutes. Let them cool before serving.

❖ Hot Fudge Sundaes

For some of us, it's hard to think of anything more satisfying than biting into cold, dense ice cream under a blanket of warm, chewy fudge and billows of whipped cream. I like to keep a container of fudge in the refrigerator so that it's ready for last-minute company (and for me, whenever the urge strikes). If you're expecting a horde, the recipe can be doubled, tripled, or even quadrupled. MAKES ABOUT 1⅓ CUPS HOT FUDGE SAUCE, 8 TO 10 SERVINGS

4½ tablespoons unsalted butter, cut into pieces

4½ ounces bittersweet chocolate, chopped

⅔ cup sugar

¼ cup light corn syrup

Pinch of salt

1 teaspoon vanilla extract

Vanilla or other ice cream

Unsweetened whipped cream and Frosted Almonds (see page 282), or other coarsely chopped toasted nuts, strawberries, raspberries, and/or sliced bananas, as garnishes

1 Combine the butter, chocolate, sugar, corn syrup, salt, and ¼ cup of hot water in a small, heavy saucepan set over very low heat (with a heat diffuser, if possible). In about 3 minutes, when the butter and chocolate have almost melted, slowly whisk the mixture until it's well blended. Let it cook (even at the lowest heat it will cook at a low boil), whisking occasionally, until it becomes a smooth, thick, and glossy sauce, 8 to 10 minutes. Stir in the vanilla and remove the fudge sauce from the heat.

2 Scoop the ice cream into bowls and cover each serving with hot fudge sauce; refrigerate any extra. Top with whipped cream, garnish with nuts and fruit, if using them, and serve right away.

Do-Ahead Options

❧ Make the frosted almonds up to a week ahead or toast the nuts up to 2 days ahead.

❧ Refrigerate the sauce for up to a month and reheat it over gently simmering water.

APPENDICES

SOME IDEAS FOR
EASY HORS D'OEUVRES

I'm an hors d'oeuvre minimalist. Sometimes I'm so minimal I've been known to serve only drinks, then go right to dinner. But serving a few nibbles promotes relaxation and fun, and gives you more time in the kitchen if you need it. One or two easy-to-put-together bites or tempting morsels that you purchase are all you need — just enough to whet the appetite and not ruin dinner. Something as simple as a bowl of freshly toasted golden hazelnuts and a lovely, old glass plate holding glistening purple and green olives speared with tiny forks are beautiful in an understated way. Joseph, my haircutter with drop-dead taste, thinks a Campari cocktail with two huge green olives covers all the bases.

Daniel, my detail-fixated friend who, when quoting Oscar Hammerstein in an inspired songwriting moment, declares "There is nothing like an endive." Quite true. Each leaf is a crisp canoe waiting to be bedecked with a sliver of smoked trout, tiny scoop of guacamole, dab of tapenade, dainty roll of prosciutto, spoonful of golden onions in sour cream — need I go on?

I like to rummage through my plates and platters and find the dish that suits the food and signals what sort of dinner is coming, whether rustic or elegant, down home or more European. And, of course, I set everything up ahead of time so people can help themselves wherever we happen to be, whether it's in the living room in front of the fire, hanging out in the kitchen, or lounging on the patio.

I generally go with finger food or spreads and dips, or little bits on picks, the operating principle being that it has to be comfortable for guests to handle and able to be downed in one or two bites. Occasionally I serve something more elaborate, like stuffed mushrooms with chorizo or with a good melting cheese like Italian Fontina or French Gruyère, but even then, a small appetizer plate and a fork aren't too much to deal with. After all, we're talking about small gatherings and we're usually sitting down.

Vegetables

- Fresh raw peas in the pod to snap open, cooked edamame in the pod (or any already shelled), and grape tomatoes make pop-in-your-mouth nibbles that require no work at all
- Roasted Sweet Peppers with Olive Vinaigrette (page 62), cut into strips
- Roasted Mushrooms with Lemon Oil (page 56; tossed in some of the oil) served warm or at room temperature

Nuts and Nibbles

- Toasted hazlenuts and pumpkin seeds in a Venetian glass bowl, if there happens to be one around. (Why? Because once I had perfect hazelnuts while overlooking the Grand Canal. So, get the bowl and a Grand Canal, if you can.)
- Whole blanched almonds, deep-fried until golden, then salted (they're a wonderful classic Spanish tapa)
- Shelled pistachios in a vibrant earthenware bowl
- Wild rice toasted raw in vegetable oil like popcorn over medium heat. (It will become very crisp and light, but won't fluff open. Careful, though — it can burn quickly.)
- Stuffed grape leaves, made or purchased
- Pappadums (Indian lentil wafers) toasted over a burner, crisped in a moderate oven or toaster oven, or deep-fried for a few seconds. Serve them as a cracker.

Olives, from Tiny to Huge and Green to Black

◆ A rustic bowl or jar of them just as they come from the barrel or jar

◆ Marinated in olive oil with sprigs of fresh thyme, rosemary, and crushed garlic

◆ Marinated in olive oil with cumin, oregano, and strips of fresh orange peel

Dips and Spreads for Raw Vegetables, Croutons, Crackers, and Bread-Type Things

◆ A sort of Persian yogurt: plain yogurt drained in cheesecloth in the refrigerator overnight, then mixed with chopped ginger, scallion, cumin seed, and diced cucumber and sprinkled with pistachios. Serve with warm onion naan or pita triangles

◆ Goat cheese log marinated in olive oil, chopped fresh herbs, ground coriander seed, and freshly ground pepper

◆ Toasted walnut bread spread with a soft mild goat cheese, topped with a slice or two of fresh fig, a few drops of balsamic vinegar, and fresh thyme leaves

◆ Feta Cheese with Tahini and Walnuts (page 60)

◆ Roasted red pepper and olive dip from Artichokes with Roasted Red Pepper and Olive Dip (page 50), served with cooked artichoke bottoms, marinated artichoke hearts cut into chunks, or shrimp; stirred into roasted, chopped eggplant and seasoned with mint, garlic, and Spanish smoked paprika, if you have it

◆ St. André or other triple-crème cheese softened and mixed with Kalamata olives, capers, and herbs and served with slices of French bread or focaccia cut into finger-size pieces. Or use purchased fromage blanc or puree one part plain yogurt with three parts fresh ricotta in the food processor

◆ Feta Cheese and Roasted Red Pepper Pesto Spread (page 107)

◆ Ricotta pureed very smooth in the food processor, with pieces of smoked salmon added to taste, plus fresh dill and grated lemon rind, seasoned with salt and pepper; serve it sprinkled with salmon roe or tiny capers

Meats

- A selection of thinly sliced Spanish serrano ham, prosciutto, or Westphalian ham (loosely folded to pick up), and sliced Spanish chorizo, good salami, or French-style sausage

- Fresh fig quarters or papaya slices wrapped in Serrano ham, prosciutto, or another good ham

- Mini-antipasto with marinated, preserved (or roasted; see page 56) mushrooms, chunks of pricey Italian or Spanish canned tuna or dry-cured or smoked tuna, and one kind of salami or cured meat, such as coppacola or bresaola (air-cured beef)

- Home-roasted or purchased sliced roast beef (or filet), spread with blue cheese softened with a little milk or cream and a few drops of brandy, then rolled; a strip or two of roasted pepper could go inside, too (with or without the cheese)

- Steamed or sautéed Asian pork dumplings (purchased), with soy sauce for dipping

- Italian-style sandwiches (*panini*) filled with a thin slice of prosciutto, ham, salami, or pâté and a thin slice of Asiago, Fontina, or other cheese, then press-grilled in your waffle iron (without brushing them with oil) and cut into small triangles

- Grilled Rib-Eye Kebabs, Satay Style (page 148), in smaller pieces

- Soy and Spice Marinated Grilled Lamb (page 134), in smaller pieces

- Veal meatballs (made smaller) from Veal Meatballs with Fresh Dill (page 142)

Seafoods

- Small slices of smoked salmon spread with a little crème fraîche or sour cream, sprinkled with dill or fresh tarragon and fresh pepper, and rolled around thinly sliced cucumber; or spread with a bit of wasabi paste and rolled around a sliver of pickled ginger

- Small slices of gravlax drizzled with prepared honey mustard and rolled around a peeled slice of crisp apple

- Stone crab claws served with the roasted red pepper pesto from Grilled Tuna with Roasted Red Pepper Pesto (page 106)

- Grilled Littleneck clams with lime wedges

- Shrimp

  Roasted in Olive Oil with Rosemary and Lemon (page 68)

  Grilled, then sprinkled with coarse salt and fresh pepper and Spanish smoked paprika (*pimentón*)

  Boiled or grilled and served with the mint-ginger sauce from Stir-Fried Shrimp with Mint-Ginger Sauce and Mango (page 108)

  Steamed or sautéed Asian dumplings (purchased) with soy sauce for dipping a *banderilla* (see below)

Skewered Tidbits

A typical Spanish tapa called *banderilla* has a piece or two of meat, fish, and/or vegetable on a pick. Use a long wooden skewer — it's more fun and dramatic.

- Cube of Spanish Manchego cheese, slice of chorizo, and an olive

- Smoked chicken cut into cubes, speared, and served with Roasted Red Pepper and Olive Dip (page 50) or Feta Cheese and Roasted Red Pepper Pesto Spread (page 107) as a dip

- Fresh sausages and wursts broiled, grilled, or sautéed, cut on the diagonal, and speared with a piece of sun-dried tomato, olive, or roasted pepper

- Grilled or sautéed small shrimp or sea scallops, cut in halves or quarters and served with hoisin sauce or the Roasted Red Pepper and Olive Dip (page 50)

- A tiny ball of fresh mozzarella sandwiched between one small red and one small yellow cherry tomato drizzled with basil in olive oil (or plain olive oil and a leaf of basil next to the cheese)

❋Ingredients and Techniques for Foolproof Baking

Ingredients

Butter

I like unsalted butter best. To my taste, its flavor is purer at the start than the salted, and when well wrapped and stored in the refrigerator or freezer, it is less likely to pick up off-tastes. In dessert recipes, unsalted butter is the only one to use. Though small in actual measurement, salt plays an important role in bringing out both the sweetness and the flavor of the dessert, but I like to be in charge of how much goes in, without guessing how much the butter is adding.

Eggs

All the recipes that call for eggs mean large eggs unless they specifically say "extra-large." However, here's a handy conversion table so you can use whatever size egg you happen to have in the house (the measurement is after the eggs have been lightly beaten):

   1 large egg = 3¼ tablespoons

   2 large eggs = ¼ cup + 2½ tablespoons

   3 large eggs = ½ cup + 1¾ tablespoons

   4 large eggs = ¾ cup + 1 tablespoon

   5 large eggs = 1 cup + 1 scant teaspoon

Most of the recipes call for eggs at room temperature, but if you're making a recipe at the last minute or you forgot to take them out, slip the eggs into a bowl of very warm, but not hot, water while you measure the other ingredients.

Milk

Milk in a recipe means whole milk. Reduced fat (2%) or low-fat (1%) milk can be used, though it will give a less tender and rich result.

Heavy Cream

The most luscious (and easily whipped) cream comes from cream that hasn't been ultra-pasteurized, which is a cooking process done at extremely high temperature in order to kill pathogens and extend shelf life. While that's good for stability, it isn't good for flavor. It can be difficult to find a brand that hasn't been subjected to this process, but it's worth looking for.

The most efficient way to whip cream is in a chilled stainless-steel bowl using a chilled whisk or beaters. As soon as you start a recipe, toss the bowl and whisk into the refrigerator or freezer, so they're cold when you're ready to make it. Whip the cream until it's softly mounded and voluptuous, never stiff and firm (which is the step before becoming butter). I don't add sugar because for me, unsweetened whipped cream shows off desserts best, and I love its pure taste.

Bittersweet and Bitter Chocolate

Chocolate just got more exciting, if that is possible. And more complicated. Store shelves these days are tempting us with a multitude of dark bittersweet chocolates with a dizzying range of higher cocoa butter percentages, which make the chocolate firmer and give it more melt-in-the-mouth quality.

Like wine, chocolate reflects the soil and environment where the cocoa beans were grown, their variety, and their curing, roasting, and blending style. Each manufacturer blends beans to create tantalizing flavor nuances, such as fruitiness or nuttiness, or a floral quality. (Some manufacturers produce more than one style of bittersweet, and they give each a name.) In addition, there are single-estate and single-variety chocolates such as Criollo, which is considered the ultimate bean. Sweetness levels can vary, too, depending on the amount of sugar that has been added, as well as the vanilla.

Callebaut, Scharffen Berger, Lindt, El Rey, Valrhona, Guittard, and Ghirardelli are some high-quality brands that are available in stores and by mail order. Looks like you'll just have to conduct your own chocolate tastings to find your favorites (not too sad, that).

And if it isn't already clear, they all make great munching, straight from the bar.

What doesn't make great munching, however, is *bitter* chocolate, which is chocolate in a pure state — a mixture of cocoa butter and cocoa solids with no sugar. Years ago at a well-known specialty food store, I was rifling their shelves for bittersweet chocolate and couldn't find any. I was erroneously informed that bitter and bittersweet were the same. Obviously that person had never tried a taste of the bitter, because tasting it is remembering it forever.

And finally, if you're a chocolate dessert lover, why not chop a whole lot to keep around for convenience. It's good for months.

Techniques
How to Measure Dry Ingredients

Professional bakers weigh their ingredients for accuracy, but when you're not weighing, follow these pointers for dependable results. Use a wire whisk to easily and thoroughly combine a mixture of dry ingredients in a bowl.

Flour

When the Recipe Does Not Call for Sifting: If your flour is sitting in its original bag, pour it into another container for storage (it will have compacted from sitting). This simple process alone will aerate the flour. Had you measured it directly from the bag, each cup could weigh up to ½ ounce more, and that could make a big difference in the result.

Use the spoon-and-sweep method for measuring flour, cocoa, and sugar. Use metal nesting-type measuring cups (glass and plastic cup measures are for moist or liquid ingredients). Set the cup on a sheet of waxed paper and spoon the ingredient into it to overflowing. Then, without shaking the cup or otherwise settling the ingredient, sweep across the top with a straight-edged tool that's wider than the cup — such as an icing-type spatula, chopstick, or the blunt edge of a knife — to level it. The paper is convenient because you can then use it to pour the excess flour back into its container.

When a Recipe Calls for Sifting: 1 cup of *sifted flour* is more than 2 tablespoons less flour than 1 cup of *flour, sifted*. The two measurements aren't interchangeable, and using one for the other will more times than not give you a disappointing result. Here's how each is done:

Sifted flour is sifted and measured at the same time. For example, flour is sifted directly into a 1-cup nesting-type measuring cup set on a sheet of waxed paper until it's over-flowing. Then, without shaking the cup in any way, use a straight-edged tool to sweep across the top of the cup to level it; pour the excess flour on the paper back into its container.

1 cup flour, sifted, is flour measured into a cup first by the spoon-and-sweep method. Then the flour is sifted onto a piece of paper or into a bowl.

Salt

Salt is no longer just salt (as if life weren't complicated enough). A teaspoon of one type can be much saltier than a teaspoon of another, not to mention the differences in crystal size and taste because of mineral content. But where this matters most is in baking, where specific amounts of salt are called for.

I prefer kosher salt, and it's the one that I've used for all the recipes in this book. So if you use common salt — or fine sea salt, which is also generally saltier — I suggest you use a little less than what I've called for in the baking recipes.

Common supermarket salt is fine grained, almost harshly salty, and contains iodine and additives. Kosher salt, on the other hand, is medium-coarse with a less salty, more gentle, taste and it's unadulterated. An equal amount of common salt (and some sea salts) gives a saltier result than the same of kosher salt because of its tiny grains and intensity.

Baking Powder

I use an aluminum-free baking powder because aluminum imparts a somewhat harsh, metallic flavor to baked goods. It's easy to determine if a brand has aluminum in the mix by just reading the label. I buy the Rumford brand at a local health-food store and others are available by mail order.

❋ Mail Order Sources

Here are some respected sources for foodstuffs that may not always be available in your local markets. A few offer exceptional products that are theirs alone.

Baking Products

CAKE FLOUR

NONALUMINUM BAKING POWDER

SALT

VANILLA EXTRACT AND BEANS

- The Baker's Catalog
  P.O. Box 876, Norwich, VT 05055-0876
  800-827-6836
  www.kingarthurflour.com

- Walnut Acres Organic Farms (for baking powder)
  Penns Creek, PA 17862-0800
  800-433-3998
  www.walnutacres.com

Chiles

ANCHO CHILES

CHIPOTLES EN ADOBO (a canned product)

- Kitchen/Market
  218 Eighth Avenue, New York, NY 10011
  212-243-4433

- Adriana's Caravan
  409 Vanderbilt Street, Brooklyn, NY 11218
  800-316-0820
  www.adrianascaravan.com

- a cook's wares
  211 37th Street, Beaver Falls, PA 15010-2103
  800-915-9788
  www.cookswares.com

Chinese/Japanese Products

CHINESE HOISIN SAUCE

DRIED BLACK FOREST MUSHROOMS

JAPANESE MIRIN

JAPANESE PANKO BREAD CRUMBS

ASIAN SESAME OIL

- Adriana's Caravan (see CHILES)

- The CMC Company
  PO Box 322, Avalon, NJ 08202
  800-262-2780
  www.thecmccompany.com

Chocolate

- Corti Brothers
  5810 Folsom Boulevard,
  Sacramento, CA 95819
  800-509-FOOD

- La Cuisine
  323 Cameron Street, Alexandria,
  VA 22314-3219
  800-521-1176
  www.lacuisineus.com

- Williams-Sonoma Food
  P.O. Box 7456, San Francisco, CA
  94120-7456
  800-541-1262
  www.williams-sonoma.com

- Sweet Celebrations Inc. (and for
  mocha coffee beans and cocoa nibs)
  P.O. Box 39426, Edina, MN 55439-
  0426
  800-328-6722
  www.sweetc.com

- Kitchen/Market (see CHILES)

Grains, Rice, and Beans

COARSE BULGUR WHEAT

- Adriana's Caravan (SEE CHILES)

ISRAELI COUSCOUS

- Indian Harvest Specialtifoods, Inc.
  P.O. Box 428, Bemidji, MN 56619-
  0428
  800-294-2433
  www.indianharvest.com

- Dean and DeLuca Catalog Center
  2526 East 36th North Circle,
  Wichita, KS 67219
  800-221-7714
  www.dean-deluca.com

FRENCH LENTILS

- Indian Harvest
  (see ISRAELI COUSCOUS)

- Dean and DeLuca
  (see ISRAELI COUSCOUS)

- Adriana's Caravan (see CHILES)

RISOTTO-STYLE RICE

- Corti Brothers (see CHOCOLATE)

- Adriana's Caravan (see CHILES)

- Zingerman's
  422 Detroit Street, Ann Arbor,
  MI 48104
  888-636-8162
  www.zingermans.com

BASMATI RICE

- Indian Harvest Specialtifoods, Inc.
  (see ISRAELI COUSCOUS)

- The CMC Company (see CHILES)

Dried Herbs and Spices

- Penzey's Spices
  P.O. Box 933, W19362
  Apollo Drive, Muskego, WI 53150
  800-741-7787
  www.penzeys.com

- Dean and DeLuca
  (see ISRAELI COUSCOUS)

- Adriana's Caravan (see CHILES)

PAPRIKA, HUNGARIAN

- a cook's wares (see CHOCOLATE)

- Adriana's Caravan (see CHILES)

PAPRIKA, SPANISH *PIMENTÓN*

- La Tienda
  888-472-1022
  www.tienda.com

- Adriana's Caravan (see CHILES)

- Zingerman's (see ARBORIO RICE)

Mascarpone

- Vermont Butter & Cheese Company
  Websterville, VT 05678
  800-884-6287
  www.vtbutterandcheeseco.com

Meat

BACON

- Niman Ranch
  1025 E. 12th Street, Oakland,
  CA 94606
  866-808-0340 or 510-808-0330
  www.nimanranch.com

- Nodine's Smokehouse
  P.O. Box 1787 Torrington, CT
  06790
  800-222-2059
  www.nodinesmokehouse.com

LAMB AND PORK

- Niman Ranch (see BACON)

SPANISH CHORIZO

- La Tienda (see SPANISH PAPRIKA)

- Corti Brothers (see CHOCOLATE)

- The CMC Company (see CHILES)

Piquillo Peppers

- La Tienda (see SPANISH PAPRIKA)

- Zingerman's
  (see RISOTTO-STYLE RICE)

Sherry Vinegar

- La Tienda (see SPANISH PAPRIKA)

- a cook's wares (see CHOCOLATE)

- Zingerman's
  (see RISOTTO-STYLE RICE)

Tamarind Paste

- Kitchen/Market (see CHILES)

- The CMC Company (see CHILES)

- Adriana's Caravan (see CHILES)

Asian Fish Sauce

- The CMC Company (see CHILES)

- Adriana's Caravan (see CHILES)

- Kitchen/Market (see CHILES)

❖ Bibliography

Batmanglij, Najmieh. *New Food of Life.* Mage Publishers. 1998.

Bugialli, Giuliano. *The Fine Art of Italian Cooking.* Times Books, 1977.

Dent, Huntley. *The Feast of Santa Fe.* Simon & Schuster, 1985.

Foods of the World, Pacific and Southeast Asian Cooking. Time-Life Books, 1970.

The Good Cook. Time-Life Books: *Soups,* 1979; *Pork,* 1980; *Classic Desserts,* 1980; *Dried Beans and Grains,* 1982.

Hazan, Marcella. *The Classic Italian Cook Book.* Harper's Magazine Press, 1973.

Kennedy, Diana. *Recipes From the Regional Cooks of Mexico.* Harper & Row, 1978.

Margen, Sheldon, M.D., and the Editors of the University of California at Berkeley Wellness Letter, *The Wellness Encyclopedia of Food and Nutrition.* Rebus, 1992.

McDermott, Nancie. *Real Thai.* Chronicle Books, 1992.

Rombauer, Irma S., and Marion Rombauer Becker. *Joy of Cooking.* Bobbs-Merrill, 1983.

Sahni, Julie. *Classic Indian Vegetarian and Grain Cooking.* William Morrow, 1985.

Schmidt, Arno. *Chef's Book of Formulas, Yields and Sizes.* Van Nostrand Reinhold, 1990.

Schneider, Elizabeth. *Uncommon Fruits and Vegetables: A Common Sense Guide.* Harper & Row, 1986.

Stevens, Molly. "Does Egg Size Matter?" *Fine Cooking* magazine (May 2002).

Thorne, John and Matt. *Simple Cooking* newsletter 44 (Autumn 1995).

Valera, Gregorio. *Frying Food in Olive Oil.* Madrid Complutense University, International Olive Oil Council, 1994.

✣ Index